FOR DUMMIES

COMPUTER
BOOK SERIES
FROM IDG

TurboTax For Windows® For Dummies

M000288008

Keyboard Shortcuts

To Do This . . .	Type This . . .
Start a new tax return	Ctrl+N
Open an existing tax return	Ctrl+O
Print a tax return	Ctrl+P
Undo your last action	Ctrl+Z
Cut	Ctrl+X
Copy	Ctrl+C
Paste	Ctrl+V
Prepare an itemized statement	Ctrl+I
Save a tax return	Ctrl+S
Flip to EasyStep from Forms mode	Ctrl+R
Close a tax return	Ctrl+F4
Close TurboTax	Alt+F4
Flip from one error to another on an actual form	F7
Get help (in EasyStep)	Alt+H
Access the Calculator (in EasyStep)	Alt+A
Do a Summary (in EasyStep)	Alt+S
Override the calculated amount (in Forms mode)	Ctrl+D

Important Dates to Remember

January 16, 1996	4th quarter 1995 Estimated Tax due
April 15, 1996	Federal Income Tax return (Form 1040) due
April 15, 1996	1st quarter 1996 Estimated Tax due
June 17, 1996	2nd quarter 1996 Estimated Tax due
August 15, 1996	Form 1040 due if filing time was extended by four months
September 16, 1996	3rd quarter 1996 Estimated Tax due
January 13, 1997	4th quarter 1996 Estimated Tax due

*Note: IRS agents get very angry when they see the words *cheat* and *taxes* on the same page. We're not suggesting that you cheat on your tax return; instead, use these tricks to make preparing your tax return so easy that you don't even have to think about cheating.

. . . For Dummies: #1 Computer Book Series for Beginners

FOR DUMMIES

COMPUTER
BOOK SERIES
FROM IDG

TurboTax For Windows® For Dummies®, 2nd Edition

Cheat Sheet

Using the TurboTax Calculator

Double-click here to make your calculator disappear

Figure C-1: Use your mouse or the numeric keypad to work the Calculator.

✔ Click any number to enter that number into the accumulator (the black bar on the top where the numbers appear).

✔ Click an *operator* to perform a mathematical function:

- ÷ = divide
- * = multiply
- − = subtract
- + = add
- = = equals (finish each calculation with an =)
- +/− = change sign (negative to positive or vice versa)

✔ Click Back to erase the most recently typed digit.

✔ Click CE to clear the current entry.

✔ Click Clear to clear the entire current calculation.

✔ Click . to receive a decimal point.

✔ Click Paste to copy the current number into your tax return.

✔ Double-click the Control bar (or press the Esc key on your keyboard), and the Calculator vanishes into thin air.

Things to Collect While Getting Ready to Prepare Your Tax Return

✔ Last year's tax return

✔ W-2 forms

✔ 1099 forms of all kinds

✔ Schedules K-1

✔ Year-end bank, savings and loan, and credit union statements

✔ Brokers' statements and other summaries of stock and bond purchases and sales

✔ Closing statements on the purchase or sale of the home or other property you own

✔ Record books or financial statements for businesses or rental properties that you operate

✔ Statements of benefits that you receive from your employer

✔ Medical expense receipts

✔ Receipts for real estate and property tax payments

✔ Federal and State income tax estimated tax vouchers

✔ Mortgage loan statement (Form 1098)

✔ Receipts from charities indicating date and cash amount given (or description of noncash items donated)

✔ Insurance claim forms for casualties or thefts

✔ Evidence of unreimbursed business-related expenses incurred as an employee

COMPUTER BOOK SERIES FROM IDG

References for the Rest of Us!®

Are you intimidated and confused by computers? Do you find that traditional manuals are overloaded with technical details you'll never use? Do your friends and family always call you to fix simple problems on their PCs? Then the . . .*For Dummies*® computer book series from IDG Books Worldwide is for you.

. . .*For Dummies* books are written for those frustrated computer users who know they aren't really dumb but find that PC hardware, software, and indeed the unique vocabulary of computing make them feel helpless. . . .*For Dummies* books use a lighthearted approach, a down-to-earth style, and even cartoons and humorous icons to diffuse computer novices' fears and build their confidence. Lighthearted but not lightweight, these books are a perfect survival guide for anyone forced to use a computer.

> *"I like my copy so much I told friends; now they bought copies."*
>
> **Irene C., Orwell, Ohio**

> *"Quick, concise, nontechnical, and humorous."*
>
> **Jay A., Elburn, Illinois**

> *"Thanks, I needed this book. Now I can sleep at night."*
>
> **Robin F., British Columbia, Canada**

Already, hundreds of thousands of satisfied readers agree. They have made . . .*For Dummies* books the #1 introductory level computer book series and have written asking for more. So, if you're looking for the most fun and easy way to learn about computers, look to . . .*For Dummies* books to give you a helping hand.

IDG BOOKS WORLDWIDE™

TurboTax®
FOR
WINDOWS®
FOR
DUMMIES®
2ND EDITION

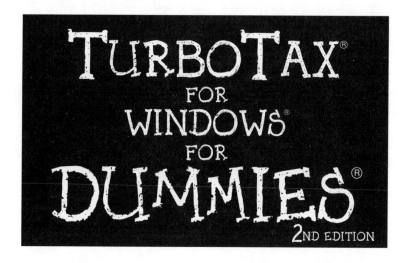

TurboTax® FOR WINDOWS® FOR DUMMIES®
2ND EDITION

by Gail Helsel, CPA

IDG Books Worldwide, Inc.
An International Data Group Company

Foster City, CA ♦ Chicago, IL ♦ Indianapolis, IN ♦ Braintree, MA ♦ Dallas, TX

TurboTax® For Windows® For Dummies®, 2nd Edition

Published by
IDG Books Worldwide, Inc.
An International Data Group Company
919 E. Hillsdale Blvd.
Suite 400
Foster City, CA 94404

Library of Congress Catalog Card No.: 95-81432

ISBN: 1-56884-948-6

Printed in the United States of America

10 9 8 7 6 5 4 3 2 1

2A/RW/RR/ZV

Distributed in the United States by IDG Books Worldwide, Inc.

Distributed by Macmillan Canada for Canada; by Computer and Technical Books for the Caribbean Basin; by Contemporanea de Ediciones for Venezuela; by Distribuidora Cuspide for Argentina; by CITEC for Brazil; by Ediciones ZETA S.C.R. Ltda. for Peru; by Editorial Limusa SA for Mexico; by Transworld Publishers Limited in the United Kingdom and Europe; by Al-Maiman Publishers & Distributors for Saudi Arabia; by Simron Pty. Ltd. for South Africa; by IDG Communications (HK) Ltd. for Hong Kong; by Toppan Company Ltd. for Japan; by Addison Wesley Publishing Company for Korea; by Longman Singapore Publishers Ltd. for Singapore, Malaysia, Thailand, and Indonesia; by Unalis Corporation for Taiwan; by WS Computer Publishing Company, Inc. for the Philippines; by WoodsLane Pty. Ltd. for Australia; by WoodsLane Enterprises Ltd. for New Zealand.

For general information on IDG Books Worldwide's books in the U.S., please call our Consumer Customer Service department at 800-762-2974. For reseller information, including discounts and premium sales, please call our Reseller Customer Service department at 800-434-3422.

For information on where to purchase IDG Books Worldwide's books outside the U.S., contact IDG Books Worldwide at 415-655-3021 or fax 415-655-3295.

For information on translations, contact Marc Jeffrey Mikulich, Director, Foreign & Subsidiary Rights, at IDG Books Worldwide, 415-655-3018 or fax 415-655-3295.

For sales inquiries and special prices for bulk quantities, write to the address above or call IDG Books Worldwide at 415-655-3200.

For information on using IDG Books Worldwide's books in the classroom, or ordering examination copies, contact Jim Kelly at 800-434-2086.

For authorization to photocopy items for corporate, personal, or educational use, please contact Copyright Clearance Center, 222 Rosewood Drive, Danvers, MA 01923, or fax 508-750-4470.

About the Author

Gail Helsel is a CPA who has been sticking her nose in other people's income taxes since 1975. She spent several years in the Chicago tax department of Deloitte Haskins and Sells (now Deloitte & Touche), learning the ropes of tax preparation and generally getting in everyone's hair.

Gail teaches computer classes for the Indiana CPA society (including TurboTax) and is coauthor of *WordPerfect for Windows Super Book*. When not wrapped up with being a mom, writing, computerizing, and futzing with taxes, she day-dreams about playing the fiddle with a bluegrass band.

Welcome to the world of IDG Books Worldwide.

IDG Books Worldwide, Inc., is a subsidiary of International Data Group, the world's largest publisher of computer-related information and the leading global provider of information services on information technology. IDG was founded more than 25 years ago and now employs more than 7,700 people worldwide. IDG publishes more than 250 computer publications in 67 countries (see listing below). More than 70 million people read one or more IDG publications each month.

Launched in 1990, IDG Books Worldwide is today the #1 publisher of best-selling computer books in the United States. We are proud to have received 8 awards from the Computer Press Association in recognition of editorial excellence and three from Computer Currents' First Annual Readers' Choice Awards, and our best-selling ...*For Dummies*® series has more than 19 million copies in print with translations in 28 languages. IDG Books Worldwide, through a joint venture with IDG's Hi-Tech Beijing, became the first U.S. publisher to publish a computer book in the People's Republic of China. In record time, IDG Books Worldwide has become the first choice for millions of readers around the world who want to learn how to better manage their businesses.

Our mission is simple: Every one of our books is designed to bring extra value and skill-building instructions to the reader. Our books are written by experts who understand and care about our readers. The knowledge base of our editorial staff comes from years of experience in publishing, education, and journalism — experience which we use to produce books for the '90s. In short, we care about books, so we attract the best people. We devote special attention to details such as audience, interior design, use of icons, and illustrations. And because we use an efficient process of authoring, editing, and desktop publishing our books electronically, we can spend more time ensuring superior content and spend less time on the technicalities of making books.

You can count on our commitment to deliver high-quality books at competitive prices on topics you want to read about. At IDG Books Worldwide, we continue in the IDG tradition of delivering quality for more than 25 years. You'll find no better book on a subject than one from IDG Books Worldwide.

John J. Kilcullen

John Kilcullen
President and CEO
IDG Books Worldwide, Inc.

Dedication

To my extremely patient children, Katherine and Georgia.

Acknowledgments

Several people played key parts in putting this book together in seemingly record time. I want to thank my editor, Pam Mourouzis; Guy MacNeill, who took time he didn't have to help me learn the new features of TurboTax; Eric Heinemann, the middle-man between me and the IRS; Matt Wagner; Dan Bieger; and all the folks in Production.

(The Publisher would like to give special thanks to Patrick J. McGovern, without whom this book would not have been possible.)

Credits

Contents at a Glance

Cartoons at a Glance

By Rich Tennant

page 18

page 197

page 221

page 259

page 204

page 140

page 7

page 41

page 244

page 153

Table of Contents

Introduction

I attended my first computer classes at Indiana University in the early '70s, when there was one computer on campus and we neophyte geeks prepared our computer programs on punch cards, tediously keypunching into the long hours of the night. We would turn in our stack of punch cards to the computer operator, who would diligently feed them to the big computer that took up an entire climate-controlled room. About 24 hours later, we would see the printed output, which typically would be followed with revisions to the program, another late night of punching holes in cards, another stack of cards to the operator, another 24 hours, and so on and so on.

Fast-forward to today. These little computer boxes now sit in our living rooms, effortlessly calculating while visions of fireworks or flying toasters dance across the idle screen.

Sometimes you may question your investment in all this equipment. You hope that no one is peeking over your shoulder when you think of how much money you paid in order to play a game of solitaire without using a deck of cards. Some of the programs that you run on your computer may be frivolous, but so what? When a program like TurboTax comes along, you find yourself nodding and smiling, knowing that all the cost was worthwhile.

TurboTax can save you hours, money, and frustration all at the same time. Think of it: No more trying to figure out which tax forms you need, no more scrounging around trying to find those forms, no more paying professional tax preparer fees, no more feeling helpless while trying to understand IRS instructions, and no more headaches. This is what computers were made for.

And after you complete your income tax return and send it off in the mail, confident that all the forms have been filled in correctly, don't feel guilty about rewarding yourself with a nice game of computer solitaire.

About This Book

This book is a guide to using TurboTax. It's also a reference that you can use while preparing your income tax return. In addition to giving step-by-step instructions for working with the TurboTax program, this book is filled with explanations of just what the IRS is asking for, written in easy-to-understand English with just a touch of humor to make the whole tax process easier to swallow.

Don't expect to be overwhelmed by convoluted tax instructions or confusing computer terms. This book isn't written for the people who want to speak the lingo and sound like the pros. Instead, you'll find friendly, conversational descriptions and easy-to-understand information about such topics as the following:

- Putting the TurboTax program on your computer
- Figuring out which expenses you can deduct from your income
- Preparing more than one tax return with TurboTax
- Getting yourself out of TurboTax-related computer trouble
- Organizing your tax records for using TurboTax next year

Preparing income tax returns is often a lonely business. The very nature of the material that it deals with is private and personal, so you probably won't invite the neighbors to help like you might when you whitewash the backyard fence. Instead, you can think of this book as the good friend you invite over while you prepare your income tax return. Ask your questions and expect neighborly chatter and useful hints.

How to Use This Book

As you use TurboTax to prepare your income tax return, you can follow along from the front of the book to the back, skipping the sections that don't apply to you. Or, if you prefer, use the table of contents and the extensive index to help you find exactly the information that you need. Whichever approach you take, be sure to spend a few minutes enjoying the cartoons along the way!

Don't worry about trying to memorize the information in this book. Leave that to the folks who eat and breathe computer jargon and to those high-paid tax accountants who leave for vacation on April 16. This book isn't going anywhere. Keep it by your side and refer to it as often as you like.

When you use TurboTax, you have to type things, press certain keys, or point with your mouse and click buttons on-screen in order to accomplish tasks. The following conventions used in this book help you to recognize what to do in different situations. For example, when you need to type something, like your full name, you see a sample in boldface that looks like this:

Jane Eyre

With the sample is a description of what you should type so you'll know exactly which information TurboTax expects you to provide.

Messages that appear on-screen are in this typeface:

    Turbo Tax message

Instructions that require several sequential steps appear in a numbered list, with the actual steps you perform in boldface and any explanatory text in regular type. The following example gives the steps for printing a 1040PC tax return:

1. **When you finish preparing your tax return, save it by choosing File⇨Save on the menu bar or by pressing Ctrl+S on your keyboard.**

2. **Choose File⇨Print or press Ctrl+P on your keyboard.**

3. **Click the Tax Return for Filing and 1040PC Format for Filing buttons.**

4. **Click the Print button.**

   TurboTax checks your tax return for potential problems or missing items. If it finds a problem, it tells you about it. You can then fix the problem and return to step 1.

In addition to step-by step instructions and typed examples, I include pictures of actual TurboTax screens so that you'll know what to expect when you click a button or perform some other procedure in the program.

Wondering why some keys in these steps are underscored? Well, those keys are called *hot keys,* which work in conjunction with the Alt key on your keyboard. To access the Save command in the File menu, for example, just press and hold down Alt, then press F, and then press S. These keyboard shortcuts appear in the book like this: Alt+F,S.

You'll also run into Ctrl+[*some specified key*] shortcuts, such as Ctrl+O. Press the Ctrl key and, while still holding down that key, press the key that follows the plus sign; this is a quicker way of accessing frequently used commands.

That little arrow thingy between the words *File* and *Save,* and also between *File* and *Print,* tells you to click the word *File* and then to click the menu choice that follows the arrow (*Save* or *Print*). Sometimes you may see two or three arrows, which indicate that you have to click two or three consecutive menu choices.

Who Are You?

You've decided to use TurboTax software, maybe for the first time or maybe not, and you've got Windows running on your computer. (For specifics on the version of Windows you should be running and the hardware considerations that will keep your computer running while you're using TurboTax, take a look at "Hardware Requirements: 286, 386, 486, Hike!" in Chapter 1.) Most importantly, you've got yourself a tax return to prepare and, like it or not, you've got to get it done. You always have the option of packing up the whole mess and letting someone else do it for you. But if you really wanted to do that, you probably wouldn't be holding this book.

How This Book Is Organized

For the most part, this book follows the order in which you prepare your tax return. First, you figure out how to get TurboTax running on your computer, then you gather all your receipts and tax documents, and then you think about reporting all your income on the tax return. Next, you frantically try to reduce that income with deductions. Calculating tax is next, and then you put everything together and stick it in the mail. Finally, you sit back and hope that the IRS doesn't audit you. The following sections show how all these concepts fit together in *TurboTax For Windows For Dummies,* 2nd Edition.

Part I: It All Starts Here

This part helps you get to know TurboTax and clues you in to recent changes in the tax laws that may affect you. You can also pick up some hints about how to go about gathering all the forms and receipts that may not have any bearing on your income tax, but, hey, they're fun to save and make a great trash-can fire when you're all finished. Get the lowdown here about what tax is and why you pay it year after year, ad infinitum.

Part II: Tax Preparation Can Be Fun

I've been told that going to the dentist can be fun, too, but you can't believe everything you hear. Putting your tax return on your computer may not qualify as fun in your book, but at least this section tries to make it entertaining. Familiarize yourself with examples of income and deductions — the stuff IRS agents' dreams are made of — and then find out where to put those items on your tax return.

Part III: You Owe How Much Tax?!?

I can't predict whether this section of the book will provide you with good news or bad news. I can say, though, that between your TurboTax program and this book, you have a chance to catch every possible way in which you can keep your tax bite to a bare minimum.

Part IV: The Land Beyond 1040

Browse through this section to see how the IRS regards your tax return. Read about who gets audited and why and what to do if you become one of the chosen. This part also includes neat ideas about how to get yourself organized (sometimes everybody needs a little nudge in that direction) and what you can do now to get ready for this whole process to kick in again next year.

Part V: The Part of Tens

This part contains lists, lists, and more lists of ten or so things that help you save time and make you appreciate the wonderful tax preparation program that you purchased: ten keyboard shortcuts for tired mice, ten things to do if you're audited, ten things you can do now to make life easier next year, and more.

Appendixes

Appendix A gives you the particulars on installing TurboTax on your computer. Appendix B provides you with a sample Form 1040 that you can use as a cross-reference to sections in this book.

Icons Used in This Book

Watch for these little pictures; they point the way to important information as you go along.

Having trouble getting to sleep at night? These items should do the job. These pieces of techno information tell you why TurboTax is doing what it is doing or what the programmers intended when they created a particular aspect of the software. Drop one of these bits of technical jargon and computerese on the floor, come back in the middle of the night and turn on the light, and watch the computer geeks scatter in all directions.

Tips can help you work smarter and faster. Watch out: Learn too many of these and you'll be pegged an expert before you can say TurboTax backwards. (You tried to say it, didn't you?)

 This icon saves you the trouble of digging out your yellow highlighter. If you can't remember these key points, it doesn't matter. Just remember what the icon looks like and find it when you need a memory refresher.

 If you neglect to pay attention to these sections, I get to say "I told you so" when things go wrong.

 You can chew on these heavy-duty chunks of technical tax information if you're really hungry. You may never need to know these things — for the most part, they're only here so you won't think that I made up all these crazy tax rules.

Where to Go from Here

This is it, your last pat on the back before you begin preparing The Tax Return. Dig in and have a good time. TurboTax is only as daunting as you want it to be; whenever the program seems to get out of hand, pick up this book and shake it at your computer. Better yet, look up the problem area, find your solution, and we can wave at each other across the beach after April 15.

Part I
It All Starts Here

The 5th Wave   By Rich Tennant

"I THINK 'FUZZY LOGIC' IS AN IMPORTANT TECHNOLOGY TOO. I'M JUST NOT SURE WE SHOULD FEATURE IT AS PART OF OUR TAX PREPARATION SOFTWARE."

In this part...

Once upon a time, tax returns were three-page items — one page for income, one page for deductions relating to that income, and one page where you added it all up and multiplied by the "normal" tax rate of 1 percent. The idea of using a computer and a sophisticated computer program to figure this out would have been ludicrous.

Today, *not* using some kind of tax aid seems to border on the demented. When tax laws fill volumes and legal cases that fine-tune those laws fill libraries, and when the available tax forms and their accompanying instructions fill three three-inch three-ring binders, who can be expected to know where to begin?

This part of the book is as good a place as any to start your tax preparation adventure. Read up on what TurboTax can do for you, learn about recent changes in the tax laws (like we really need *more* laws), and treat yourself to a brief foray into the logic behind our tax system. (Is that a contradiction in terms?)

Chapter 1
Making Friends with TurboTax

- -

In This Chapter

▶ How the HeadStart version differs from the Final version

▶ What TurboTax can and can't do

▶ What type of computer equipment you need

▶ How to start up TurboTax from the Windows Program Manager or from Windows 95

▶ Which extra little TurboTax gimmicks you'll find

- -

*B*y the time you finish using TurboTax to prepare your income tax return, you're going to know it pretty well. So unwrap the box, shake hands, and make a conscious decision to like this program. You don't have to set a place for it at the dinner table or put it on a leash and take it for a walk around the neighborhood or anything. But give it a chance, and you may find that this tax return preparation business can actually be fun — well, at least tolerable.

Ready, Set, HeadStart

If the TurboTax box that you brought home from the store says HeadStart Version in the lower-left corner (chances are that it does if you bought your program prior to January 15), you do not have the Final version of TurboTax. If the box is long gone, you can check your version from within the TurboTax program by clicking the <u>H</u>elp menu, followed by <u>A</u>bout TurboTax for Windows.

"So what if I bought the HeadStart version?" you ask. Well, for one thing, the IRS won't accept your tax return if you print it from the HeadStart version. Just in case you try to do so, TurboTax prints nasty DO NOT FILE comments all over your forms.

The problem is that the tax laws and tax forms can change right up to the end of the year. It would be irresponsible for any tax preparation program to issue its final version before the folks in Washington finish tweaking the tax laws for the year. So we all have to wait.

Meanwhile, over at the TurboTax offices, those hard-working programmers frantically add new laws and last-minute changes to IRS forms to their program so that your tax return will be up to date. As soon as they make all the changes, they let loose on the marketplace the Final version of TurboTax, which replaces the HeadStart version on store shelves.

If you bought the HeadStart version, the people in the shipping department at TurboTax are ready to send you a copy of the Final version at no extra charge. See "When Will I Get the Final Version?" in Chapter 18 and also the following sidebar to find out how to make sure that you get the Final version.

What to Expect from TurboTax

You can do all kinds of cool things with TurboTax. Here are some of the coolest, in my opinion:

- ✔ You can save lots of money by not having to pay a tax service or an accountant to prepare your tax return.

- ✔ You can prepare your tax return in the privacy of your home — and you don't even have to pick up the newspapers and dirty laundry.

- ✔ You can print out professional-looking forms, and if you spill coffee on one of them, you can just print another.

- ✔ You don't have to figure out whether you need a Schedule SE, Form TD F 90–22.1, or Schedule PT-109 — TurboTax does that for you.

- ✔ You can change a number on one page and be confident that the number will flow to all the related forms — much easier than erasing until you make holes in the paper.

- ✔ You can experiment. Maybe you didn't really win $20,000 at the racetrack, but with TurboTax, you can plug that figure into your tax return and see how much tax you'd have to pay.

Where's my program?!?

Be sure to register your program by filling out and sending in the registration card as soon as you open the HeadStart version. After you do that, if January has come and gone and you are still waiting for the Final version of TurboTax to come in the mail, it's time to get on the phone. Call TurboTax directly at 520-295-3100. The shipping people at TurboTax are usually on their toes when it comes to sending out the Final version, so if yours hasn't appeared by February 1, your registration card may not have made it to the right place or somehow may have gotten misplaced.

It's also reasonable to expect a tax return program to give you an error-free product. If you enter accurate information, you can count on TurboTax to give you an accurate tax return.

Putting in the right numbers is *your* job. Because TurboTax can't reach out of the disk drive, grab your W-2 form, and read the numbers, it relies on you to feed it. Give it a healthy diet of income and expenses, and it coos like a baby and burps out a nice, clean tax return.

What Not to Expect from TurboTax

Although TurboTax does all the basic tax return stuff, it considers some things above and beyond the call of duty. Not only will this program not do the dishes or empty the trash, a few times you may feel the need to call in the heavy artillery in the form of professional tax accountants, or at least professional hand-holders:

- ✔ **TurboTax doesn't do audits.** If you happen to be one of those lucky taxpayers who gets chosen for an IRS audit, I'm afraid that the TurboTax people will not be joining you, much as they might like to. Intuit, the company that makes the software, is not responsible for the tax return that you mail to the IRS. Sorry.

- ✔ **Sticky tax situations sometimes require in-depth research into the bowels of the U.S. Treasury Regulations.** Now there's a disgusting thought. When the going gets tough, TurboTax steps aside and leaves the heavy-duty research to the pros. You should, too. Don't be afraid to call on a tax accountant if you don't find the answers you need.

Don't call us and we won't call you

You're kind of out there on your own with this tax return. The makers of this program have included all kinds of disclaimers in their program material about not being responsible for the accuracy or adequacy of positions taken by the taxpayer using this program. If the program goofs up on a math calculation and says that $10,000 plus $5,000 equals $2,000 and you don't catch it but the IRS does, then Intuit will pay you back for any penalty you may incur. That's about as far out on a limb as the company is willing to go, however, so beware! Transcribe numbers carefully and read the on-screen directions, along with guidance from this book, cautiously and completely.

It's okay to call a tax accountant with one question — even if they are not preparing your entire tax return, most accountants will probably be willing to do a little work for you. Tax accountants bill by the hour. Before calling, prepare your tax return as best you can and have a precise question ready. The accountant can give you a quicker (that is, less expensive) answer if you organize your information first.

Hardware Requirements: 286, 386, 486, Hike!

Before you load TurboTax onto your computer, it's important to figure out whether your computer is up to the task. There's a lot of talk out there about 386 this and 486 that, Pentium processors and Windows 95, not to mention all that talk about hundreds of megabytes, 55 mph speed limits, and 366 days in leap years. The numbers never stop bombarding us.

According to the folks at TurboTax, your computer should have these numbers — and these are the *minimum* requirements — in order to make a successful go of the program:

- ✔ 4MB of RAM (memory)
- ✔ One floppy disk drive
- ✔ A 386 processing unit
- ✔ Microsoft Windows Version 3.1
- ✔ 15MB of available hard disk space
- ✔ A mouse
- ✔ A laser, ink-jet, PostScript, or 9- or 24-pin printer (if you plan to print the forms yourself)

The higher those numbers get, the faster and more efficiently TurboTax runs. If you want to know more about what all those words and numbers mean, grab a copy of Dan Gookin and Andy Rathbone's *PCs For Dummies,* 3rd Edition (IDG Books Worldwide, Inc.)

Don't know the specs on your computer? No worries. Check the covers of the manuals that have been gathering dust under your computer desk, read the messages that race by on your computer screen when you first turn it on, look on the outside of your computer or printer for hints about what it is, or open the front door, grab an 11-year-old off the sidewalk, and have her take a look.

Getting TurboTax Up and Running

If you consider yourself a veteran Windows user, skip this section. If you're not a Windows veteran, read on.

To run TurboTax, you need to be running Windows. Windows is the program that puts all the cute little pictures of filing cabinets and card decks on your screen and then forces you to drag a creature called a mouse around in order to do all the neat stuff.

In Windows 3.1

The Windows Program Manager is the backbone of any program running in the Windows 3.1 environment. When you're using Windows, you're using the Program Manager, which pretty much takes care of itself and you. It contains program-starting icons for all the programs that you've loaded on your computer. Like a good traffic cop, it keeps your programs coming and going and makes sure that they don't run over each other. When TurboTax or any other program is running, so is the Program Manager, hiding behind your TurboTax screen and keeping the peace among your various pieces of software.

To start TurboTax from the Windows Program Manager, follow these steps:

1. **Find the TurboTax for Windows program group — the square that contains the TurboTax icons — and double-click it.**

   If it is not visible on your screen, click the <u>W</u>indow menu and then choose TurboTax for Windows (if you don't see it there, click <u>M</u>ore Windows and scroll through the list until you find it).

2. **Find the picture of a little red-white-and-blue top hat (see Figure 1-1), point to it (not with your finger but with the arrow that the mouse controls), and then click your heels together, saying, "There's no place like TurboTax," over and over again.**

   If that doesn't work, try clicking the left mouse button twice rapidly. Be sure that you don't push the mouse around on the desk while you're trying to click — this is the downfall of many otherwise perfectly capable mouse baiters.

   If you click and click and the little hat keeps running away from you, sliding around on-screen, click the hat icon once and then press the Enter key.

Figure 1-1:
The
TurboTax
top hat icon.

In Windows 95

If you installed TurboTax through Windows 95 (installation procedures are described at the back of this book in Appendix A) and are running that nifty new system, you can find the TurboTax program by following these steps:

1. **Click the Start button.**

2. **Choose Programs.**

3. **Choose TurboTax from the menu that appears.**

After you successfully complete this operation in either version of Windows, you enter the TurboTax program.

TurboTax, as depicted in Figure 1-2, greets you with a friendly message and an inviting Next button, which you can click if you want to explore. If you aren't yet ready to play around in the program, choose File⇨Exit. TurboTax asks whether you want to save changes before exiting. Say NO at this point.

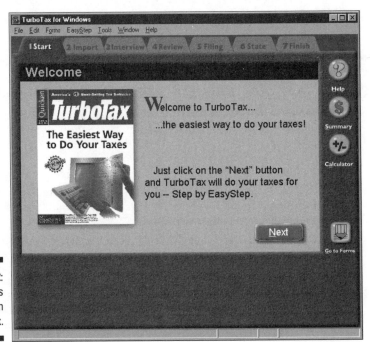

Figure 1-2:
Greetings
from
TurboTax.

Extra, Added Attractions

Over the years, TurboTax has added all sorts of neat little gimmicks that look good on-screen and may or may not strike your fancy. Herewith is a brief summary of these odds and ends.

Graphs

Have you ever wanted to see a real, almost-live image of just how the federal government uses your money? I agree: depressing thought. You can see exactly why it's so depressing by looking at Figure 1-3. See "Wow! Graphing Your Results" in Chapter 12 for a description of how these graphs work, what you can do with them, and what information you can get from them.

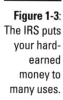

Figure 1-3: The IRS puts your hard-earned money to many uses.

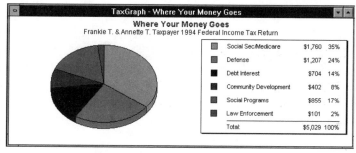

Deduction Finder

Wondering whether you caught every possible deduction? Some expenses that you can deduct from your income may be obvious to you, like mortgage interest or charitable contributions, but you may not be aware of others. This neat little TurboTax tool appears as part of the TurboTax review process; you can see the whole process in Figure 1-4, a picture of the TurboTax `Reviewing Your Return` screen. The Deduction Finder checks for obvious and not-so-obvious deductibles that you may have overlooked. Take a look at "The Deduction Finder" in Chapter 8 for all kinds of information about this slick feature.

The Deduction Finder reminds you that the
swimming pool you installed in your backyard
may qualify as a medical deduction

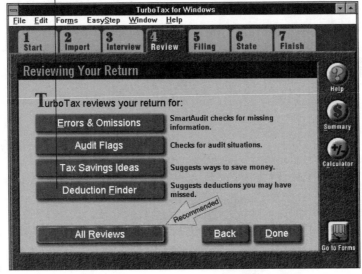

Data transfers

If you use a computer program like Quicken for recording personal or business
financial information, you can avoid having to make entries in TurboTax that
you have already entered in Quicken or another program. Information saved in
many of the leading personal finance programs transfers into TurboTax with a
little massaging of the numbers. See Chapter 5 for the scoop on information
transfers.

Data untransfers

Perhaps as significant as transferring data from Quicken or some other personal
finance package is the capability to change your mind. If you transfer data into
your income tax return and then decide that the data is incomplete, or maybe
you fear that you may be duplicating the transferred data when you enter
information from your receipts, you can undo the transfer at any time. Chapter 5,
which describes income transfers, also tells you how to get out of transfer trouble.

Electronic filing

Send your tax return on a mission through space. It's a bird! It's a plane! It's Super Tax Return! You can file your return electronically either by sending the IRS a disk or by wiring them a file via modem. This process cuts down on the human factor of processing your tax return and, as a result, can cut several weeks off the processing of your refund. Note that (so far) you can't send the IRS an electronically filed return by yourself — you need an officially sanctioned electronic-filing place (like TurboTax or any of a number of banks and tax preparation services) to do the job for you. Returns that you want TurboTax to file electronically for you get sent to one of the following addresses:

For first-class mail:

TurboTax Electronic Filing Center
P.O. Box 10388
Green Bay, WI 54307-0388

For overnight delivery:

TurboTax Electronic Filing Center
3130 S. Ridge Rd.
Green Bay, WI 54304-5625

Check out the details of preparing your return for electronic filing in Chapter 13.

Tax planning help

TurboTax helps you look at next year and beyond with its tax planning features. Find out what the IRS looks at in determining which returns qualify for audits. Find out how to avoid an audit. Discover tools you can use to save tax dollars down the road. Check out "Tax Saving Suggestions" in Chapter 15.

State tax preparation

In the old days, you were on your own when it came to preparing your state income tax return (unless, of course, you lived in one of those states that didn't even have income tax). Now TurboTax offers software that sucks information out of your federal income tax return and sticks it on your state tax return. TurboTax has software available for all states that assess an income tax. You must purchase the state program separately from the federal program, but they work together as one program once they're on your computer. Check out Chapter 13 for more information about preparing state income tax returns.

The 5th Wave By Rich Tennant

"MISS LAMONT, I'M FILING THE CONGREGATION UNDER 'SOULS', MY SERMONS UNDER 'GRACE' AND THE FINANCIAL CONTRIBUTIONS UNDER 'AMEN'."

Chapter 2

Attention Seasoned Veterans: Changes Since Last Year

. . . .

In This Chapter

▶ Changes to TurboTax since last year

▶ Changes in tax laws since last year

▶ The goods on TurboTax state tax return software

. . . .

*I*f you used TurboTax in years past, you may be curious to know what's new this year. Each year, the program gets updated because tax forms change, along with many of the tax laws that you spent hours memorizing last year. In this chapter, see at a glance — or several glances — which scintillating changes have occurred since you last fired up this program. (Or if you're a new TurboTax user, see how lucky you are to have switched to this method of tax preparation this year.)

Shiny New Features

At first blush, TurboTax looks pretty much the same as last year. But dig in a little and look at all these nice new features the program has to offer:

✔ You can get around easier now in TurboTax than ever before. Use the Interview Navigator, a button on the EasyStep Interview screen, to view a list of all the information you've already entered in your tax return (see the example in Figure 2-1). Click an item and you can either go right to the part of the Interview that introduced that item or go directly to the form on which the item appears.

Figure 2-1:
The
Navigator
guides you
through
all the
TurboTax
forms and
helps you
easily find
where you
want to go.

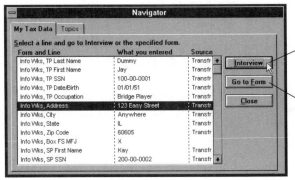

Click any entry and then click
here to go to the selected
place in the Interview

Click any entry and then click
here, and TurboTax beams you
over to the proper form

✔ The Fast Track is a new feature that helps streamline the EasyStep Interview. Choose Fast Track early in the Interview process, and TurboTax asks you a series of questions designed to weed out the parts of the EasyStep Interview that don't apply to you. When you complete the Fast Track questions, TurboTax proceeds with the Interview, asking you only the questions that it thinks are appropriate to your tax situation.

✔ TurboTax's help system got a face-lift this year. All help is located in the same window. This way, you only have to scream for help once and all the services — fire department, police, ambulance, coast guard — come to your rescue at the same time. Once you're surrounded by the help ground forces, just click one of the tabs to call on the kind of assistance you want. Choose from among IRS Instructions, Program Help, Tax Help, and Cross Reference (see Figure 2-2).

Click these tabs for different types of help

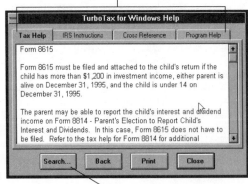

Figure 2-2:
HELP!

Click here to go to the general list of help topics

✓ Get a list of the active forms in your tax return while you're working in the Forms mode. Click the button that is labeled `Show all forms in your current formset` — it's the one that looks like several pieces of paper — and display a list of all the forms available for your tax return. While in this Forms window, click the Show My Return button to display a list of just the tax forms in your tax return.

Tax Laws Come and Tax Laws Go

Some things are better left alone — and then there are tax laws. One of these days, the tax gurus in Congress may get it right, but don't bet the farm on it. Imagine how folks in 1913, the first year of federal income taxation, would have laughed if someone from 1995, traveling in some sort of tax evasion time warp, landed on their front porch and tried to describe TurboTax. "I'm sure," an old-timer would have said skeptically (everyone was an old-timer in 1913), or whatever the equivalent slang of 1913 may have been.

As always, new surprises await you in the tax laws this year. Even as this book went to press, Congress was busy futzing with changes to tax laws, so there may be even more items to consider beyond this list. Check the front pages of the booklet the IRS sends you in the mail around New Year's Eve, which will list all the up-to-the-minute changes the tax folks voted in this year. The following brief summary of tax law changes that were in place early in the fall of 1995 includes references to the places in the book where you can find the details.

✓ **The "Nanny" Tax:** An old tax but a new change to the income return. Congress has provided taxpayers with an opportunity to remit withholding from wages of household employees right on the income tax return — what a nice time-saver. You prepare Schedule H (which TurboTax does for you) and report the wages paid to your household employee for the entire year, the taxes withheld, and your share of social security and Medicare taxes. You can compute Federal Unemployment Tax on this form, too. All these taxes get added up and placed on a new line on Form 1040 (see the 1040 cross-reference in Appendix B — take a look at line 53).

And on the subject of household employees, the IRS has eased off on tax payments for teenage babysitters and yard workers. Hire an under-18-year-old babysitter or yard worker, and that person is no longer subject to social security taxes. (***Exception:*** If the teenager works full-time, year-round as a babysitter or yard worker as opposed to working part-time while a student, then social security taxes apply.)

✔ **Treatment of Health Insurance for the Self Employed:** Last year, there was a lot of controversy right up to the last minute and beyond about whether self-employed people (Schedule C filers) could take part of their medical insurance as an adjustment on page one of their income tax return, or whether they had to report the entire amount on Schedule A as an itemized deduction. Finally, this law has been made (more or less) permanent.

Self-employed individuals can take 30 percent of their health insurance costs as an adjustment on page one of their tax return. The remaining 70 percent goes to Schedule A for consideration as a medical itemized deduction. TurboTax asks you about self-employed health insurance in the EasyStep Interview while it questions you about other Schedule C items. See Chapter 7 for more information about filling out your Schedule C.

✔ **Personal exemptions** (those deductions you get to take for each of your dependents) have increased this year. In 1994, an exemption was worth $2,450. For 1995, the value has increased to $2,500. Chapter 6 explains how to figure out who your dependents are.

✔ **Social security numbers** are now required for everyone — even newborn babies. Babies born prior to November 1, 1995 need to have social security numbers. This rule will make employment forms much easier to fill out in case your infant gets a job before celebrating that one-month birthday.

✔ **Mileage deduction goes up again:** The standard deduction for business-related auto mileage has increased from 29 cents to 30 cents per mile.

Affairs of the State

TurboTax now provides software for all state income tax returns. Not only that, using the software is much easier this year than it has been in past years. Previously, you had to work with your state tax return in a separate file, saving and exiting your federal return before you could play with the state taxes. Now state income taxes blend seamlessly with the federal version. Your entire tax return, federal and state, is saved in one file, no matter how many states you need to include (in case you like to move a lot and have to file several state tax returns in one year). Just choose Go to State from the File menu, and your federal income tax information gently drifts over to the state tax return.

Remember that, just as in past years, the state income tax return software is a separate purchase from the federal software.

Chapter 3

Assembling Your Data

● ●

In This Chapter

▶ Collecting all the stuff that goes on your tax return

▶ W-2s, 1099s, and K-1s: Understanding what all those forms represent

▶ Remembering the most important thing: last year's tax return

▶ Maintaining a calm frame of mind

● ●

*P*erhaps the most daunting part of preparing a tax return is gathering up all the little notes and papers that accumulate during the year, being certain all the while that you'll miss Something Major. This chapter assumes that you have not spent the year preparing for this moment. But from this point forward, you should plan to do some advance preparation. You're stuck being a taxpayer for the rest of your life; make it a tolerable experience by planning for the future. For specific pointers on getting your tax life in order, see Chapter 16.

Knowing what to save is half the ball game. Being able to find it in time to include it in your tax return is the other half. You need some physical way to group your receipts and other tax papers — be it in shoeboxes, file folders, big envelopes, three-ring binders, paper bags, abandoned fish tanks, buried pumpkins, whatever — just as long as it's a place that you can remember when the time comes to retrieve the information. Think of it as your Designated Tax Papers Place.

Little envelopes come in the mail throughout the spring with the friendly words `Important Tax Document Enclosed` printed on them. All of these things should go in the Designated Tax Papers Place.

When it comes time to actually prepare your tax return, you should get out all your tax papers and begin sorting them into groups of similar types of items. Look for a unifying thread in organizing piles of receipts. Documents reporting income, for example, such as W-2 forms and 1099 forms, should be put together in one group, receipts for charitable contributions in another, records of child care expenses in another, and so on. Depending on how many items you have in one group, you may want to consider subgroups — breaking up the income forms into groups of W-2 forms, 1099-Interest forms, and 1099-Dividend forms, for example.

The following section gives you a handy checklist that you can use to determine what kind of paperwork you ought to be collecting. If receipts are required but have disappeared, you can often use canceled checks in place of lost receipts.

Checklist of Receipts and Paperwork to Assemble

This list helps you assemble information that you will need to prepare your tax return. By grouping tax receipts and documents together, you'll have a major head start on your tax return. The list is arranged pretty much in the order in which these things get listed on your tax return. Gathering up all this stuff at once may seem like a headache-provoking chore, but doing it before you actually sit down and begin preparing your tax return will actually save you many bottles of aspirin in the long run.

Some of these things may not apply to your personal situation. If something on the list doesn't mean anything to you, you probably don't have that type of item, so just ignore it and go on to the next one.

❑ **Last year's tax return**

Don't leave home without it. And don't attempt to prepare this year's tax return without it, either.

❑ **W-2 forms**

If you had a job and an employer for any part of last year, you get this form in the mail; it tells you how much you earned.

❑ **1099 forms of all kinds**

This category includes 1099-INT (interest income), 1099-DIV (dividend income), 1099-MISC (miscellaneous income), and anything else that starts with a 1099. Sometimes you have to hunt in every nook and cranny of the form you receive to see what kind of form it is. Banks are notorious for typing the form number in the tiniest print possible and hiding it in secret places on their forms. Any form you get in the mail that reports some kind of income will have a form number on it. If you can't find the form number and you're not sure what type of income the form represents, call the company that made the form and ask.

❑ **Schedules K-1**

These forms come in all shapes and sizes and represent your portion of ownership of a small business, trust, or partnership. Sometimes these schedules arrive in great fold-out maps with ten-page legends and plenty of confusing numbers on them. Other times, they're pretty manageable. Just for the record, they're all the same to TurboTax.

❑ **Year-end bank, savings and loan, and credit union statements**

If the statements from your money institutions reflect interest income, they may have the number 1099 etched on them, in which case you probably have already put them in the 1099 category. If you still have some uncategorized bank statements, now's the time to gather them up.

❑ **Brokers' statements and other summaries of stock and bond purchases and sales**

Information relating to any stock or bond you bought or sold this year goes in this pile. If you sold investments that you purchased in an earlier year, get the original purchase information and put it here, too. If you can no longer find that information, ask your broker to dig it out. (That's what brokers get paid for.) If you sold stocks, ask while you're on the phone with your broker whether any *stock dividends* were paid in the year(s) you owned the stocks, when they were paid, and what their value was at the time of payment.

❑ **Closing statements on the purchase or sale of the home or other property that you own**

If you sold a home, find the closing statement from the time when you bought it as well. This goes for your main home, a summer home, or any kind of home you own, whether or not you live in it.

❑ **Record books or financial statements for businesses or rental properties that you operate**

You may have an accountant who prepares statements for you, or you may do them yourself. In any case, you need a year-end summary of the income and expenses that occurred in your business during 1995.

❑ **Statements of benefits you receive from your employer**

This category includes such stuff as retirement contributions, your personal use of a company car, and moving expense reimbursement. Your employer includes these amounts on your W-2 form and sometimes gives you a separate statement that summarizes them.

❑ **Medical expense receipts**

Doctors, dentists, hospitals, labs, prescriptions, eye doctors, glasses, hearing aids, medical insurance, the number of miles you drove to take advantage of any of these services — this pile includes medical stuff for you and all your dependents.

❑ **Receipts for tax payments (real estate and property)**

Besides property tax statements, if you paid *state* income tax beyond what was withheld from your paycheck (for example, if you sent money with last year's state tax return), that amount counts in this group.

❑ **Federal and State income tax estimated tax vouchers**

If you paid quarterly estimated taxes, you should have one of the following: a copy of the voucher that you sent with your taxes, a paper that summarizes what you paid, or canceled checks.

❑ **Mortgage loan statement (Form 1098)**

❑ **Receipts from charities indicating date and cash amount given or description of noncash items donated**

For noncash donations that exceed $250 in value, you must have a receipt signed by the organization receiving the donated items.

❑ **Insurance claim forms for casualties or thefts**

❑ **Evidence of unreimbursed business-related expenses incurred as an employee**

If you drive your car during the workday, running errands for your boss, and don't get reimbursed for the mileage, you are allowed to take a deduction for that driving, along with unreimbursed parking expenses and tolls. Other expenditures you incurred on behalf of your tightwad boss, like buying the office postage stamps or picking up a new desk calendar, are all things that the IRS wants to hear about.

As you lay out all your tax receipts and statements, ready for the task of preparing your income tax return, consider the juxtaposition of the place where you will be working and the normal use of that location. If you plan to work on the dining room table, think about how long your stacks are going to have to remain on the table. You may want to consider working in a low-traffic area so that you don't have to worry about clearing off your papers before you're finished.

Before you put out your tax papers, make sure that no one will have to pick up the stacks to clear the table until the tax return is finished, the cat won't jump up and skate across the papers, the wind from an open window won't give wings to your receipts, the ceiling won't collapse, and the kids won't need the space for their homework. Come to think of it, unattended stacks, particularly if they are not weighted down, are risky.

The Search, Step One: Don't Panic

The calm approach to assembling information for your tax return is always the best, if you have the time. If it's too late to be calm and hysteria has already set in, see the next section, "The Search, Step Two: Forget Step One — Call 911."

Try to have an organized method of searching for tax receipts and statements (for example, finish one file cabinet drawer or one desk drawer full of crumpled pieces of paper before going on to the next) so that you can cover as many bases as possible in the first pass. The preceding checklist has some ideas for determining the order in which you should search for things.

Your employer, former employer, or other organization that pays you fees must mail official tax forms such as W-2s and 1099s by January 31. Therefore, if January comes and goes and you have not received a form that you are expecting, get on the phone early in February and find out where it is.

Collecting data should be fun, like a scavenger hunt. Once you know what you need, first think of all the places those things may be. Then start thinking of more obscure places. Year-end interest statements from the bank, for example, may have gotten stuck in the same envelope as your monthly bank statements. W-2 forms may have ended up in the place where you save payroll check stubs. Ask family members whether they have seen particular items. Wondering where you put the mortgage statement from the bank? Call a few friends and ask where they keep their statements. Doing so may give you some ideas.

Try to do some of your statement- and receipt-gathering on a weekday during business hours in case you have to make some telephone calls to track down copies of lost or never-received receipts. (See "Finders Keepers, Losers Weepers," later in this chapter.)

The Search, Step Two: Forget Step One — Call 911

April is fast approaching and you still can't find that elusive W-2 form that you know arrived earlier this spring? Maybe a little panic is in order after all. By now, it's time to get serious about making sure that you have everything that you're going to need. If you're convinced that something is hopelessly lost, make arrangements to replace it *now*.

Check out these information-gathering tips before you start pulling out hair, biting off your fingernails, or generally inflicting bodily harm. There are ways to deal with missing information that usually don't involve physical pain. Try these methods:

- ✔ An employer can photocopy a W-2 form for you.

- ✔ Banks and credit unions can give you the amounts of interest earned or paid over the telephone.

- ✔ Corporations paying dividends to shareholders can probably give you earnings information over the telephone. If you have trouble finding available figures for dividend payments, check out a book called *Moody's Dividend Record.* This book, which should be available at your local library, tells you how much in dividends per share a company paid. In fact, if you call a library's reference desk, you can probably get the dividend information from particular companies over the telephone.

- ✔ Partnerships, trusts, and S-corporations issuing K-1 forms are notoriously late in sending out these forms. You are really at their mercy, because the information presented on these forms is available nowhere else. If you are waiting for a K-1 form, you may have to rely on pressuring or pleading with the company issuing the form. Have a little patience if you can — the form is probably in the hands of the company's accountants. If you can't wait any longer for the information the K-1 form holds, try bribing someone with a freshly baked cake, a lawn-mowing offer, or whatever it takes.

 If all else fails and you are missing a K-1 form and can't locate a source for finding out which numbers should go on the form, don't use that as an excuse not to file your tax return, as tempting as it may be to put off the inevitable. You may have to leave off the information from the missing K-1 form; or if you or someone at the company issuing the form can estimate what the amount should be, go ahead and use the approximation.

An alternative to filing the tax return with a potentially incorrect amount on it is to file an extension form in its place, in which case you pay any tax that you may owe but reserve the right to file the actual tax return later in the year. See "How to File a Late Return (Legally)" in Chapter 12 for information about extending the due date of your tax return. The IRS is pretty sticky about that April 15 deadline; tax returns that are filed late without being properly extended are subject to penalties. See "The Cost of Filing Late" in Chapter 12 for the price tag on a late return. If you choose to file the tax return with an approximation of a number and then realize that you need to change the number, you can do so by amending the tax return. See "Changing Your Tax Return After You File It," again in Chapter 12.

Finders Keepers, Losers Weepers

Receipts once misplaced can often be re-created. If you've looked in all the obvious places — under the bed, at the bottom of the bird cage, behind stuffed drawers — check with the source: stores are often willing to provide a hand-written receipt to replace a misplaced one of the computer-generated variety. You may not even need hard evidence of your purchase. If all you need is the amount, a simple phone call may get it for you.

Don't forget the obvious when looking for evidence of deductions: Your check-book, credit card statements, canceled checks, and club records are great sources of evidence regarding amounts that you have paid.

Funny Little Forms That Come in the Mail

January is so much fun. All those little envelopes telling you how much you earned and how much interest you paid provide countless hours of entertain-ment. Never any cobwebs in the mailbox in January. Don't toss these forms. Put them in the big envelopes, shoeboxes, file folders, or whatever receptacle (except that round one in the corner) you have selected as the Designated Tax Papers Place. Save everything that comes in the mail in January — even the ads for that island resort. (Tax return preparation sometimes leaves people with the feeling that they should slip quietly out of the country.)

The following list tells you which forms you should look for and what they represent. Basically, any envelope marked with the `Important Tax Docu-ments Enclosed` notation deserves your attention (in recent years, I've noticed that contest and other promotional junk mail arrives with a similar message, so beware!). Watch for these forms:

✔ **W-2 Wage and Tax Statement**

This form, prepared by your employer, summarizes your wages for the year and the taxes and other items that were withheld from them. You should receive at least one of these forms from each job you held, even if you worked for only a few days. The exception is if your employer paid you in cash or did not withhold taxes. In that case, see the next item.

✔ **1099-MISC Statement of Miscellaneous Income**

Companies or organizations that pay you money for services send out this type of form. This form reports the amounts that you received that were not subject to withholding. These amounts include the following types of income:

- **Fees for work that you performed from which no tax was withheld**
- **Royalty income**
- **Rent income**
- **Other miscellaneous income**, such as jury duty fees or recoveries of amounts deducted in prior years (for example, an insurance reimbursement for a medical expense deducted last year)
  - **Prizes and awards** — either the dollar amount of cash prizes or the cash or resale value of goods received

If you didn't get a 1099-MISC in the mail even though you received money or property during the year, it doesn't mean that you've pulled one over on the IRS. It's still your responsibility to report and pay tax on all the income you receive, so if you don't have the form, just note what you received on a piece of paper and stick it in the miscellaneous income pile for your tax return.

✔ 1099-INT Statement of Interest Income

Earnings on savings accounts or other forms of cash investments with fixed returns produce interest, which this form reports.

✔ 1099-DIV Statement of Dividend Income

If you own shares of stock in a corporation, this form reports the income you earned on those shares.

✔ 1099-R Retirement Plan Distributions

Retirement plans are required to send you one of these forms if you are getting proceeds from such a fund.

✔ 1099-OID Statement of Original Issue Discount

This statement reflects the interest you earned on bonds (or notes) that you purchased at less than face value. As the value of the bond increases over time relative to its face value, you report the interest earned each year.

✔ 1099-G Statement of State Income Tax Refund

If you received a refund from last year's state income tax return, you should receive one of these statements. The amount listed on the statement should match the amount on your state return.

✔ 1099-B Proceeds from Sales of Securities

If you sold bonds or stock or even unloaded shares in a money market fund, you should get one of these forms reflecting how much you received.

✔ 1098 Statement of Mortgage Interest

This form reports the amounts that you paid a bank or other lending institution for interest on a mortgage.

Get those forms!

Employers are required to furnish W-2 forms by January 31. If you haven't received yours, follow up on it. Call the employer. The same goes for 1099 forms: Check with the person or company who paid you if you're expecting a 1099. Sometimes companies don't realize that they are supposed to issue this form. The rules (there's never just one) are as follows:

✔ If you earned at least $600 last year for work you performed for someone else, that person or company is required to give you (and the IRS) a 1099-MISC form reflecting those earnings.

✔ 1099-INT forms must be issued by any institution or organization paying you interest that exceeds $10 per year.

The person or company that paid you less than $600 doesn't have to send you a 1099. That, however, doesn't relieve you of your responsibility to report the income. Likewise, in the case of 1099-INT forms, even if you earned less than $10 and you didn't get a 1099-INT, you still have to report and pay tax on the income.

✔ **K-1 Partner's/Shareholder's/Beneficiary's Share of Earnings**

If you are a partner in a partnership, a shareholder in an S-Corporation, or a beneficiary of a trust, you should receive a K-1 form, which lists your share of the organization's financial activity for the year.

✔ **Chain letters**

"Send $500 to the person whose name appears at the top of this list and then mail this letter to the five people whose tax returns you'd most like to see audited. . . ." Shame on you for even thinking about mailing a chain letter to your ninth-grade math teacher.

Last Year's Tax Return

Don't even think about preparing your tax return without last year's return by your side. Your single best resource for preparing an income tax return is last year's work. You can see what kinds of income that you had and the types of expenses that you deducted. The old form can help jar your memory banks when you start pulling out receipts (and your hair).

Keep last year's form with you at all times during the process of assembling data and preparing your return. Make yourself look back at every single line of information on that form. You'll be amazed at how much it helps you to have a completed form as a reference.

The "It's April 15 and I Haven't Started My Tax Return" Nightmare

Cold sweats . . . huge tax return forms enveloping you in your bed . . . a giant Uncle Sam standing atop the Empire State Building with a tiny you in his grip. . . . Sitting upright with a start, knowing that you sealed the envelope and stuck it in the mail but forgot to attach the W-2 form . . . and forgot postage . . . and forgot to put the tax return in the envelope. . . . It's just like those final exam nightmares that plague the student in everyone. But *this* nightmare comes only in April.

So how do you fend off these frightening thoughts that haunt your dreams? I have a few suggestions (you knew I would):

✔ **As the Girl Scouts say, Be Prepared.**

Don't wait around until the last minute. Gather up your information in January, pick a cold Saturday afternoon, and get the thing over with and into the mail. I know, easier said than done, but preparing your tax return won't be any easier if you wait until April.

✔ **Save stuff.**

It's better to save too many slips of paper than to throw away things that will be difficult to replace. If there's a number on it, chances are that you want to keep it. Pitch the stuff you don't need *after* you prepare your tax return, not before you start.

✔ **Organize your tax information.**

I can't repeat this tip often enough. If you have a system for keeping track of all those miscellaneous receipts, you can be confident that you haven't missed any important items that need to be included in your tax return. You can also rest easier knowing that the chance of losing something is greatly diminished if every receipt and statement has a place to call home. See Chapter 16 for some pointers on putting your tax house in order.

Chapter 4

Income Tax 101: Basic Facts

. . . .

In This Chapter

▶ How we pay taxes

▶ What does and doesn't get taxed

▶ Which expenses reduce the income that gets taxed

▶ Other taxes we pay in addition to income taxes

. . . .

*W*hat is tax, anyway? The 16th amendment to the Constitution gives Congress the right to extract money from hard-working, wage-earning, red-blooded American citizens at a pace no one could have envisioned when the law was written. Income taxes have been around since 1913 and show no sign of going away, no matter what the rumblings are in the Republican Congress.

Like it or not, we live with income taxation. It helps to have a handle on some of the basic ingredients that make up the federal tax system.

Why We Pay Taxes

Why? Well, for goodness' sake, we pay taxes so that we won't have to go to jail, of course.

There are other reasons, too. The government was established to accomplish things with our money that individuals would have a difficult time accomplishing themselves. Many people feel that programs such as national defense, public education, social welfare, public roadwork, the postal service, and law enforcement (as well as financing the national debt) must be handled by the government instead of by private organizations. In order to finance these and other programs, the government taxes its citizens.

How We Pay Taxes

We pay all kinds of taxes ourselves — sales tax, property tax, and the income tax we may have to remit with our annual tax returns — and our employers help pay several of our other taxes. Most people don't see the taxes they pay. Sales tax is added to the price of goods we buy; property tax is often paid by our landlords or our mortgage companies; income tax is withheld from our paychecks and sent off to the federal, state, and local governments by our employers. *Half* the social security and Medicare taxes we pay is withheld from our paychecks and remitted by our employers; the other half is paid directly by our employers and not even listed on our paycheck stubs. Federal and state unemployment taxes are also paid directly by the employer in almost every state. It's as if we never owned much of this money in the first place.

This carefully orchestrated method of taxation disguises the true amount of tax we pay. If we had to write the checks for all these taxes, perhaps we would pay closer attention to how much taxation really costs us and how our tax dollars are being used. Just look at the list in Table 4-1, which lists the income-based taxes we pay. This table does not include taxes that we pay on items we purchase.

Table 4-1	Taxes That Are Based on Income
Type of Tax	*How We Pay It*
Federal Income Tax	Withheld from our paychecks, paid by us in the form of estimated payments, or paid with our tax returns.
State Income Tax	Withheld from our paychecks, paid by us (not applicable in the form of estimated payments, nor paid in some states) with our tax returns.
Local Income Tax	Withheld from our paychecks, paid by us (not applicable in the form of estimated payments, nor paid in some localities) with our tax returns.
FICA (Social Security Tax)	Half is withheld from our paychecks, and the other half is paid on our behalf by our employers. Self-employed individuals pay both halves themselves either through estimated payments or with the tax return.
FUTA (Federal Unemployment Tax)	Paid on our behalf by our employers.
SUTA (State Unemployment Tax)	Paid on our behalf by our employers. (There are exceptions here — a few states allow employers to withhold SUTA from employees' wages, but most states do not.)

What Kind of Income Gets Taxed?

You didn't really think that you could baby-sit the neighbor's pet snapping turtle and not tell the IRS about it, did you? The rule of thumb is this: If you did something to earn it, you pay tax on it. Also, if your investments earn money, you pay tax on those earnings.

You can earn some minimum amounts without paying tax. If your total income is less than the amounts listed in the following IRS Stuff, you won't owe any income tax and don't have to file a tax return. If, however, taxes were withheld from your income and your income still falls under the amounts listed here, you are entitled to a refund of the taxes withheld, but you must file a tax return in order to receive that refund.

The following list gives you a fairly comprehensive summary of items that are subject to income tax. See the IRS Stuff that follows the list if you think that, by some chance, you may not even have to pay the tax.

- ✔ Wages and salaries
- ✔ Interest earned on investments
- ✔ Dividends earned on investments
- ✔ Receipts from a business you own
- ✔ Rent from property you own
- ✔ Fees for services you have performed
- ✔ Royalties on things you have created, such as books
- ✔ Prizes won in contests, raffles, lotteries, and so on
- ✔ Gambling winnings
- ✔ Your share of earnings from partnerships in which you are a partner
- ✔ Your share of earnings from S-Corporations in which you are a shareholder
- ✔ Your share of earnings from trusts in which you are a beneficiary

Basically, the logic here is that if you did something that generated income or invested in something that earned income, you are responsible for reporting those earnings to the government and paying tax on them.

The main thing to remember, however, is that TurboTax asks you all the right questions to get you through this list of taxable items. You don't have to keep track of what's taxable.

You don't have to pay any income tax at all, nor do you have to file an income tax return, if your total income for 1995 is not higher than the thresholds listed in Table 4-2:

Table 4-2	1995 Filing Requirements
If You Are	*File a Tax Return if Your Income Is at Least*
Single	$6,400 ($7,350 if you were at least 65 on 12/31/95)
Married filing jointly	$11,550 if both spouses are under age 65
	$12,300 if one spouse was at least 65 on 12/31/95
	$13,050 if both spouses were at least 65 on 12/31/95
Married filing separately	$2,500
Head of household	$8,250 if under age 65
	$9,200 if at least 65 on 12/31/95
Widowed in 1993 or 1992 with a dependent child	$9,050 if under age 65 $9,800 if at least 65 on 12/31/95

Does Anything Not Get Taxed?

Some income that comes in actually stays in rather than turning around and heading out the door and down the street to your friends in Washington, DC. Income that you didn't ask for, for example, like stuff from that gift horse you keep hearing about, is not subject to income tax. (It may be subject to gift tax, but that's not your problem — the giver pays the gift tax.)

If you invest your income in certain organizations that the IRS looks upon favorably, your earnings may slide by without being taxed. Qualifying investments include state or municipal bonds and tax-exempt mutual funds and municipal bond funds. In addition to being exempt from federal income tax, income from municipal and state bonds is exempt from state income taxation in the state in which the bonds are issued.

Obligations issued by the federal government, such as treasury bonds, treasury notes, and U.S. savings bonds, produce income that is subject to federal income tax but is exempt from state and local income taxes.

Other bits and pieces of income are not subject to tax, but most of what you find here are just small exceptions to the rule that comes down from Uncle Sam: "Every time you earn a dime, save a piece for me." (Doesn't that sound like a title for a country song? Are you listening, Garth?) If you are uncertain about whether an item is subject to income tax, call the agency or organization paying the income and ask. Somebody there should know.

Put away your checkbook! The following are the most common items that don't get taxed:

- ✔ **Cash gifts**

    If gift tax applies, the person giving the gift pays the tax.

- ✔ **Inheritances**

    The estate, not the beneficiary, is liable for inheritance tax.

- ✔ **Earnings on investments in state or local municipal bonds or bond funds**

    Just to be on the safe side, however, check with the organization or municipality issuing the bond or with the administrator of the bond fund to make sure that the IRS has approved the tax-free status of the bond. In particular, check whether the bond is subject to income tax in your state. Earnings on bonds are not subject to state income tax in the state in which they are issued.

    A bond fund can invest in bonds from many states, so it is quite possible that at least part of the earnings from a bond fund is subject to income tax in your state.

- ✔ **Social security earnings**

    Actually, only *part* of your social security earnings is tax free if your income is over a certain level and the moon is full (see Chapter 8 for more information about social security).

- ✔ **Child support received under a divorce or separation decree**

- ✔ **Proceeds from retirement funds to which you have contributed**

    If you have already paid tax on the amount you contribute, you don't pay tax again when you withdraw the funds.

Expenses That Reduce Taxable Income

The real fun starts after you figure up all your income. Now you can chip away — the more you chip, the lower your tax.

Just what is a deduction, anyway?

A *deduction,* according to my good friend and late-night companion, Noah Webster, is "something that is or may be subtracted, as in 'deductions from taxable income.'" Well, that seems pretty clear. It's just a crying shame that old Noah couldn't have helped write the IRS instructions.

You may wonder why some expenses are deductible and others are not. Or maybe you don't. If you care, here's the scoop: The income you earn is taxable. To the extent that it costs you money to earn that income, some kind-hearted lawmakers decided that you shouldn't have to count that cost when figuring your taxable income. So you add up all your income, deduct what it costs to earn that income, and — voilà! — you have your taxable income.

Deductions that endure

Way back in 1913, when the first official income tax form was created, six basic categories of expenses could reduce income before tax was applied. These categories, as set out in the following section, have withstood the test of time and are all amazingly still intact, although somewhat altered. (The tax return *instructions,* however, have not exactly held up with the same stamina; instructions for the first tax return were printed on one page, and now they fill volumes.)

Herewith, the allowable deductions as presented on the first federal income tax return in 1913:

1. The amount of necessary expenses actually paid in carrying on business, but not including business expenses of partnerships, and not including personal, living, or family expenses

2. All interest paid within the year on personal indebtedness of taxpayer

3. All national, State, county, school, and mu-nicipal taxes paid within the year (not including those assessed against local benefits)

4. Losses actually sustained during the year incurred in trade or arising from fires, storms, or shipwreck, and not compensated for by insurance or otherwise

5. Debts due which have been actually ascertained to be worthless and which have been charged off within the year

6. Amount representing a reasonable allowance for the exhustion (sic), wear, and tear of property arising out of its use or employment in the business, not to exceed, in the case of mines, 5 percent of the gross value at the mine of the output for the year for which the computation is made, but no deduction shall be made for any amount of expense of restoring property or making good the exhustion thereof, for which an allowance is or has been made

That seemed easy enough in 1913. Back then, that's about all anyone needed in terms of directions for filling out the tax return. But it didn't take long for big-hearted senators and congressmen to figure out that they could win votes by pushing new deductions into tax law, making things more and more complex until we have what we have today — enough tax laws to choke a woolly mammoth.

Living expenses

In addition to taking deductions for the costs of earning a living, you are allowed to reduce your income by certain costs of living. One of the major things you get to deduct from your taxable income is the cost of borrowing money to purchase a home. And there's no rule about what kind of home you have to buy. Big, little, cheap, expensive — if you borrow money to buy it, you can deduct from your income the interest on the amount you borrow. See "Interest(ing) deductions" in Chapter 8 for the nitty-gritty on deducting interest expense. You can also deduct the cost of taxes that you pay for property you own. Read all about it in the "Tax deductions" section of Chapter 8.

Business-type expenses

If you operate a business of your own, whether it's large or small, the costs associated with that business, such as advertising, printing, office rent, and myriad other things, are allowed as deductions. The logic here is that business expenses are legitimate deductions if they are a required part of conducting your business. Who decides what constitutes required parts of doing business? The IRS, of course. See Chapter 7 for more information.

Special Tax Bonuses

In addition to deductions from your income, you can reduce your tax bite, such as it is, in special ways. These little tricks are known as *tax credits* (see Chapter 12). A tax credit is a direct reduction of your income tax as opposed to a reduction of your income. The child and dependent care credit is an example. Once the amount of the credit is calculated, it reduces your income tax dollar for dollar.

Income Tax 101: Semester Review

You could pore over tax laws for years and still come away utterly confused and not much better off than you are right now in terms of being ready to confront your tax return. The laws change regularly, the interpretation of the laws changes even more frequently, and the bottom line is, with TurboTax, you don't need to know much beyond the basics.

Understand the premise that incoming money is potentially subject to taxation and that expenditures are potentially allowed as means for reducing the taxable income, keep these facts in mind as you go through the year earning money and spending it, and save receipts; and you should be able to look your tax return packet in the eye rather than hiding it under the newspapers, hoping that it will get taken out with the trash.

Part II
Tax Preparation Can Be Fun

The 5th Wave   By Rich Tennant

Dave gets ready to prepare his tax return

In this part...

This part takes you by the hand and leads you right through the entire process of getting information from that formidable pile of receipts on the table into the TurboTax program.

Before you launch into this process, it's probably time to order a nice, big pizza (sausage and extra cheese, if you don't mind) and lay in a supply of your favorite cold, fizzy soft drink. Save the filet mignon and the bottle of red wine for the stick-that-tax-return-in-the-mail celebration.

Chapter 5
Revving Up TurboTax

· ·

In This Chapter

▶ Choosing between EasyStep and direct access to forms

▶ Hearing a voice from the grave: last year's tax return

▶ Jumping from TaxLink to Quicken

▶ Moving around in the TurboTax Interview

▶ Flitting from form to form

▶ Recognizing menus and buttons

▶ Fooling around in the File Cabinet

▶ Saving your tax return

▶ Doing slick things with your mouse

▶ Getting out of TurboTax

· ·

*T*urboTax: The very name conjures up images of high-speed chases around the Indianapolis 500 Motor Speedway track. And just like those finely tuned Indy cars that circle the track each May, TurboTax as a computer program can be tweaked and tuned until it, too, runs like a champ. Knowing how to do it takes a little start-up time, however — a pace lap or two, if you will. Consider this chapter your resource when the engine sputters rather than hums.

On Your Mark, Get Set . . .

To start the TurboTax program and get things rolling, double-click the Uncle Sam hat icon on your Program Manager screen. From Windows 95, click the Start button, select Programs, click the TurboTax for Windows folder, and then click TurboTax for Windows.

The following list takes you through the start-up steps of getting your tax return preparation underway with TurboTax:

1. **Click Next on the initial TurboTax screen to get things moving.**

2. **Click Continue EasyStep to get things moving a little further along.**

   Be sure to take a moment to appreciate the cool floating yellow arrows that TurboTax has created for your viewing pleasure (see Figure 5-1).

Figure 5-1:
Imagine if
you will
another
universe,
one in which
arrows float
across your
screen
seemingly
unrestricted
by
gravitational
forces....

Cool floating yellow arrow

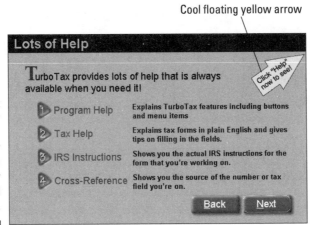

3. **Click Next to really get things moving.**

4. **Click Next again.**

   Things should be moving along any time now.

5. **Click Name Your Tax Return.**

   TurboTax gives you a chance to name your tax return and save it. The program has already chosen the name UNTITLED.TAX for you. If you like that name, although I can't imagine that you would, click OK; otherwise, type the name of your choice in place of UNTITLED.TAX. Keep your tax return filename to eight or fewer letters or numbers. (Of course, if you're using Windows 95, you can use more than eight letters for your filename.) Click OK after you finish naming the baby.

6. **Import information from last year's version of TurboTax, Quicken, or another personal finance program.**

   (See "Quicken and Other Transferable Programs" later in this chapter for further information about this option.) If you prepared your tax return with TurboTax last year, you can click Import from TurboTax and save yourself a lot of work by bringing in tons of information from last year's return. Click Skip if you're not going to import.

7. **Click Next to proceed into the Interview.**

   Here TurboTax asks you probing questions about how much money you made last year and what you spent it on.

8. **Click Start Interview to start the Interview a little more.**

9. **Click Let's Get Started to really start the Interview.**

Two-Step, Sidestep, EasyStep: Choosing between EasyStep and the Forms Method

The first important decision you have to make with TurboTax is whether to use the EasyStep method for preparing your tax return or the you're-on-your-own classic approach, otherwise known as the *Forms method*.

EasyStep is a method that takes you by the hand and leads you through your tax return, line by line, form by form, asking sensible-sounding questions and directing you on a straight path through the melee of taxland. It's hard to miss a form needed for your tax return if you answer all the EasyStep questions truthfully.

The *Forms method* lets you pick and choose the forms you think you need for your tax return, and then it lets you fill out those forms one line at a time with no guidance. Use the Forms method only after your tax return is basically completed, when you have to go back and add one thing to your tax return and you're sure you know where that one thing goes. Read about moving in and out of EasyStep and the Forms method later in this chapter in "Getting Around in TurboTax."

There's just no downside to preparing your tax return with EasyStep. Leave the Forms method for the folks who think that they know more about preparing taxes than this program does.

 There are three different types of federal income tax return forms: 1040EZ, 1040A, and the regular 1040. The 1040EZ and 1040A are simplified versions of the 1040. You don't have to know the difference between these forms, nor do you have to make a choice. TurboTax keeps an eye on the information you give it, and if you qualify to file one of the simpler forms, then TurboTax prepares that form for you. It's all automatic.

Back to the Future: Importing from Last Year's Tax Return

Before you dig into preparing your 1995 tax return, you have a chance to import information from your 1994 tax return or from Quicken. If you prepared your tax return with TurboTax last year and want to save yourself the time and effort of retyping lots of basic information, choose Import from TurboTax. Then click Start TurboTax Import, and up pops a box from which you can choose the file containing last year's return.

The process of importing information from last year's tax return transfers things like your name, address, social security number, information about your dependents, your employer's name, names of places that paid you income in 1994, and amounts from last year's tax return that have a place on this year's return as well. It's a big time-saver.

If you can find your way to last year's tax return from the pop-up box that stares at you from center-screen, select the filename, click OK, and go on to the section, "Name, Rank, Serial Number, Please," in Chapter 6. If you're still looking for last year's tax return file, the next couple of paragraphs tell you how to find lost files.

Figure 5-2 shows you a rendition of what you may see on your screen. The name of the current 1995 tax return file you are working on, as well as any others you may have saved for this year, is listed on the left side of the box with *.TAX* added to the name.

Figure 5-2:
Looking for
last year's
tax return
file.

Select Return to Transfer from		?☒
File name:	Folders:	OK
*.tax	d:\tax95w	Cancel
dummies.tax	🗀 d:\	Network...
dummies1.tax	📁 tax95w	
garbage.tax	🗀 1040_95	
List files of type:	Drives:	
Tax Files (*.tax)	💾 d: gap2	

In the middle of this box, you can see your current drive, the TAX95W directory, and the 1040_95 directory under it. Change the directory so that you are looking at the TAX94 directory. To change directories, point to the current drive with your mouse arrow (mine is D:\) and then click twice on the drive letter. Doing so drops down a list of the names of all kinds of directories that live on that drive. Scroll down through this list, as shown in Figure 5-3, until you see TAX94.

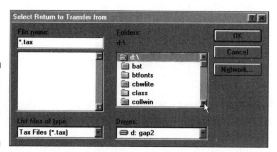

Figure 5-3:
Find the
TAX94
directory.

Click twice on the TAX94 directory name, and your 1994 tax files appear on the left side of the box. Click the filename over on the left and then click OK.

Taxpayers who use Quicken and other personal finance programs can import 1995 financial information directly into their tax returns. If you fall into this category and want to find out more about this process, see the following section.

If you plan to import last year's tax return from TurboTax and also plan to import this year's financial information from Quicken or some other personal finance program, perform the TurboTax import first.

Quicken and Other Transferable Programs

Quicken is a finance program that is at home dealing with both your personal finances and your business, if you have one. It keeps track of day-to-day monetary transactions and enables you to produce summary reports that give you the perspective to make intelligent financial decisions. From a tax stand-point, Quicken is a winner: You've already got a huge head start on the prepara-tion of your tax return if you use Quicken all year to track your income and expenses (translate: deductions).

Quicken isn't the only financial-planning program on the market. Several programs produce information similar to Quicken. The biggest advantage to using Quicken in conjunction with TurboTax is that the programs are made by the same company and there is a direct link between the two programs. You can view your Quicken information on-screen from TurboTax and even make changes to Quicken via TurboTax. You'll find, however, that most of the major competing products also can create files that TurboTax can read, so don't feel that you have to trash a program you already have.

Check the documentation that comes with your finance program. See whether it includes a chapter on sending information to tax software — look in the index under topics such as *tax, export,* and *TurboTax.* If the financial program can communicate with a tax program like TurboTax, chances are it will tout that fact.

If you use Quicken, it doesn't matter which version you use — they all provide information that you can import into TurboTax and meld with your tax return.

To import information into TurboTax from Quicken or another financial program, follow these steps:

1. **Before you try to bring the information into TurboTax, assign your account categories to tax lines within the financial program.**

   This procedure varies among programs, but you should be able to find it in the same area where you create or edit account names. Look at the financial accounts and figure out where on your tax return they would appear: Medical expenses go on Schedule A for itemized deductions, interest income goes on Schedule B, business expenses go on Schedule C, and so on.

2. **If you are using Quicken 4 or 5 for Windows, you can exit the Quicken Program and proceed to step 3. If you are using any other program, follow the procedures in the financial program to create a tax report, a tax export file, or a TXF (tax transfer) file.**

   Remember the name that you give to the tax file.

3. **Turn on your TurboTax program.**

4. **From the Import tab of EasyStep, choose Import from Quicken.**

5. **If you are using Quicken 4 or 5 for Windows, click TaxLink.**

   TurboTax displays the name of the Quicken file you most recently used. If that is the correct file, click Continue. If you want a different Quicken file, click Browse. Find the correct file on the Open file window that TurboTax displays, click OK after designating the correct Quicken file, and then click Continue. See step 6 for the cool stuff you can do with TaxLink.

   or

5. **If you are using a program other than Quicken 4 or 5, choose Import from other (TXF), click Report Ready, and then select the TXF file from the Select TXF File for Import window that opens on-screen.**

   Make sure that you select the correct filename for the file containing your tax data (you deposited that filename in your brain bank in step 2, remember?) and click OK.

With Quicken Versions 4 and 5, you get to take advantage of TaxLink, the TurboTax feature that gives you access to your Quicken files from within TurboTax. In the TaxLink screen, you see a display of all your Quicken categories. You can expand a category to see the individual transactions within it, view the categories that have been assigned to lines in your tax return, assign a category (or even a specific transaction within a category) to a particular tax line, and unassign a category from a tax line. Figure 5-4 displays the TaxLink arena. After you're finished playing with TaxLink, click the Close button to send your Quicken data racing to your tax return.

Click here to see all
the categories that
are linked to tax lines

Click here to see
all the categories
in your Quicken file

Click here to see all the
categories that are not
linked to tax lines

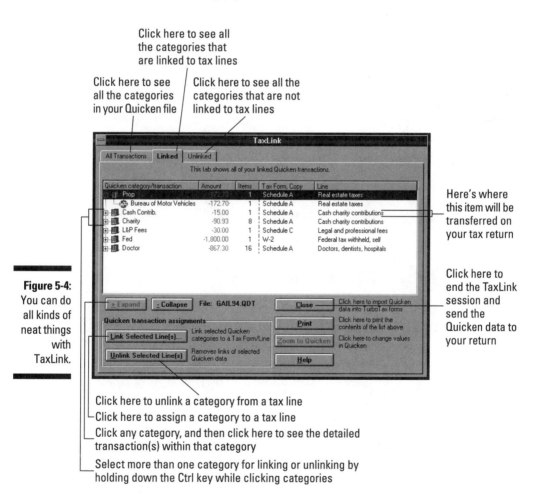

Figure 5-4:
You can do
all kinds of
neat things
with
TaxLink.

Here's where
this item will be
transferred on
your tax return

Click here to
end the TaxLink
session and
send the
Quicken data to
your return

Click here to unlink a category from a tax line

Click here to assign a category to a tax line

Click any category, and then click here to see the detailed
transaction(s) within that category

Select more than one category for linking or unlinking by
holding down the Ctrl key while clicking categories

At this point, the data from your financial planning program has been incorporated into your current year tax return.

TurboTax gives you an extra-added bonus if you use Quicken 4 or 5 for Windows. The little TaxLink button at the top of the EasyStep screen allows you to communicate directly with Quicken from within TurboTax. Click this button, and you are transported back to Quicken and given an on-screen display of your Quicken files and the tax lines to which they are linked. You can add or change these linkages from this screen. When you're finished playing in Quicken, click the Close button, and you're back at TurboTax. Any changes you make to tax lines in Quicken update your TurboTax program when you close TaxLink. Information that you have already imported from Quicken is not duplicated.

If you decide that you don't want to perform the import transplant while you're still looking at the Quicken screen, *don't click the Close button.* Instead, click the control bar (the little minus sign in the upper-left corner of the window) and choose Close. Or press Ctrl+F4. Or press Esc. Or scream, "Wait a minute! I don't want to do this!" One of these choices is sure to get you out of the import process without a scar.

After you transfer information from Quicken, you may have a change of heart. If you decide that you don't want the Quicken (or other financial software program) information in your tax return (if, for example, you are afraid of duplicating Quicken's imported information with original data you type in your tax return), you can *unimport* the information. Click the File menu and choose Remove Imported Data. Presto! The imported information vanishes.

Getting Around in TurboTax

It's pretty easy to move from one place to another in TurboTax. Say you're answering questions in the EasyStep Interview and you remember something that you forgot to include on a prior screen. You can hop from one place to another in a couple of ways — without ever leaving the Interview.

✔ Click the Back button or press Alt+B on your keyboard. Either option backs you up one screen at a time.

✔ Click the Interview Navigator button at the top of the screen (as indicated in Figure 5-5) or press Alt+V. At the My Tax Data tab (see Figure 5-6), you see all the information you have entered in your tax return thus far. Click the item you want to revise. Click the Interview button, and TurboTax returns you to the precise point in the Interview where you entered this information. Click the Go to Forms button, and TurboTax sends you out of EasyStep to the actual tax form where you can enter additional information.

Figure 5-5:
Click the
Interview
Navigator
button to
relocate
yourself
within
TurboTax.

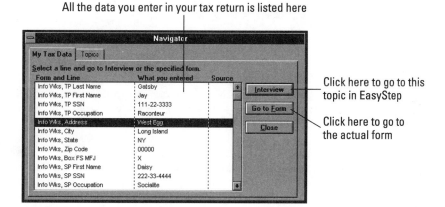

All the data you enter in your tax return is listed here

Figure 5-6:
TurboTax's
spiffy new
Navigator.

Click here to go to this
topic in EasyStep

Click here to go to
the actual form

✔ To get to a particular part in the Interview process, with the Interview
Navigator open, click the Topics tab. You can select from the entire
spectrum of tax form topics available to you in the Interview process. As
illustrated in Figure 5-7, the checked boxes indicate topics that you have
completed, and unchecked boxes indicate topics that you still need to
complete or that might not apply at all to your tax return.

Figure 5-7:
Click any
topic and
then click
the
Interview
button, and
TurboTax
transports
you to the
Interview
questions
about the
selected
topic.

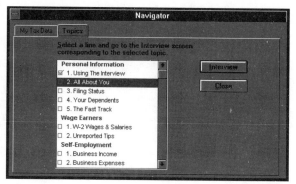

Jump around in the Interview to prior topics if you forgot something, but then go right back to where you left off. You can tell where you left off by the check marks on the Interview Topics drop-down menu.

Don't skip sections of the Interview. The Interview asks so many pertinent questions that it's foolish to skip sections. Even if you're certain that a particular section doesn't apply to you, play along and let TurboTax do the thinking for you.

You can leave the Interview entirely and venture out into the land of choosing your own forms by clicking at the bottom-right corner of your screen on the little Go to Forms button — the one that looks like a preschooler's fat pencil — or by pressing Alt+G on your keyboard.

Anytime you're in the Forms mode and want to return to the safety of the Interview, find the EasyStep button at the top of the Forms screen (it looks like footprints) and click it. Clicking this button gives you a choice of going into the EasyStep Interview for the form you are currently working with or resuming EasyStep at the place you left off.

Pick a Form, Any Form

When you're using the Forms method, you can select any form — either to observe or to edit — by clicking the Forms button at the top of the screen (the one with the little blank pages on it). Clicking this button pops up a list of *all* available forms — not just the ones that might be appropriate to your tax return. Click the one that interests you; then click OK to open that form. You can select only one form at a time from this list, but you can go back to the list as many times as you like, opening many forms one on top of another. You also have the option of showing a list of just the forms in your tax return. Click the Show all forms in your current formset button to display the tax forms in use on your tax return. Then click the Show My Return button in the Open Form window that appears. If you plan on opening several forms, you can keep this window on-screen by clicking the Keep this Open checkbox.

When multiple forms are open in the Forms mode, flip among them by clicking the Window menu and selecting the form you want to have on top. Choosing Window⇨Cascade lets you see all the forms nicely layered with their title bars showing in flirtatious display. Just click a title bar to yank that form out of the stack and put it on top of the pile.

Too many forms cluttering your screen? Close a form by double-clicking the control menu, the little minus sign in the upper-left corner of the form. Doing so doesn't remove the form from your tax return, but only clears a little space for you on-screen.

I'll Have a Tuna on Rye: The Menu System

As if there aren't enough choices for you on-screen, between all the buttons and drop-down lists, you can look to the menus for more options. Some of the menu items may appear gray from time to time; when a menu item is gray, that item is not currently available to you. You may find it available by switching modes. Some choices are available only in the Forms method, while others apply only to EasyStep.

You can access each menu choice in one of two ways: either by clicking it or by pressing the Alt key on your keyboard followed by the underlined letter of the menu item.

For an example of the second option, you can select Show My Return from the Forms menu by pressing Alt+O,M. Pressing Alt activates the menu bar, *O* is the underscored letter in *Forms,* and *M* is the underscored letter in *My.* As I discuss the menu options, I indicate the letters that you can press from the keyboard by underscoring them (for example, Forms⇨Show My Return).

Don't hold down the Alt key while you are pressing underscored letters; you'll just confuse poor TurboTax. Press and release Alt and then press underscored letters to activate menu choices. And if you get caught in menu limbo — if, say, you've already pressed the Alt key but now you've changed your mind and want to leave the menus — either press the Esc key twice or click the mouse button with the pointer on the actual tax form.

Here's a brief survey of your menu choices:

The File menu, shown in Figure 5-8, includes the New, Open, Save, Print, and Exit stuff that you see in many Windows programs, along with a few unique items:

File	
New Tax Return	Ctrl+N
Open Tax Return	Ctrl+O
Save	Ctrl+S
Save As	
Goto State	
Remove State ...	
Transfer '94 ...	
TaxLink	
Import...	
Remove Imported Data	
Print...	Ctrl+P
Print Setup	
Electronic Filing	
1 DUMMIES1.TAX	
2 GARBAGE.TAX	
Exit	

Figure 5-8:
The File menu.

- ✔ **Goto State** takes changes that you've made to your federal tax return since you prepared your state return and relays those changes to the state return.

- ✔ **TaxLink** lets you into your Quicken program to assign items to tax forms (see the section on "Quicken and Other Transferable Programs" earlier in this chapter for more details about Quicken TaxLink).

- ✔ **Import** lets you import tax-related information from Quicken or other financial planning programs.

- ✔ **Remove Imported Data** removes information imported from Quicken and other financial planning programs.

- ✔ **Electronic Filing** prepares the form needed to accompany the electronic transmittal of your tax return. See Chapter 13 for information about how electronic filing works.

Basic Windows operations like Undo, Copy, Cut, and Paste appear on the Edit menu, as in Figure 5-9 — and so do the following TurboTax features:

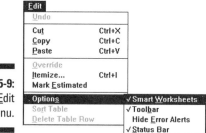

Figure 5-9:
The Edit
menu.

✔ **Override:** Use this operation (at your own risk) to ignore TurboTax's calculation and insert one of your own.

✔ **Itemize:** Create a detailed schedule of what makes up a particular number on your tax return with the Itemize feature. You'll also find this option on a button at the top of the Forms mode screen (don't sweat this one yet; the section later in this chapter called "Buttons on the Toolbar" covers itemizing in detail).

✔ **Mark Estimated:** If you're plugging indefinite numbers in your tax return, you can use this option to mark a number as "estimated." The number appears in italics on your return to remind you that you have not entered the final number. In addition, items that you've marked as estimated show up on your error list so you won't forget and leave them in the return. After you indicate a number as estimated, this menu choice changes to Unmark Estimated. You can remove the italics when you're ready.

✔ **Options:** TurboTax displays a lot of cool timesaving stuff on-screen, like the toolbar buttons across the top of the Forms screen, a feature called Smart Worksheets that gives you live access to the details that make up a number on your tax return, error alert messages that pop up on your screen when you're not looking, and the status bar that appears across the bottom of your screen and shows the name of the tax form currently displayed. Control the display of these features with the Options option.

Items on the Forms menu, shown in Figure 5-10, are available to you only when you are in the Forms mode. They help you select and move around in various forms.

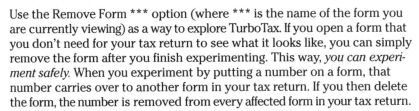

Figure 5-10:
The Forms
menu.

✔ **Show All Forms:** Choose any form you like from a master list of all available forms.

✔ **Show My Return:** See a list of all forms currently in use in your tax return and choose any one of them to view. If you open a form that is missing information, press the F7 key; TurboTax whisks you to the first line that needs information. Pressing F7 over and over again takes you through the entire form to each incomplete line.

✔ **QuickZoom to:** Click a number on a tax form and notice QuickZoom at the bottom of the screen on the right side in the status bar. You can quickly access the input worksheet or tax form that the number comes from either by selecting this menu choice or by double-clicking the number.

✔ **Remove Form 1040:** Remove Form 1040? What? Actually, whichever form is currently displayed on your screen will be listed here as Remove Form ***, and you can select this menu item to zap an unwanted form into oblivion.

Use the Remove Form *** option (where *** is the name of the form you are currently viewing) as a way to explore TurboTax. If you open a form that you don't need for your tax return to see what it looks like, you can simply remove the form after you finish experimenting. This way, *you can experiment safely.* When you experiment by putting a number on a form, that number carries over to another form in your tax return. If you then delete the form, the number is removed from every affected form in your tax return.

✔ **Link Field:** If more than one place in your tax return could be a logical source of a given number, this option lets you designate the place where TurboTax should look for the number.

✔ **Select Line:** Use this option to select a specific line number on the currently displayed form. Type a line number, click OK, or press Enter, and presto! Your cursor goes to that line.

✔ **Form Errors:** Select this option to display a list of all errors and problem areas in your tax return. Then double-click any item in the list to go directly to that part of your tax return.

✔ **Find Next Error:** When you need to find open, unfinished items on a form, or items that don't make sense to TurboTax (things that generate error messages), select this menu option (or press the F7 key) with a form showing on-screen. Your cursor jumps to the first unfinished (or incorrect) item. Select this menu choice again and move to the next item. Keep going until you get a congratulatory message from TurboTax telling you that all the open items on that form have been fixed. When you see this message, you'll know that you've filled in all information to TurboTax's satisfaction.

✔ **Magnify:** Zoom in or out depending on whether you prefer a close-up view or a bird's-eye view of your tax return. Choose from Thumb to 200% and many points in between.

The items on the EasyStep menu, shown in Figure 5-11, give you the option of moving from one tabbed heading to another in EasyStep. Choosing one of these seven choices — Start, Import, Interview, Review, Filing, State, and Finish — is the same as clicking the appropriate tab. While you're in the Forms mode, choose Go to EasyStep to return to EasyStep. If you're already in EasyStep, Go to Forms takes you back to the forms (it's the same as clicking the big pencil at the bottom-right corner of the screen).

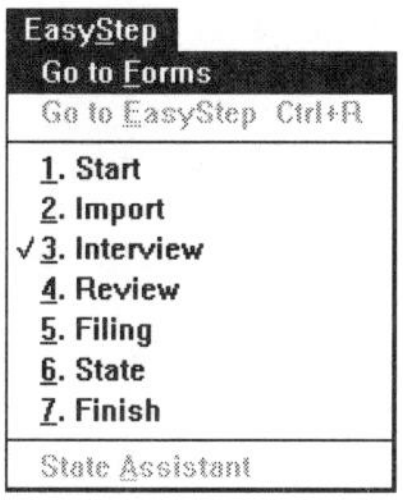

Figure 5-11:
The
EasyStep
menu.

EasyStep
Go to Forms
Go to EasyStep Ctrl+R
1. Start
2. Import
✓ 3. Interview
4. Review
5. Filing
6. State
7. Finish
State Assistant

The State Assistant option on the EasyStep menu is available only when you are working on a state tax return. Click this option when your state return is displayed, and TurboTax shows you its state checklist feature. The checklist is full of questions that refer to information that TurboTax needs to complete your state tax return — information that it couldn't find in your federal tax return. Read the items on the checklist and fill in the blanks.

The Window menu provides standard Windows stuff for dealing with multiple windows — Tile, Cascade, and Arrange Icons — and lets you view several windows in different ways. At the bottom of this menu, you see a listing of all currently open forms that you can select by number or by clicking the form name (four forms are open in the example in Figure 5-12; the form on top of the screen is the one checked).

Figure 5-12:
The Window
menu.

The Tools menu choices (see Figure 5-13) that relate specifically to TurboTax include the following:

Figure 5-13:
The Tools
menu.

✓ **My Tax Data:** Choose this option to go to the listing of every item you've entered in this tax return. Click an item and then choose Go to Form to go to the form on which that item is entered.

✓ **Final Review:** This takes you to the Review tab in the EasyStep method.

✓ **File Cabinet:** Choose File Cabinet to display a list of income and expense categories. Select a category that fits one of your miscellaneous receipts and find yourself whisked to the appropriate form for that item.

✓ **Calculator:** Pop up a calculator on-screen.

✓ **Tax Summary:** Access the pop-up analysis of your tax liability and refund or balance due. This summary is updated continuously as you enter information into your tax return and is accessible both in the Forms method and EasyStep (in EasyStep, you can just click the Summary button on the right side of the screen).

✓ **What-if Worksheet:** Select this option to experiment with different tax scenarios. How much tax will you pay if you get a raise? How will your tax differ if you prepare your return using the Married Filing Separate status instead of Married Filing Jointly?

✓ **History Worksheet:** See how your tax returns compare over time. This option is only available if you imported tax information from last year into this year's tax return.

✔ **Plan Mode:** Use this feature to experiment with your 1996 tax return and estimate what your 1996 tax situation will be. Plan Mode takes your 1995 tax return numbers and throws them into a 1996 setting based on whatever was known about 1996 tax laws when the TurboTax program was finalized.

Save your 1995 tax return in a separate file before you begin playing with Plan Mode. Plan Mode overwrites your 1995 numbers with a 1996 scenario. This experiment should be performed in a file separate from your actual 1995 tax return. Even if you're finished with your 1995 return, you still should keep it in a separate file so that it will be available for importation into next year's TurboTax program.

✔ **Tax Graphs:** Take a look at graphical on-screen displays of Income Sources, Deductions, Tax Analysis, and Where Your Money Goes.

Get on-screen help either in the form of general tax assistance (Tax Help) or TurboTax guidance (Program Help) from the Help menu, shown in Figure 5-14. But be forewarned: Some items on the Help menu don't appear at all times.

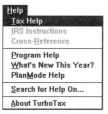

Figure 5-14:
The Help
menu.

✔ **IRS/State Instructions** gives you the official word from the tax authorities about the form displayed at the top of your screen. (This option is not available in the HeadStart version.)

✔ **PlanMode Help** provides assistance with the TurboTax Plan Mode, a method of tax planning for 1995. (This option also is not available in the HeadStart version.)

✔ **Cross-Reference** is handy if you're stumped about how in the world TurboTax came up with a particular number. Click a number while in the Forms mode, and then choose Cross-Reference from the Help menu to see which form generated the number.

✔ **Search for Help On** displays a comprehensive list of TurboTax topics. Scroll through the list or type the topic of your choice at the top of this help window. When you find the topic about which you want help, click Display to show the help information on-screen or Print to print a hard copy of the information.

> ✔ **What's New This Year** gives you a capsule summary of changes in the tax
> laws since you prepared your 1994 tax return.
>
> ✔ **About TurboTax** tells you which version of the software you're using.

Secret Messages on the Status Bar

The TurboTax status bar appears at the bottom of your screen. In the right
corner of this bar, TurboTax frequently displays a message that describes the
source of a particular number on your tax return. Click a number or other piece
of information on your tax form; then look at the right side of the status bar to
see one of the following messages:

> ✔ QuickZoom means that the selected item on the form comes from another
> form. Choose Cross-Reference from the Help menu to find out where the
> item originated.
>
> ✔ Calculated Value means that the TurboTax program has calculated
> the number.
>
> ✔ Text Input Field means that you have to type *text,* such as your name,
> from the keyboard — this is the original entry spot for text information.
>
> ✔ Numeric Input Field means that you have to type *numbers,* such as
> income, from the keyboard — this is the original entry spot for numerical
> data.
>
> ✔ Estimate means that you designated this field as an estimated value.
>
> ✔ Itemized Value means that you requested an itemized statement
> supporting a field (by clicking the Itemize button in either the Forms
> method or EasyStep when it is not dimmed); this message tells you that
> itemized details support the number.
>
> ✔ Overridden Value means that you've chosen to override a calculated
> value or an amount that carried from another form (by choosing Override
> from the Edit menu while in Forms mode).

Buttons on the Toolbar

The TurboTax toolbar, as pictured in Figure 5-15, provides you with shortcuts to
some of the more commonly used menu selections. This bar is available only
when you are using the Forms method. See the name of each toolbar button as
you pause your mouse pointer over the button.

The following buttons inhabit the toolbar.

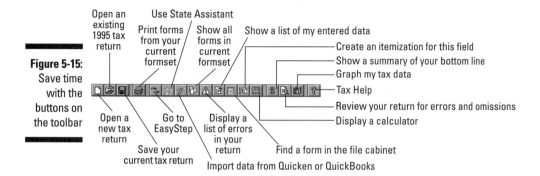

Figure 5-15:
Save time
with the
buttons on
the toolbar

Open an
existing
1995 tax
return

Use State Assistant

Print forms
from your
current
formset

Show all
forms in
current
formset

Show a list of my entered data

Create an itemization for this field

Show a summary of your bottom line

Graph my tax data

Tax Help

Review your return for errors and omissions

Display a calculator

Open a
new tax
return

Go to
EasyStep

Display a
list of errors
in your
return

Save your
current tax return

Find a form in the file cabinet

Import data from Quicken or QuickBooks

File It Here: The File Cabinet

Say your tax return is nearly complete, yet you still have some scraps of paper hanging around, property tax paid when you bought your auto license plates or dues paid to a professional organization. You may be a prime candidate for poking around in the File Cabinet.

Using the Forms method, from the Tools menu, you can choose File Cabinet. Start typing the topic you're looking for, and the list advances to that part of the alphabet (for example, begin typing **professional organizations**, and by the time you type **pro** you'll be at the Professional Organizations topic). Or, if you prefer the slower route, you can scroll through the available choices. Click a different drawer to get a different part of the alphabet.

Click the topic you want and then pick Select. TurboTax opens the appropriate form.

Protect Your Precious Data

Your tax return information is only as safe as the disk you save it on. And if you don't save it on a floppy disk, there may be trouble right here in River City. One little electrical storm or a friendly power surge, and your hard drive may take its place on the Frisbee field. To avoid having to kick yourself several times while you re-create hours of data, say Yes every time TurboTax asks whether you want to save your tax return, and remember to save to a floppy disk once in a while.

Each time you leave TurboTax — even if you only came in to peek and didn't change a single digit of a single number — TurboTax gives you the chance to save the return. Do it. It can't hurt.

Sneaky Mouse Tricks — Eeeek!

Your mouse may not be able to find its way out of a maze or deftly remove a bit of cheese without tripping the mousetrap, but that little critter *can* do some tricky things.

✔ Right mouse clicks open up a shortcut menu when you're using the Forms method. Depending on what you're up to on-screen, the menu choices may differ. Select a menu choice by clicking with the left mouse button.

✔ You can uncheck boxes on the tax return forms that have been checked (for example, the `Do you want $3 to go to the Presidential Election Campaign Fund?` box on page 1 of the 1040) simply by clicking them again with the mouse.

✔ Double-clicking any number on the tax return automatically opens the form that generated that number — assuming, of course, that the number came from another form. If the number was originally entered on the form, then a double-click opens an Itemization form on which you can enter details about the number.

✔ When you try to enter information directly on the forms in TurboTax (instead of using the EasyStep method), sometimes your pointer looks like an arrow and sometimes it looks like an I-beam (see Figure 5-16). When the pointer is an arrow, you are trying to type a number in a field that TurboTax wants to calculate for you, and TurboTax doesn't want you to mess with it. Using your mouse pointer, point at the space where you want to enter something and click. If the mouse pointer turns into an I-beam, thousands of coins will start falling out of your disk drive in the next five minutes. If I'm wrong, go ahead and enter your information. The I-beam means that you have the right-of-way to enter what you want. If the mouse pointer remains an arrow shape, you're out of luck on both counts.

Figure 5-16:
Either you can enter information directly onto the tax forms or you can't.

If you hope to enter information and click a space, and the mouse pointer remains shaped like an arrow, then TurboTax figures out the information for that space itself, either by computation or by carrying numbers over from another form. If you're determined to ignore what TurboTax wants to put into that space, you can *override* the entry by choosing Edit⇨Override from the menu or pressing Ctrl+D on your keyboard. Then you can enter your own number in the space. The number appears in red on a color monitor. Change your mind and want to undo an override? Choose Edit⇨Cancel Override, and the number reverts to whatever TurboTax thinks it should be.

Overriding a computation made by TurboTax is dangerous. TurboTax knows *much* about taxes, so be sure that you know what you're doing and that you understand thoroughly how TurboTax computed a number before you change it. And remember: TurboTax's guarantee of correct computations on your tax return no longer applies if you override numbers.

Finished for the Day

It's time for a good night's sleep, and you're ready to get out of TurboTax. Here's some good advice: *Always exit TurboTax properly.* Don't just turn off your computer if TurboTax is still on-screen. Leave the right way. Choose File⇨Exit or press Alt+F4 from the keyboard. When asked to save your return, click an emphatic *Yes,* and you're out. From the Windows Program Manager, you can choose how to end your day. You can leave the computer running or not, and you can exit Windows or not. As long as you leave the TurboTax program the right way, you're in no danger of suffering loss to your tax return data.

Chapter 6

Basic Training

• •

In This Chapter

▶ Putting basic information onto your tax return

▶ Picking a filing status

▶ Determining whether you can take the exemption given to senior citizens and the legally blind

▶ Figuring out who's a dependent and who's not

• •

I've done a great deal of talking about what TurboTax is and what it can do, and I've talked about what a tax return is and why we file the darn things. Now it's time to put the key in the ignition and see whether this baby can fly.

When you use the EasyStep method, TurboTax asks you lots of questions on the top half of your screen. The answers that you provide get dropped into your tax return on the bottom half of your screen.

This chapter deals with all the stuff that appears on the top half of the first page of your tax return — the nosy stuff like where you live, how many kids you have and how many months you let them live in your house, and whether you're married or at least acting like it.

All this information is vaguely related to how much tax you owe. Read on to see how you can get all this information into TurboTax and still have time to go out and catch a movie later.

Name, Rank, Serial Number, Please

When you begin preparing a tax return in TurboTax and get past all the intro-ductory stuff (see Chapter 5), TurboTax asks this question: Who are you preparing this return for? (The grammar may not be the greatest, but TurboTax gets the point across.) Your choices are Yourself or Yourself & Spouse.

If you choose Yourself, the program asks many of the ensuing questions in the second person: `Do *you* have any dependents to claim? Would *you* like to donate $3.00 to the Presidential Election Campaign Fund? Is there anything else *you* would like to tell the IRS before you're notified of your audit?` **(Just kidding.)**

Choose Yourself & Spouse, and TurboTax rewords its questions to accommodate the fact that this tax return is for two people.

The program then asks for the full name of each taxpayer. Move from one block to the next (such as First Name to M.I.) by pressing Enter or Tab. Move backward with Shift+Tab. After you enter full names, TurboTax asks you to provide a nickname for each person. I'm not joking. If you are filling out a tax return for your parents, for example, you may want your mother's and father's names to appear properly on all the forms. If you tell TurboTax at the nickname section that the tax return is for Mom and Dad, as shown in Figure 6-1, you start seeing questions like, `Did Mom and Dad have any gambling winnings in 1995?` or `Please enter the total amount Mom received, if any, for custom hire (machine work).`

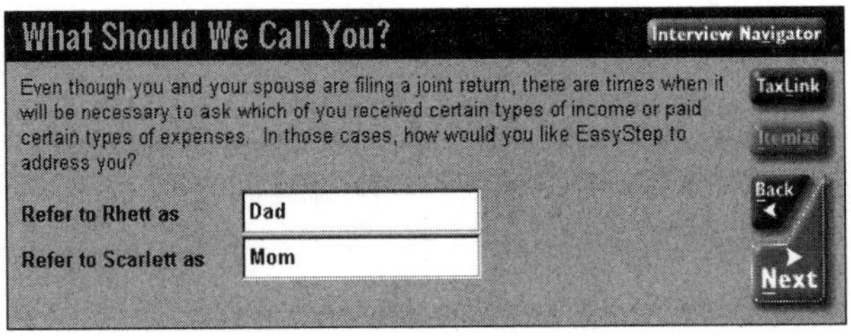

Figure 6-1:
TurboTax
uses
nicknames
to make tax
preparation
less formal.

What can I say? It's a friendly program.

What's in a number?

It's social security number time. Some people can recite their social security numbers forwards, backwards, and while standing on their heads. Others have to flip through all the cards in their wallet each time someone asks for the number. Card flippers will really appreciate the fact that TurboTax asks you only *once* for your social security number. Your social security number, by which you are known in all the major agencies of the U.S. government, must appear on every single tax form.

Of course, most people have better things to do with their time than type nine-digit numbers over and over again, trying to get the little dashes in just the right places. This is one of the reasons we have computers. Type the number once and then put the little card away. In fact, if you continue to use TurboTax in the future, you never have to type the number again — it carries over from one form to the next, from one year to the next. Such a luxury!

Home sweet home in a post office box

When TurboTax asks for your address (or Dad and Mom's address, as the case may be), the program is looking for your *mailing* address. This is the address to which your future tax returns, big refund checks, and all other correspondence with the IRS should be mailed. Some people use post office boxes or mailing companies that rent boxes for receiving mail, and that's okay with the IRS. Whatever address you would put on a telephone bill or a cereal mail-in offer is the address to put on your tax return.

Let me just say a word about that sticky mailing label that comes in the mail on your IRS booklet. The IRS mails your tax form and instruction booklet to you with a peel-off label attached to the front. You can take this label off the booklet and stick it on the top of your tax form when you are ready to send in your form. This label saves the IRS lots of time that it would otherwise use foolishly. If the stick-on label has the wrong address printed on it, the IRS would like you to cross off the wrong address, write in the correct address (good luck finding room!), and stick the corrected label on your tax return.

The problem with this label is that after you stick it on your return, you're stuck with it, so to speak. TurboTax will gladly print a new copy of your tax return if you change your mind about something, but then you've got the label stuck on the old return instead of the new, revised version. You have to peel the label off, maybe in a few pieces, find the Elmer's glue, and glue the pieces onto the revised tax return. Then maybe you decide to change something else in your tax return. Pretty soon, the stick-on label looks like it has seen better days — many of them.

Actually, if you look at the stick-on label, you see that it contains all sorts of secret codes that only the IRS understands. The tax form booklet that the IRS sends tells you what you need to know about these codes. Personally, secret IRS codes always worry me.

My advice on the matter of the label is this: Use the label if you want to, and don't if you don't want to. But don't stick it on until you have the final, final, final tax form that you want to turn in. And that's final.

Anyway, whether you use the label or not, TurboTax still waits patiently for you to enter your address. Go ahead and type your mailing address. Even if you plan to cover up the typed address with the label when you file your tax return, other forms that go with your tax return may require an address. This way, your address carries over to everyplace else.

Follow your mailing address with other requested information: telephone number, occupation, and so on. Some of this information is optional, but leaving it out generates an error message, so go ahead and answer all the questions now — this way, they won't come back to haunt you.

What Are You Going to Be When You Grow Up?

One of the snoopier questions asked on your tax return is the Occupation question. Just what do you call yourself, anyway? You may be tempted to pick some kind of exotic profession, such as King of England, Belly Dancer Extraordinaire, or Famous Sous Chef (what do sous chefs cook, anyway?). The tax return, however, is probably not the best place to play jokes. Go ahead and answer this question with as accurate a description as possible in the tiny space allotted. You've only got about 20 to 25 characters in which to describe your job, so be succinct. Your title at work may be General Manager of International Sales Operations, but Sales Manager is about all that will fit on this line.

Beechwood Aging and Fuzzy Vision

Not exactly well known for its generosity and kindness, the IRS shows its gentle side when giving consideration to taxpayers who are over 65 or have weak vision. An extra exemption is available for people who fall into this category.

What all this really means is that if you qualify as *elderly* (see the following section, "Will you still love me when I'm 65?") or *blind* (see the section, "Doctor's orders"), just answer affirmatively the questions posed by TurboTax. The program figures out how much that Yes answer is worth on your tax return.

Will you still love me when I'm 65?

Are you 65 years old? Sounds like an easy question. But nothing is easy when the IRS is concerned. TurboTax figures out whether you meet the requirements of this exemption when you fill in your date of birth in the section where you give your name and address. To qualify for an over-65 exemption, you must be at least 65 years old on January 1, 1996. Notice that's *1996,* not 1995. Just one of those extra little benefits for New Year's Day babies. You probably got your picture in the paper on the day you were born, too.

Doctor's orders

Sometimes you may feel like you're blind (especially when you ran into the back end of that pickup truck last week), but in order to answer the `Were you legally blind as of December 31, 1995?` question, you must meet at least one of the following tests:

- ✔ You are completely blind.
- ✔ Your vision is no better that 20/200 in your best eye while wearing your glasses or contact lenses, as attested to by your eye doctor.
- ✔ Your field of vision is 20 degrees or less, as attested to by your eye doctor.

You have to have a statement signed by your eye doctor supporting either the second or the third item. Attach a copy of this statement to your tax return in the first year that the situation applies. In future years, attach a statement of your own to your tax return saying that you sent the eye doctor's statement in a previous year.

Who's Taking Care of Whom? Being Claimed as a Dependent

TurboTax asks whether you (or Mom, or whomever you are preparing this return for) can be claimed as a dependent on someone else's return. Again, please?

Suppose you had a rough year and moved in with your folks, and they supported you for, say, eight months until you managed to get back on your feet. Based on the rules of claiming dependents (see "The Great April 14 Search for Dependents," later in this chapter), your parents can say that you are their dependent. If they are going to take advantage of this option, in addition to giving them extra nice presents on their birthdays, answer an emphatic Yes to TurboTax's question about being claimed on someone else's return (see Figure 6-2) by clicking the Yes box.

Figure 6-2:
Tell the truth: Is someone else claiming you as a dependent?

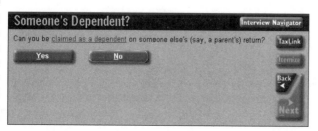

If a parent or anyone else has the right to claim you as a dependent (even if they don't actually claim you), you must answer this question affirmatively. Otherwise, pick No.

The Prez Campaign: Will They Call It Off If We All Agree Not to Contribute?

One of the strangest things to be added to the federal income tax return in recent years is the right to designate $3 of your tax money to the Presidential Election Campaign Fund. When TurboTax asks you whether you want to contribute to this fund, it states that making this contribution neither increases your tax nor reduces your refund.

What the heck does that mean? Here's a little illustration to show you how it works.

Amount	What Happens to It
$5,000	Withholding
$4,500	Tax liability
$500	Refund due to you

Say your total income tax for the year is $4,500 and that $5,000 was withheld from your paycheck during the year. As a result, you can look forward to a refund of $500.

If you check No to the presidential relief fund question, you get $500 and the government gets $4,500 to do with as it pleases. If you check Yes, you still get $500, the coffers of the Presidential Election Campaign Fund are fattened by $3, and the government gets $4,497 to spend as it sees fit.

Does it make sense now? Do you care? It always seems to me that presidential candidates spend what they want to whether they have my $3 or not, but hey, what do I know?

Unidentified Flying Electronic Tax Returns (UFETRs)

At an early stage in your tax return preparation, TurboTax asks whether you want to file your tax return electronically. Being able to file an electronic tax return simply means that you have the right to have your tax return dispatched

A TurboTax space odyssey

Jules Verne, who took a journey inside the human body in *Fantastic Voyage* and toured the bowels of Earth in *Journey to the Center of the Earth*, could surely have done something creative with the concept of tax returns zooming through the telephone wires, bouncing off satellite dishes, and causing major traffic accidents as they careen across highways.

But alas, he's gone, and you're stuck with me. Let's see. Imagine if you will a spring morning: birds chirping, flowers blooming, and children rushing off to school. Suddenly, school buses full of innocent children and carpools full of business-suited ladies and gentlemen begin veering right and left, dodging great flying sheaves of tax return forms shooting through the air at lightning speeds. Birds are knocked down out of the sky, covered with tiny paper cuts on their wings. Forest fires in the western states are ignited and then ravage out of control, consuming thousands of important tax documents in their wake. Trains derail. Airplanes crash. Riverboats capsize. The electronic tax returns! They're everywhere!

All right, so it needs a little work.

from one computer (that of the dispatcher) to another (that of the IRS). If you've ever sent anything over telephone wires by using a modem, then you can probably envision that of which I speak. It's not anything you can see — it's all done by magic.

At this point, answering affirmatively doesn't start sending tax waves out of your computer; it merely primes TurboTax to prepare the correct forms that accompany the electronic transfer of your tax return.

Just for the record, you are still required to send in signed paperwork with your electronically filed return.

For more information about preparing and sending your tax return electronically (and safely), see Chapter 13.

1040PC: A Politically Correct Tax Return?

The 1040PC is the IRS's acknowledgment that people everywhere are learning about and using personal computers. That's right: PC stands for *personal computer*, not *politically correct* and not *popcorn*. You can prepare a standard

1040 form by using TurboTax, or you can prepare your return in *1040PC format.* The 1040PC format is a series of coded pages that can be read through scanners into the IRS's computer.

Why would you want to file your file in this format? Don't ask me. It seems like a great deal of trouble. You still have to print the darn thing and mail it in, just like any other tax return. The theory is that some computer at the IRS will suck it right in, rather than having to wait for real people to type in your numbers, and maybe you'll get your refund a little quicker.

If you want to give it a try, go ahead and continue to prepare your tax return in TurboTax the way you normally would. After you are finished, proceed to the EasyStep Filing tab and select the 1040PC option. See the section in Chapter 13 called "Partial High-Tech with the 1040PC" for further instructions.

TurboTax Does State Tax Returns

Okay, I know it costs a little extra, but one of the nicest things TurboTax does for taxpayers is to provide software for state tax returns. For 1995 tax returns, TurboTax has a software program for every state that has state income tax. You have to buy the program separately, but you may find it worth the additional cost (go to the same store that sold you the federal version of TurboTax, or order it directly from Intuit — an order form comes in the box that contains your federal program). If you decide to use TurboTax to prepare your state income tax return, click Yes when asked, Are you planning to use this program to prepare your state return? TurboTax then lets you indicate your primary state of residence. (If you lived in more than one state in 1995, you will have an opportunity when you prepare your state return to indicate the other state(s) in which you lived.)

Using TurboTax to prepare your state tax return can save you lots of time. You can rely on TurboTax to accurately transfer amounts from your federal return to your state return. If an amount changes on your federal return, you can request that your state return be updated, too. See Chapter 12 for information about using the state tax software.

Married Filing Jointly, Single Filing Separately, Separate Filing Together — What's the Deal?

As you proceed through the questions TurboTax asks, you come to the question about filing status. This is the IRS's way of finding out whether you are single, married, or somewhere in between. Did you ever wonder whether that nice couple down the street is really married or just happily coexisting? The IRS knows.

Once again, this is a good time to look at last year's tax return. Chances are, you are still of the same status as last year. If the situation has changed and you are uncertain just what category you fall into, check the following IRS Stuff.

Your filing status helps to determine the rates at which your tax is assessed, so pay close attention and pick the one that describes your situation:

✔ **Single:** You were not married as of December 31, 1995, or you were legally separated as of December 31, 1995, according to a divorce or separate maintenance decree.

✔ **Married Filing Jointly:** You were married as of December 31, 1995.

✔ **Married Filing Separate:** Same rules as for Married Filing Jointly.

It is sometimes advantageous to file separately even though you qualify to file a joint tax return. If one spouse can claim a great deal of itemized deductions, such as medical expenses, that would be limited by the combined Adjusted Gross Income were both spouses to file jointly (see

Can you officially file as a head of household?

In order to file your tax return as a head of household, you must be paying at least half the living expenses for one of the following:

✔ **A parent:** The parent does not have to live in your home, but you must be able to claim the parent as your dependent. (See "The Great April 14 Search for Dependents.")

✔ **An unmarried child:** The child does not have to be your dependent but must have lived with you in your home for at least half the year.

✔ **A married child:** The child must be your dependent and must have lived with you in your home for at least half the year.

"Have Deductions, Will Itemize" in Chapter 8), their tax rates will be lower if they file separately. If you think that this situation may be applicable to you, go ahead and use TurboTax to prepare separate returns for you and your spouse and compare the tax rates with those calculated in a jointly filed return.

✔ **Head of Household:** You were not married as of December 31, 1995 (or you were separated and lived apart from your spouse for at least the last half of 1995) *and* you paid over half the cost of keeping up a home for all of 1995 for your parent or your child(ren). This head-of-household stuff gets hairy. If you think that you qualify, see the following IRS Stuff sidebar for the nitty-gritty.

✔ **Qualifying Widow(er):** Your spouse died in 1993, 1994, or 1995, and you did not remarry by December 31, 1995. You have a child whom you claim as a dependent, the child lived in your home for all of 1995, you paid over half the cost of keeping up your home for the child, and you could have filed a joint return in the year in which your spouse died.

The Great April 14 Search for Dependents

You probably already know how many dependents you have. If you filed a tax return last year, check page 1 of your old return and see whether any of the players have changed. Chances are, you just have to copy those names when TurboTax asks you to list your dependents.

If you used TurboTax last year, the program carries your dependents forward to this year's tax return. Magic! You need only enter new dependents or delete those who no longer qualify. If nothing has changed, skip this entire section.

The next few paragraphs tell you what kinds of things to expect from TurboTax when you are entering your dependents. The rest of this section deals with how to figure out who your dependents are. If you already know who's who, move on.

All dependents present and accounted for

Most of the time, entering your dependents into TurboTax requires only knowing how to spell their names. The EasyStep Interview asks you a few simple questions and then puts the names where they belong: on page 1 of your 1040. Fill in the dependent's social security number and relationship to you. If the appropriate relationship (great-grandmother, for example) does not appear on the pop-up list, pick Other and type in the relationship yourself. The IRS also wants to know how many months the dependent lived with you during 1995.

Help is on the way

If you don't know whether or not to count as a dependent the next door neighbor's child, who seems to spend more time at your house than his own, click Guide Me, as shown in Figure 6-3. TurboTax walks you through a series of questions geared toward helping you determine who is — and isn't — a dependent.

Figure 6-3:
TurboTax can help you figure out who your dependents are.

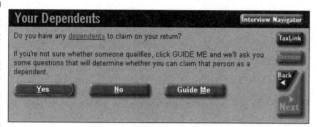

After you pick Guide Me, answer all the questions. Skip one and you're looking for trouble.

You can always click the Back button to go backward if you change your mind or make a mistake.

This Guide Me section tells you whether or not a person qualifies as a dependent — and then it gives you the option to add that person to your list of dependents on your tax return.

Big Brother is watching

You are required to list the social security numbers of all your dependents over the age of one. The IRS can impose a $50 fine for each omitted number. If you just applied for a number and haven't received it yet, enter **Applied For** in the box where the number goes.

Oops! Backing up a step

Suppose you realize that you added someone twice to your list of dependents or listed somebody who really doesn't belong there. When this happens, you need to back things up in order to remove the intruder.

The easiest way to remove someone from the list of dependents on page one of your tax return is to click the Interview Navigator button, click the child's name from the My Tax Data list, and then click the Go to Forms button. Doing so removes the EasyStep question zone from the top of your tax return and lets you have at the actual tax forms. Select the name of the unwanted dependent by clicking it and purge it with the mighty Delete key. Poof! (Make sure that you click the rest of the stuff associated with that dependent, such as the social security number, the number of months that the dependent lived in your home, and so on.)

Return to EasyStep by following these steps:

1. **Click the EasyStep button at the top of the screen (or choose Easy_Step from the menu bar).**

2. **Click _Resume (see Figure 6-4).**

Figure 6-4:
Making your
way back to
EasyStep.

The joys of dependency

You may not appreciate having to support people the rest of the year, but when it comes time to file your income tax return, you'll wish that you had said yes when your Great Aunt Isabel asked to move in with you.

According to the IRS. a *dependent* is someone for whom you provided at least half the support during the year being taxed. If the person is not a relative, he or she had to have lived in your home all year. The easiest way to figure out how many dependents you have is to take a head count around the dinner table.

If your dependent passed away during the year but met all dependency tests for the part of the year that he or she lived, you may claim the dependent for the full year.

Friends, neighbors, casual acquaintances, and so on can count as dependents if you provided more than half their *support* and they lived in your home for the entire year. Support means money. You pay, you get the exemption. Fair's fair. When you're trying to calculate the percentage of support you paid on behalf of your dependent(s), count things like education costs, medical expenses, food, lodging, clothing, transportation, and even fun stuff like going to the movies. Compare this amount to how much the likely dependent paid (or others who may be able to claim the exemption). If you paid more than half, you are entitled to the exemption.

To count as a dependent, a person has to pass all five of these formidable tests:

Test #1: The person must be a *relative* or live in your house all year. See the next IRS Stuff to figure out when a relative is a relative, as opposed to someone who just comes to your house for Thanksgiving dinner.

Test #2: The person must be a citizen of the United States.

Test #3: The person cannot file a joint return with anyone. That's right, your spouse is *not* your dependent.

Test #4: The person has to have earned less than $2,500 in gross income during 1995. This doesn't mean that you can't claim someone who is getting social security income or who has funds tied up in tax-exempt bonds. Gross income for this test means only income that can be taxed. Also, children (*your* children, that is) don't have to pass this test. They can earn more than $2,500.

Test #5: You have to provide more than half the cost of day-to-day caretaking of this person.

Either your blood or that of your spouse has to be surging through the veins of anyone who can count as a relative. That means parents, children, their parents, their children, and also everybody's brothers and sisters. In-laws count, but your aunt's husband doesn't. Cousins don't count, nor do fake relatives like that nice neighbor everybody calls Uncle Bud. The exceptions to the blood rule are legally adopted children and the parents who legally adopted you. The following rules also apply:

✔ If you divorce, your former in-laws are no longer considered your relatives by the IRS.

✔ Babies born right up to the last second of December 31 count as dependents for the whole year, so synchronize your watches if you're counting down more than the Big Apple drop. Stillborn babies do not count, but if the child was born alive and died immediately thereafter, dependent status applies.

✔ Foster children count only if they lived in your home for the entire year.

✔ Boarders who work at your home for their support do not qualify as dependents.

✔ The number of dependents that you report determines the number of exemptions you get on your tax return.

What is an exemption, anyway, and why would you want to be (or have) one? An *exemption* is the special deduction you get for doing nothing other than owning up to all the people you took care of during the year. Go ahead, take it. How many times do you get presents from the IRS?

Chapter 7

From Where Does Your Income Come?

In This Chapter

▶ Income from jobs

▶ Income from your own business

▶ Income from selling miscellaneous things

▶ Income from retirement funds

▶ Income from investments

▶ Income that really isn't income (as far as the IRS is concerned)

▶ Income that really isn't income (as far as you're concerned) but that really *is* income (as far as the IRS is concerned)

*H*ere begins the meaty dollars-and-cents part of the book. In this chapter, I look at all the main ways that people get income. I talk about how you enter all this income into TurboTax so that it appears properly on your tax return, and I discuss the items that may seem like income but that you don't have to report on your tax return.

Income comes in many shapes and forms. Sometimes it's easy to recognize it for what it is: money you received that you have to share with the IRS. For example, if you get a paycheck from a job and at the end of the year you get a W-2 form that shows what you earned, it's pretty easy to figure out that the amount you earned is income and that the IRS wants to hear about it. Other times, though, figuring out what is and isn't income is not so obvious.

Whenever money comes into your life, the official act of Receiving Income occurs. The two big questions you have to ask yourself are, "How am I going to spend it?" and "Do I have to tell the IRS about it?"

After a year has passed, remembering everything that transpired in terms of your income can be difficult. That's when good record-keeping comes into play. Check out Chapter 16 for some pointers on keeping track of your financial life throughout the year.

After you answer TurboTax's questions about who you are and where you live, TurboTax is ready to receive information about your income. Before proceeding, you must choose either to follow the entire course of TurboTax Interview (in which you'll be asked questions about every single item that could potentially feed into your income tax return) or to use the Fast Track.

The Fast Track

Welcome to one of TurboTax's slickest new features: the Fast Track. If you've used TurboTax in prior years, you probably remember spending lots of time answering questions about things that didn't apply to your personal tax situation. The people who created this computer program are sensitive to the time you spend on preparing your tax return and have figured out a way for you to avoid all those unnecessary questions.

Choose Fast Track when given the opportunity and find yourself presented with several screens full of check boxes. These check boxes refer to the different types of income, deductions, taxes, and credits that you may have on your tax return. Simply check the boxes that apply to you. When you finish all the check boxes, the TurboTax Interview proceeds. But instead of asking you all sorts of picky questions about farm income, royalties from your oil wells, gambling losses, and credits for diesel-powered highway vehicles, TurboTax only bothers you with questions about the items you checked.

Use the Fast Track method to save yourself literally hours on the preparation of your tax return.

The Fast Track method is great and a welcome addition to TurboTax. However, if you don't understand some of the topics you see in the Fast Track check boxes, you'll probably be better off running the entire Interview. Sure, you can save some time with Fast Track. You can also miss something important that should have been in your tax return. Using the full Interview process ensures that you are asked detailed questions about every possible tax situation that may affect your tax return. And at each topic, you can request help (or look in this book) to find out exactly what information is requested.

Those Pesky Little W-2 Forms

Okay, it's time to talk dollars and cents. The TurboTax Interview takes you to the W-2 Wages & Salaries topic and asks: `Did you receive any W-2 Forms that reported wages or tips?` You should receive a W-2 form from each employer you worked for in the past year. If you didn't get a W-2, or if you think that the information on the form is wrong, you must contact your employer. It's your responsibility to follow up on problems with your W-2.

The W-2 form gives you important information about how much you earned during the past year and how much you didn't get to put into your pocket due to various and sundry withholdings such as these:

- ✔ Federal income tax
- ✔ FICA (pronounced *fike-uh*; it's just a fancy name for social security tax)
- ✔ State income tax
- ✔ Local income tax
- ✔ Health insurance
- ✔ Office coffee fund
- ✔ Company car reimbursements

The W-2 form also contains stuff like your name, address, and social security number. Make sure to glance briefly at these things to verify that you didn't get your boss's form by mistake.

When responding to the TurboTax question about whether or not you have wages reported on a Form W-2, notice that the words *W-2 forms* are not the same color as the rest of the text on the TurboTax screen. Whenever you see words that appear on-screen in color (or in gray if you are using a monochrome monitor), click the words to pop up a help screen that gives you a detailed description of the highlighted words.

Selecting Yes when TurboTax asks you whether you have W-2 forms brings up a pro forma W-2 form, which TurboTax fills in with information that you give it from your W-2. If you used TurboTax last year, then last year's employer(s) is already in place, as illustrated in Figure 7-1. You can start by selecting a former employer(s) and filling in the 1995 income amounts if your employer(s) didn't change. If you do have a new employer, choose New W-2 to record wages from an employer who is not on the list. Just ignore the employers on the list for whom you don't work anymore.

Figure 7-1:
If you used
TurboTax
last year,
your W-2
employers
carry over to
this year.

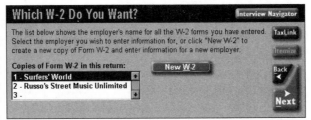

After you choose a W-2 form to work on, TurboTax takes you step by step through that entire form, requesting such information as the following:

- ✔ **Does this W-2 have an X in the "Void" box?:** What? The likelihood of your employer sending you a W-2 that should have been voided is pretty slim, but then maybe you have an employer with a very strange sense of humor. If the "Void" box is checked, by all means call your employer and tell him or her to get a new joke writer (and send you a new W-2).

- ✔ **The name and address of your employer:** Unless you choose to file electronically, filling in this information is optional — but it can serve as a handy reminder next year because TurboTax carries the information forward to your 1996 tax return.

With any information that is optional, you can click the Next button to pass over it without making an entry. TurboTax reminds you with an on-screen message if the information is not necessary.

The preceding piece of information is optional unless you are filing electronicly. If you plan to file an electronic return (see Chapter 13), you must enter every bit of information from your W-2 form exactly as it appears on the W-2 form.

From here on, the W-2 form items are not optional; enter them when TurboTax asks you to. This list describes the information that TurboTax is looking for:

- ✔ **Wages and tips**

- ✔ **Foreign source income**

Did you earn your income in another country (known as *foreign source income*)? Answer Yes or No.

TurboTax displays its famous Select a Box screen for your viewing and mouse-clicking enjoyment. Three choices appear: Next Box, Select a Box, and Done with Boxes 1–15. Click Next Box to proceed through the W-2 form input, one item at a time. You're not likely to leave anything out of your W-2 form input by using this option. Click Select a Box and choose the places you want to go in the input of your W-2 form. Just be sure that you enter all the numbers on your W-2 form. Click Done with Boxes 1–15, and TurboTax propels you past the W-2 input screen. If it turns out that you left out some important information from your W-2, TurboTax will gleefully prod you to go back and enter more information when it reviews your tax return.

✓ **Federal income tax withholding**

✓ **Social security wages**

This amount may not match the wages amount in box 1, so be sure to check your W-2 form.

✓ **Social security tax withholding (FICA)**

If you think that you may have had too much social security tax withheld (not on general principle, but under the guidelines of maximum withholding of $3,794.40), you can rest assured that TurboTax will check for you. Any excess social security tax is treated as an income tax payment and offsets the tax you may owe on your tax return.

✓ **Medicare wages**

These wages may not only differ from the wages in box 1, but they also may differ from your social security wages — *so be sure to check your W-2!*

✓ **Medicare tax withholding**

Unlike social security tax withholding, there is no ceiling on Medicare tax withholding.

✓ **Social security tips**

This amount reflects the tip income that you reported to your employer.

✓ **Allocated tips**

This amount represents tips that your employer divided among its employees.

✓ **Advance EIC payment**

EIC stands for *Earned Income Credit.* If you are eligible for this credit, you may have had part of it advanced to you by your employer. The amount that was advanced to you appears in this box. (For more information about this credit, see "Earned Income Credit" in Chapter 11.)

✓ **Dependent care benefits**

Some employers offer benefit plans that include this nice feature. Entering the amount of these benefits here doesn't necessarily mean that you owe tax on the amount, but you may. Let TurboTax figure it out. That's one of the reasons you bought this program.

✓ **Nonqualified plan**

An amount in this box represents a nondeductible contribution to a retirement plan. That's not to say that it gets added to your income; in fact, it's already included in your income. This number is just for your records, but you still need to enter it here.

✔ **Benefits included in box 1**

This box presents a summary of other benefits that your employer provided in addition to wages.

✔ **Box 13 and box 14 codes and amounts**

These figures may include personal use of a company car, moving expenses, club dues that your employer paid, or other costs picked up by the company for which you work. Enter whatever you see here (these amounts are already included in your income — these boxes are summaries). TurboTax figures out whether you can deduct something here.

✔ **Check boxes**

Click any box that is checked on your W-2.

✔ **State and local wages**

If this information appears on your W-2 form, say Yes; otherwise, say — well, I think you know.

✔ **State abbreviation**

Now this is interesting. Try typing your state's two-letter abbreviation here. Can't do it, can you? It's a trick question, and here's how it works: Type the *first letter* of your state. Keep typing that same letter until your state's abbreviation comes to the surface. Or, if you get tired of that game, press the down-arrow key or click the down arrow on-screen with your mouse and scroll (or arrow) around until you find your state.

✔ **Employer's State ID number**

Enter this number if you plan to file your tax return electronically. Otherwise, there's no reason to waste your time trying to type this number.

✔ **State wages**

Just as reported on your W-2. List information for one state at a time.

✔ **State income tax withholding**

✔ **Locality**

If you pay local taxes, click Yes and enter your local wages and withholding.

✔ **Is the W-2 related to service you provided as a member of the clergy?**

TurboTax isn't just being nosy here. You get to answer extra questions if you are a member of the clergy.

TurboTax asks you twice about state wages — only two states fit on one of these W-2 forms. If you received wages associated with more than one state and the states all appear on the same W-2 form, you need to start a new W-2 form for the third state. If your employer sent you a W-2 form that is duplicated in every way except that a different state is reported on the bottom, *don't re-enter the federal income and tax information on the second W-2 form from the same employer.* Just click through the federal stuff and stop to fill in the blanks when you get to the state section.

Follow along with your own W-2 form and type the amounts as TurboTax asks for them, and then press Enter or click the <u>N</u>ext button to move from one section to the next.

Income That Should Be on a W-2 Form but Isn't

Some forms of income are taxable and actually belong on the same line of your tax return with your W-2 income, even though they don't get reported to you on a W-2 form. Income of this sort includes taxable scholarships, fellowships, sick pay, and disability pay, to the extent that the income is taxable.

Scholarships, fellowships, ships in the night

Much later in the Interview, when you get to this topic in TurboTax, the program asks you the following question:

```
Did you receive any taxable scholarships, fellowship
grants, sick pay, or disability income NOT reported to
you on Form W-2?
```

If you received some sort of grant but aren't sure what is taxable, see the following IRS Stuff. Enter only the taxable amount.

If issued after August 16, 1986, scholarships and fellowship grants are potentially taxable. The portion of the grant used for school tuition and expenses related to school expenses, such as books and lab fees, is not taxable. The rest of the grant, including amounts used for room, board, and travel, is taxable. This breakdown assumes that the recipient of the grant is a degree candidate (including grade school and high school students). Grants issued to nondegree candidates are wholly taxable.

Grants received as compensation for teaching are taxable. If you have to teach in order to receive the grant, the grant is taxable.

TurboTax first asks you to enter scholarship and fellowship information, and then it requests disability and sick pay amounts (taxable sick pay gets entered as disability income).

Sick pay and disability payments

Amounts you received for sick and disability pay are generally taxable and are included in your W-2 form (see the following IRS Stuff for exceptions to this rule). Sometimes, though, you may receive payments for sick or disability pay from someone other than your employer, and your wages from that organization may not be included in your W-2. In those situations, you must add the amounts to your tax return in the same way that you add a scholarship. Also, you must add to your income the amounts that you received as reimbursements for medical expenses that you previously deducted. Worker's compensation payments that you may have received are not taxable and do not get added to your income. When TurboTax asks you whether you have any sick pay or disability payments that need to be included in your income, enter your taxable amount *only* (amounts not already included in your W-2 form) — then you're ready to move on to a new topic.

Suppose that you received money from an accident or health plan that you pay for yourself, either by purchasing the plan on your own or by contributing to a plan at work through payroll deductions. If such a scenario were true, the amounts that represent reimbursement for your actual medical expenses do not get included in your income unless you deduct them as itemized medical expenses. Any other amounts received from such a plan are not taxable and do not get included in income.

Some disability payments are not taxable. Payments for permanent disabilities and payments made from a plan on which the employee paid part of the premiums can be nontaxable. Check with your employer if you think that the amount on your W-2 form is wrong.

Hot Tips

You probably turned right to this section as soon as you saw it in the Table of Contents, thinking that you would discover all the special tricks that tax accountants know here. Wrong! This section is about a certain type of income known and loved by waiters and actors everywhere: tip income.

Tips are those extra bits of cash that you reluctantly part with at the restaurant, the meager amount that you dole out as you remind yourself of the cool-to-the-touch french fries you received and of all the times the waiter forgot to refill your water glass.

If you receive tips, you need to report them as part of your income. Right after quizzing you about W-2 forms, TurboTax asks whether you received any tip income that was *not* reported to your employer. (It assumes that if you reported the income to your employer, the amount was properly included on your W-2 form.) If you have tip income that didn't show up on your W-2, this is the place to report it. Click Yes on the screen shown in Figure 7-2 to record tip income that isn't on your W-2.

Figure 7-2:
Pocketed
your tips,
did you?
Here's
where you
can come
clean.

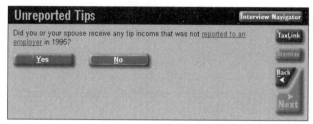

If you received less than $20 per month in tips, you are not required to report the amount to your employer. You are, however, still required to report the amount on your tax return and pay tax on it. Darn!

You're the Boss: Profit or Loss from a Business

So you finally started that lawn care business you've been talking about for years. Or maybe you're doing typesetting or computer programming, building rocking chairs, selling firecrackers and cherry bombs, providing legal services or day care, or contracting for skyscrapers. Whatever the business — whether it's your main livelihood or something you do in your spare time — if you work for yourself and are not a separate *business entity,* the income and expenses of that business get reported on your personal tax return.

A *business entity* is a business with a life unto itself. It is a separate legal entity: a corporation, partnership, or joint venture. If your business falls into one of those categories, you should file a separate tax return for it instead of using yours.

You report both business income and your related expenses on Schedule C. The net amount gets carried to page 1 of Form 1040.

Some tax forms are easy to prepare; it doesn't really matter whether you use the EasyStep feature of TurboTax or go right to the form and fill in the blanks yourself. Schedule C is *not* one of those forms. Stick with EasyStep when entering business income and expenses.

Getting started on Schedule C

If you indicate to TurboTax that you operated at least one business, TurboTax peppers you with questions about each of your businesses, one at a time. First, provide the business description and principal business code. This four-digit number code helps the IRS understand what it is you do in your business — just in case your narrative description is too vague. Also, by assigning a number to your business, the IRS can group you with other businesses of the same classification and come up with all sorts of interesting and meaningful statistics about your type of business (interesting stuff like the number of retail stores that take deductions for guard dogs or the number of Laundromats that provide video games for their customers to use while waiting). Then enter the business name, address, and Federal ID number (if you have one).

To find the principal business code that fits your business, click the words `principal business code`, which appear in the EasyStep questionnaire. You see a list of all the business codes. Find the one that comes closest to describing your business. Don't spend a great deal of time deciding which code is most appropriate. Your tax return won't be sent back to you for corrections if you mess up on choosing the code.

Let TurboTax know whether your business address is the same as your home address by answering yes or no to the address question. If your business address is the same as your home address, TurboTax runs back to the front page of your tax return, grabs the address, and copies it onto Schedule C. If you say no, you can type in the correct business address.

One of the most important things about running your own business — whether it's a weekend lawn care business or a full-time, 16-hour-a-day consulting service — is keeping good records. The significance of this advice is never more evident than at tax return time, when you must account for every dime you earned and every paper clip you purchased. Take a look at Chapter 16 for some nifty pointers on getting your records in order.

Methods of accounting

The method of accounting you use determines how some things are reported on your tax return. If you had income from this business last year, you've already chosen a method of accounting. Look at last year's return and copy the same method onto this return.

As illustrated in Figure 7-3, TurboTax shows you the choices of methods. All you have to do is choose one of them.

Figure 7-3:
Choose your accounting method here.

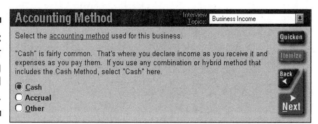

- ✔ **Cash method**

  All your receipts are recorded as income when you receive them, as opposed to when you earn them. Expenses are deducted when you pay them, rather than when you get the bill. However, if you prepay expenses that aren't yet due, you're supposed to wait and deduct them when they are actually due to be paid.

- ✔ **Accrual method**

  Receipts are recorded when earned and expenses are deducted when you contract to buy the stuff, rather than when you actually pay. If you have an inventory in your business, you have to use this method.

- ✔ **Other method**

  If a logical way to account for income and expenses that combines features from the cash and accrual methods exists, you can use it as long as you use the same method year after year. For example, if you have inventory but really prefer to use the cash method, you can use the accrual method for tracking your inventory and the cash method for everything else.

After you choose an accounting method, you can't change to another one unless you raise your hand and ask for permission from the IRS. You must prepare a Form 3115 (available at an IRS office) and send it to the IRS in order to request this change.

Stuff that you (try to) sell

Inventory, if you have some, has to be valued somehow. You can record your inventory at cost, keep track of the market value and record it at the lower of the cost or the market value, or make up some variation on the two, as long as you're consistent. When TurboTax asks how you are valuing your inventory, select one of these methods.

If you use some method other than cost or the lower figure of either cost or market value, the IRS requires that you attach a statement to your tax return indicating how you valued your inventory. TurboTax does not prepare this statement for you. You can write up your own statement and remember to include it with the tax return when you file it, or you can leave EasyStep, click the Forms button, and choose Miscellaneous Statement. Type your description on this statement and then print it out with your tax return.

If you change the way in which you value inventory at any time during the year, you have to tell the IRS about it by attaching another statement.

Changes in accounting methods and inventory valuations are serious business. Don't arbitrarily decide to change from one method to another. You should discuss any such changes with a tax accountant.

Fruits of your labors

When it is time to start entering income amounts on your Schedule C, you can proceed in one of two ways. Enter the total income when TurboTax prompts you to enter Gross Receipts. Or, if you received 1099 forms that represent the Schedule C income, TurboTax gives you a chance to enter the amounts individually from each 1099.

After you enter gross receipts, the next line you see on the Schedule C is Returns and Allowances. This line has nothing to do with the allowance you give your children on Saturday morning or the value of what they return to you in keeping their rooms clean. *Returns and allowances* refers to refunds or discounts you may give your customers. If you charge someone $10, he or she comes back and complains, and you take off $2, the $10 goes on the Gross Receipts line and the $2 gets subtracted on the Returns and Allowances line. Actually, it's easier just to put $8 on the Gross Receipts line in the first place, which is what most people do.

Sometimes your business may receive income that's not part of its normal business. If you are in the business of selling shoes and one time you decide to have a bake sale at the shoe store, the bake sale income is considered Other Income.

At-risk and material participation

The IRS wants to know whether the amounts on your Schedule C are At Risk. What they really want to know is whether you put up the money yourself for all the things you paid for in your business. If amounts on your Schedule C are At Risk, either you paid out of your business earnings or out of your own pocket, or you borrowed the money, and you are personally liable for the amount you borrowed.

Additionally, you need to figure out whether you materially participated in the business. In other words, do you do all the work, or have you hired someone to run the show while you just sit back and watch the money roll in? When TurboTax asks you about material participation, select the TurboTax option of Help. TurboTax then asks you a series of questions designed to figure out your level of participation. Work your way through the questions, and on this mini-section of your tax return you're home free.

Accounting for inventory

After you enumerate your income, TurboTax leads you to the summary of Cost of Goods Sold. In this section of the tax return, you report the value of your inventory at the beginning of the year, the cost to maintain it, and the value of the inventory at the end of the year. If you don't have any inventory to report on your Schedule C, skip past the Cost of Goods section by clicking the Next button.

It's easy to keep track of what the inventory items cost; the trick is figuring out the value of what's left after you sell some of the stuff. If this is not your first year at reporting inventory, you probably already have a way to figure out what the inventory is worth. If it is your first year, though, see the handy nearby sidebar, "The gentle art of pricing inventories," to determine how to value your inventory.

If you used TurboTax last year and carried forward your tax information, the value of your beginning inventory magically appears on your Schedule C in the Cost of Goods Sold section.

If you produce your inventory yourself rather than buy it from someone else, you should also include all labor, materials, supplies, or other costs that relate to the inventory. TurboTax asks you to supply these items when it quizzes you about the cost of your inventory.

The gentle art of pricing inventories

When it comes to putting a price tag on your inventory, you have three ways to choose from. Pick the one that sounds the easiest:

✔ **Specific Identification**

If you use this method, you keep track of the cost of each inventory item as you purchase it and specifically identify which items you sell and how much those items cost. Using this method gives you the true cost of your inventory. If your inventory includes thousands of items, however, the record-keeping for this method can get pretty hairy.

✔ **FIFO**

Using this method, you keep track of (1) how many items you purchased, (2) at what costs, and (3) on what dates you purchased them.

As you sell the items, you assume that the first item you purchased is the first sold, the second item you purchased is the second sold, and so on (FIFO = First In, First Out). This way, you don't have to identify specifically which items were sold and how much those particular items cost.

✔ **LIFO**

With this method, you again keep track of the different costs you paid for things and when you purchased them. As you sell items, you assume that the last item you purchased is the first sold, the next-to-last item is the second sold, and so on (LIFO = Last In, First Out).

Whichever method you pick, you must stick with it. You can't change to a different method without permission from the IRS.

Business deductions for people who run their own businesses

You can use all sorts of things to lower the amount of income on Schedule C, thus lowering the amount of tax you pay on your business income. These items are called *operating expenses* and include such things as the following:

✔ **Advertising** includes newspaper ads, sandwich vendors on the sidewalk, hot air balloons, promotional brochures, and so on.

✔ **Bad Debts** occur when somebody owes you money and finks out. In order to deduct it, you have to have reported this money in income somewhere along the line.

✔ **Commissions and Fees** include sales commissions, membership fees for professional organizations, and filing fees.

✔ **Depletion** occurs when coal mines, timber forests, oil wells, and other natural resources get used up. The methods for recording this depletion are complicated. See a pro.

- ✔ **Depreciation** is a way of taking a deduction for the cost of business fixtures — big-ticket items like furniture and equipment and even buildings and vehicles. Check out the particulars of this sometimes-confusing item in the section called, "Those Funny -ation Words: Depreciation and Amortization," later in this chapter.

- ✔ **Employee Benefit Programs** include health insurance, prepaid legal expenses, and education reimbursements for your employees.

- ✔ **Insurance** is not health insurance but liability insurance; insurance to protect you against loss, damage, or theft; and Workers' Compensation.

- ✔ **Interest** is the cost of borrowing money specifically for your business.

- ✔ **Legal and Professional Services:** If you hired a lawyer or an accountant, deduct the cost here.

- ✔ **Office Expenses** include costs of small equipment such as calculators, desk chairs, and other stuff that you use in your office but that is too small to depreciate and too big to call *supplies.*

- ✔ **Pension and Profit-Sharing Plans** include contributions to a retirement plan for your employees.

- ✔ **Rent or Lease Agreements** include stuff that you pay for but don't own, such as rented equipment or a warehouse to store things in.

- ✔ **Repairs and Maintenance** include repairs to things that don't work and service agreements on office equipment.

- ✔ **Supplies** include small items such as staples, paper clips, pens, pencils, coffee filters, light bulbs, and myriad other odds and ends.

- ✔ **Taxes and Licenses** include franchise taxes, payroll taxes, property taxes, and professional licenses.

- ✔ **Travel, Meals, and Entertainment** include airfare, taxi fare, lunch with clients, greens fees, and so on. Make sure that your expenses here legitimately apply to your business. You should enter business-related meal and entertainment costs in full; TurboTax (under instructions from the federal government) limits your deductions to 50 percent of these items. Membership to a country club is no longer considered a business expense.

- ✔ **Utilities** include the regular stuff: electricity, gas, and water. If you took a deduction for an office in your home, you already expensed these things. If your office or business location is separate from your home, include these expenses here.

- ✔ **Wages** are the amounts you pay employees for jobs they do.

- ✔ **And more . . .** such as contract labor, copying, postage, business seminars, and whatever else applies to your particular business.

TurboTax lists all these things for you, as you can see in Figure 7-4. Just click the items that apply to you and enter the amounts you spent.

Figure 7-4:
Choose from
loads of
standard
business
deductions.
You can
choose
Other to
report an
expense not
on this list.

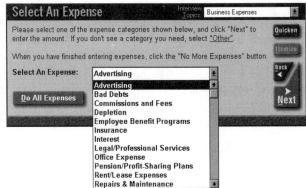

The high cost of driving

Do you use a car in your business? Remember, I'm talking about your own business, not a job for which someone employs you. If you own or lease a car or truck for your business, you can take a deduction for some of the costs of driving. If you indicate that you have car or truck expenses related to your business, TurboTax asks you about your driving record and gives you a chance to deduct automobile expenses.

Don't try to navigate your way through car and truck expenses without the aid of EasyStep. This section is tricky, and TurboTax clears through all the mess by asking the questions and figuring out what your deduction should be.

You can deduct driving expenses in two ways:

✓ **Actual Expenses method**

You have to dig up all the costs of operating your car in the past year to make this method work. You have to use this method if (a) you lease the vehicle or (b) you used this method in prior years.

✓ **Standard Mileage Rate method**

You get a flat, per-mile rate for your deduction. This method is the easiest because you don't have to keep track of all your expenses. (You can use either this method or the Actual Expenses method if (a) and (b) in the Actual Expenses method don't apply. It's your choice.)

Whichever method you choose, TurboTax figures out what percentage of the car was used for business based on the business miles you drove. Enter your mileage in answer to TurboTax's questions on the screen shown in Figure 7-5.

Figure 7-5:
Keep track of your mileage so that you can answer questions such as this one.

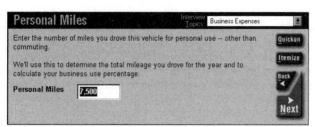

No matter which method you use, you can deduct the costs of parking, tolls, buses, taxis, train tickets, or plane tips while traveling from one business location to another. Also, you need to know the mileage that you put on the car in 1995 for both methods. One more thing: If your business takes place at one particular location outside your home (rather than at various clients' offices), you should know the distance of the commute from your house to the business location. The IRS wants you to reduce your business mileage by this amount.

If you plan to use the Actual Expenses method, gather up your automobile expense information before starting this part of the tax return so that you won't have to run around looking for insurance bills and gas credit card statements. Here's a list of the costs you should have on record in order to claim your auto or truck expense deduction under the Actual Expenses method:

- ✔ Gasoline costs
- ✔ Oil and oil change costs
- ✔ Repairs
- ✔ Auto or truck insurance
- ✔ Rental vehicle while yours is being repaired
- ✔ Tires or other new parts
- ✔ License plates
- ✔ Lease payments
- ✔ Interest on a vehicle loan

TurboTax and the IRS expect you to add up all expenses for the car, except for parking and tolls, and enter one big amount. You can, however, select an *itemization* for this amount and list every type of expense. If you do choose to itemize the list of expenses, you'll have a good guide to use in figuring out your vehicle expenses for next year's return.

You may take an optional deduction for *depreciation* of your car or truck if you are using the Actual Expenses method. If the car cost you only $100 and a new set of tires, a depreciation deduction may be negligible. If, however, the vehicle was pricey, you can get a substantial deduction by depreciating the car. But — and, yes, this is a big *but* — if you take a depreciation deduction on your car and later sell the car, you may have to add back the amount of depreciation and pay tax on it.

Don't try to figure out this depreciation business; you'll only drive yourself crazy. Let TurboTax work it out and just answer the questions as best you can. Have handy the cost of the car and the approximate date you purchased it. If you took depreciation in prior years, look at last year's return for the amount of prior depreciation expense. If you want to know a little more about depreciation, see the section called "Those Funny *-ation* Words: Depreciation and Amortization," later in this chapter.

If you choose to depreciate your vehicle, TurboTax asks you whether you want a Section 179 deduction. Section 179 allows you to deduct up to $17,500 right off the top of your asset and then spread the rest of the cost over several years. In the case of a car, you are further limited to the $2,960 maximum deduction amount. You can deduct this amount only in the first year you depreciate the vehicle. Other depreciable items also qualify for this deduction. (See "Those Funny *-ation* Words: Depreciation and Amortization," further along in this chapter.) The $17,500 limit applies to all Section 179 deductions on your entire tax return, not just the vehicle.

TurboTax then asks you for a *depreciation type.* Choose MACRS, the type already selected by default (just be glad that you don't have to know what any of this stuff means). Likewise, choose 200DB for your depreciation method.

You need to specify a *convention* for this vehicle. A convention is nothing like the one the Shriners put on. Nobody wears a funny hat (although you're welcome to do so if you want). Instead, the convention concerns the date on which you bought the vehicle. If you got it in the last three months of 1995, pick MQ. Otherwise, pick HY and don't ask.

With regard to these conventions, if you are depreciating loads of things (as opposed to just one vehicle), add up the costs of all the things you bought in 1995. Don't worry about things you bought in earlier years. Now add up all the things you bought in the *last three months* of 1995. If the second number is more than 40 percent of the first number, pick MQ for your convention. Otherwise, pick HY.

Recovery period for your vehicle = 5. Period.

Do you have evidence to support the business use of this vehicle, and is that evidence written? Yes? Good, because you need written proof if you want to take the deduction. Keep some kind of record of where you go in the vehicle.

Put a little notebook in your car and write down each time you go someplace that has a business purpose, along with the number of miles you traveled round-trip. You also can use this book to keep track of mileage for charitable and medical purposes (see the related sections about charitable and medical mileage in Chapter 8).

Answer a few other questions about ownership of the car and you're out of here.

Home sweet home as an office

After you enter automobile expenses, TurboTax gives you the opportunity to report expenses that relate to the use of your home as a place of business.

Many advantages await the person who works at home for a living: being able to take a break from work to wash the dishes, getting to answer all the irritating salespeople's calls that come in all day long, having the soft, inviting bed just a few rooms away when the urge for an afternoon nap overtakes you. . . . Actually, working at home holds many true advantages, too — such as being there when the kids get off the bus, keeping flexible hours, and substantially reducing transportation expenses.

But before you get all excited about taking tax return deductions for your home office, find out whether you actually qualify for the deductions. If you're self-employed and you use a Schedule C to report your business income, you must meet one of two conditions to be able to take deductions for home office expenses:

✔ The designated area in your home must be your principal place of business.

   or

✔ The designated area in your home must be a place where clients, patients, or customers come to do business with you.

You must use the home office exclusively for business purposes. An exception to this rule is using your home as a day care facility. The IRS lets you use all or part of your home for day care by day and personal uses by night.

If you have a place of business both outside your home and in your home, as would a doctor who practices at a hospital but does paperwork at home, the IRS does not want to hear about your home office.

Don't worry about which forms you need. That's why you have TurboTax. But, just for the record, the expenses for a home office get reported on Form 8829, appropriately called Expenses for Business Use of Your Home. Then they get carried to Schedule C or wherever else in your tax return they may belong.

Somehow, you've got to figure out how much of your home you use for business. You can get out the tape measure and count square feet. Or you can count rooms. An estimate that comes close is all you really need.

While you are entering information about using your home as an office, TurboTax asks you whether you sold your home in the past year. If you didn't, skip the rest of this warning. If you did sell your home in the past year and you are preparing your tax return with the EasyStep method of TurboTax, you won't yet have information about the gain or loss from the sale of your home. Make a note to yourself that you have to come back to Form 8829 and fill in the amount of taxable profit or loss you had on the sale (the amount will be the business percentage of the gain or loss on Form 2119).

Most likely, you'll have two kinds of expenses in conjunction with your home office expense:

- ✔ **Direct expenses** apply directly to the business area of your home, such as new carpet, repairs, cleaning costs, window coverings, and long-distance telephone calls.

- ✔ **Indirect expenses** affect the entire house. They are prorated based on the percentage of your house that applies to your business and include such things as home insurance, security systems, mortgage interest, property taxes, rent, and utilities.

In addition to all these expenses, you can *depreciate* your home and other big items such as a computer, office furniture, and other furniture or equipment that you use in your business. These big items are called *fixed assets.* For detailed information about depreciation, you can look ahead in this chapter to "Those Funny *-ation* Words: Depreciation and Amortization." Or you can try to follow along as TurboTax asks you questions about these items.

Note: If you have a net loss on your business (your expenses are greater than your income), you may not get to deduct all your home office expenses. TurboTax takes care of figuring out what is and isn't allowed, so don't worry about that. Be aware, however, that some expenses may carry over to next year's tax return. TurboTax takes care of that, too, if you use TurboTax to prepare next year's tax return. If you don't plan to use TurboTax next year, you yourself have to keep track of the amounts of things that couldn't be deducted this year, and then you have to remember to put them on next year's tax form.

Down on the Farm

If you own a farm, you need to report your farm income on Schedule F. Schedule F (one of the few forms in your tax return where the form's letter actually seems to stand for something — F = Farm) is very similar to Schedule C in terms of the types of information that go on the form. You list the different kinds of farm income you receive and the costs of running the farm.

Right after you finish answering the questions about running your own business, TurboTax gets down to the business of operating a farm. Just as with a Schedule C business, the information carries forward if you had a farm last year. Before you begin your Schedule F, TurboTax wants to know, as demonstrated in Figure 7-6, whether you want to fill in information about the farm you had last year or whether you have a new farm that you want to talk about.

Figure 7-6:
Hey Ho the
Dairy-Oh,
the farmer
picks a
Schedule F.

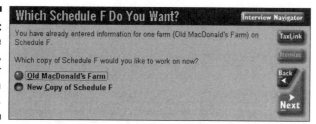

If you operate a farm, be prepared to fill in the blanks with information about your income and expenses, just as you would if you had a Schedule C business. Expenses of running a farm include all the costs of buying, planting, and caring for crops in the ground, harvesting them, raising and caring for animals, and performing general maintenance on the farm itself. Use your farm records and follow along with TurboTax to get everything listed on the tax return.

Co-ops and ag programs

A farmer's income can include federal subsidies, commodity credit (PIK) certificates, distributions from cooperatives, and insurance proceeds for damaged crops. TurboTax goes right down the list, asking you about all these items. Have your 1099-PATR or other farm income forms in front of you when you fill out Schedule F, and you can copy numbers right from those forms to TurboTax.

The silly way gas taxes get reported

If you use gasoline in tractors or other farm equipment (as opposed to using it out on the road in your pickup truck), you are entitled to take a tax credit for some of the cost of that gasoline. This way of doing things has always seemed *awfully* confusing to me, but so far no one at the IRS has asked for my opinion.

But back to reporting the gas you used on your farm. To make an accurate report, you first need to know how much of the gasoline that you purchased in the past year was used in non-highway driving — in other words, how much you used on the farm. Then you need to get Form 4136 from the IRS (alas, 4136 is one form that TurboTax does not prepare for you). Fill in the form and figure out your tax credit. Leave the EasyStep method and get yourself to page 2 of your Form 1040 in TurboTax, scan down to line 59, check off the box that says Form 4136, and type the amount on that line.

The really crazy thing is that if you took this credit last year, you have to add it back in income this year. If you find a gas tax credit amount on line 59 of your 1994 income tax return, you must list it *as income* on your farm schedule when TurboTax asks you for Other Income.

Those Funny -ation Words: Depreciation and Amortization

Because nobody really wants to know how to compute depreciation or amortization, most people want to skip this section of the book. Most people don't even want to know how to pronounce the words. If you have serious questions about this stuff, read on; otherwise, be glad that you don't have to know it.

Depreciation is the act of expensing things that cost gobs of money by spreading the expense over a period of years that represents the length of time the things should last. As you can imagine, figuring depreciation is a pretty inexact science.

Amortization is the same as depreciation, except that the things you are expensing are things you can't see or touch, such as copyrights and computer software.

Even many of the best tax accountants have long since forgotten the fancy names for the different methods of depreciation: acronyms that stand for words, such as CLADR, ACRS, and MACRS. Don't worry about remembering these names. Here's all you really need to know to get through this *-ation* business.

Whenever you purchase something for your business or your farm that costs a great deal of money (more than $250, for example, although that's just a ballpark figure), something that you expect to last a long time (say, more than two years), you are supposed to depreciate it instead of expensing the whole thing in the year you buy it.

On the various business forms (Schedule C, Schedule F, and Schedule E), TurboTax politely asks whether you have anything you want to depreciate. Say Yes, and the program asks you very specific questions about the items (called *assets*), one item at a time. To pass your catechism, be ready with the following particulars:

- ✔ **Description:** What do you call this thing that you "want" to depreciate?

- ✔ **Date Placed in Service:** Tax accountants used to call this "in place and in use." The date placed in service isn't the day you bought the item; it's the day you took it out of the box and started using it.

- ✔ **Disposed of?:** Indicate whether you sold the item in 1995 and for how much.

- ✔ **Type of Asset:** Select from a list of common asset types, or choose Other if you don't see your type here. Some of the depreciation issues that follow here in the list in this book will appear only if you choose Other.

- ✔ **Cost or Basis:** What did you pay for it? You can tack on incidentals like shipping and sales tax. However, if you are depreciating a building, be sure to remove the portion of the cost that represents the land. Land is not depreciable.

- ✔ **Percentage of Business Use:** If you use the new pickup all day long on the farm, but you also use it on Saturday night to drive to town for a nice dinner, then some small percentage becomes personal use. Estimate what percentage of the time you used the item for fun rather than profit; then subtract that figure from 100 percent. The balance is business use.

- ✔ **Section 179 Deduction:** The IRS lets you expense up to $17,500 of your assets right off the top without bothering with these nasty depreciation calculations. The $17,500 applies to all your business assets on your whole tax return added together, not to each asset individually. This deduction is purely optional, and whether or not you take it depends on whether you want bigger expenses this year or want to spread them over several years. You can take this Section 179 deduction only in the first year you purchase the asset.

- ✔ **Convention:** Add up the cost of all the assets you are depreciating this year on your whole tax return, but don't count the amounts you are taking as a Section 179 deduction (see how conversant you're becoming with tax terms?). Call this number *apple*. Now add up the cost of just the assets you are depreciating that you acquired during the last three months of the year. Call this number *orange*. Multiply apple by 40 percent (.40). Call this new number *kumquat*. If orange is bigger than kumquat, your convention is MQ. Otherwise, your convention is HY.

✔ **Depreciation Type:** TurboTax chooses MACRS for you unless the asset is land (then it chooses LAND) or intangible (such as a copyright or computer software — then it chooses AMORT).

✔ **Asset Class:** If the asset is a car, van, or passenger-type truck, choose AUTO. If it is some other kind of truck, a computer, or office equipment, choose 5. If it is office furniture, a cellular phone, or video equipment, choose 7. If it is a building that you use as rental property (such as an apartment building), choose R. If it is some other kind of building, choose NR.

✔ **Depreciation Method:** Choose 200 Declining Balance to get the highest allowable deduction in the earliest years of the asset. Otherwise, choose Straight Line, and the deduction is prorated evenly over the life of the asset.

✔ **Prior Depreciation:** If you are entering an asset that was purchased in a year prior to 1995, TurboTax asks you how much depreciation you took in previous years. Go back to previous tax returns to get this amount, or let TurboTax calculate the prior depreciation.

✔ **Recovery Period:** Look back at Asset Class. If the asset's class is AUTO, the Recovery Period is 5. If the class is R, the Recovery Period is 27.5. If the class is NR, the period is 39. If the class is 5 or 7, the Recovery Period is the same number as the class. By the time you get here, TurboTax has already made a stab at figuring out the Recovery Period. Just check it to make sure that it's right.

✔ **AMT Recovery Period:** Use the same number that you used for the Recovery Period.

✔ **Listed Property questions:** If you said that this asset is listed, you may be required to answer a few questions about who owns the asset and whether you have written records of how much of the use was business and how much was personal. *Always* make written records of personal use of your listed assets. Listed property includes automobiles, computers, and cellular phones. (*Note:* You are not required to keep written records of the use of computers and cellular phones if they were used 100 percent for business.)

1099 Miscellaneous Income

The term *miscellaneous income* conjures up images of income that is just too foolish to bother with. Wrong! If you got 1099-MISC forms in the mail, the IRS did, too — and they'll be watching to see whether you report them. You can enter the income from all your 1099-MISC forms on your Schedule C (or Schedule E or Schedule F, whichever schedule they should be associated with). When you enter income on any of these schedules, TurboTax asks if you have income from 1099s and gives you an opportunity to enter the name of the payee and the amount paid for each 1099. Some of this 1099-MISC income may belong on the Other Income line of page 1 of your 1040 (see "May I Have the Envelope, Please?" later in this chapter).

Keep all your 1099-MISC forms in front of you and follow along, entering everything on the forms, one form at a time. TurboTax asks you to enter the name of the company or person making the payment and the amounts that appear in the boxes on the form. Entering the payer address, ID number, and control number is optional.

Rental Property Rules: 14 Days, 15 Percent, 15 Days, and Other Confusion

If you own a vacation home, visit it only two weeks of the year, and rent it out the rest of the year, or if you own a little house down the street and have tenants, that rental activity is generally considered *passive income.* TurboTax asks you about rental property when it fills out your Schedule E, Supplemental Income and Loss.

If you own a vacation home, rent it out for part of the year, and use it yourself for more than the greater of *14 days in a year* or *10 percent of the total number of days it was rented,* you cannot deduct expenses on the property beyond the income. In other words, suppose that you own rental property that you rented for 90 days last year. Keep supposing, and suppose that the property generated $5,000 in rental revenue, that you had $6,000 worth of expenses, and that you slipped up and stayed on the property 15 days last year instead of your usual 14. In such a scenario, you could deduct only $5,000 of your expenses.

If you own a vacation home (or, for that matter, your main home) and you rent it out *not more than 15 days during the year,* you do not report any income on the property, nor can you deduct related expenses. It is as if the rental never happened as far as the IRS is concerned.

If you own and *materially participate* (that is, participate at least 750 hours per year) in the management of rental property and at least 50 percent of your income comes from rental activity, the income (or, for that matter, the loss) is no longer considered passive. In prior years, a rental property exception to the passive loss rule allowed taxpayers to deduct up to $25,000 in expenses in excess of income from passive rental property. Starting in 1994, that limit disappeared as long as you meet this 50 percent material participation requirement.

Costs of renting

If you rent out property, you have another whole set of records to track — not just how much rent you received during the year from tenants, but the costs of operating the property: advertising, insurance, repairs, interest on indebtedness, property tax, cleaning, utilities, decorations, landscaping, snow plowing, painting, automobile expenses, travel expenses, and more.

TurboTax prompts you for a description of the property along with its location. Your description can be as simple as *House* or *Apartment Building*. The location should include the address, city, and state. If this property qualifies as a dwelling unit (as opposed to something like a motel), you get to answer questions about how long you stayed there during the year in order to determine the 14-day/10 percent rule. TurboTax then walks you through this section by asking for your total rental revenue, letting you pick which expenses you need to report. After you enter each type of expense, click the No More Expenses box.

If you have more than one rental property, you need to keep separate records for each property. If some of the records are combined — for example, if you run one advertisement that applies to two different properties — do the best you can to split the expenses evenly between the properties.

The royal family

Royalties are a form of passive income/loss activity and can include investments in oil, gas, and mineral properties, as well as copyrights and patents. So why are they listed here with rental property? The IRS has cozied rents and royalties together and has let them occupy the same lines on the same form. It doesn't matter which you have (or even if you have both types of income); it all goes in the same place on Schedule E.

You enter royalties into TurboTax in exactly the same way you enter rents. In fact, you enter them in the same section. The program asks you whether you have any royalty income; if you answer Yes, TurboTax takes you right back to the same series of questions that you see in the Rental Income area. Go ahead and fill in income and expenses and answer the questions at the end.

Royalties that you earn as a self-employed writer are not considered passive and should be reported on Schedule C, rather than on Schedule E, as business income.

Take It to the Bank: Investment Income

If you save your money in a place that pays you for saving there, instead of just stuffing your money under your mattress or hiding it in the freezer (and you thought nobody knew about such a cool trick, didn't you?), the return on your investments is, alas, taxable income. Some investments, like municipal bonds and tax-free mutual funds, produce nontaxable interest and dividend income. Nontaxable income of this sort still gets reported on your tax return — you just don't have to pay tax on it. This section looks at the major types of investments and shows you how to report the earnings you get from those investments.

You report investment income on Schedule B of the tax return and carry it over to page 1 of your 1040. Because TurboTax knows where to put this information, all you have to do is answer the questions about your investments when you are using the EasyStep method.

Interest(ing) income

All sorts of neat investments, some of which you may own, pay interest. Answering Yes when TurboTax asks you whether you earned any interest income gives you the opportunity to enter the names of all the banks, savings and loans, investment houses, and other organizations that paid you interest just for the privilege of holding onto your money during the year. You can receive interest on all the following types of investments:

- Accounts at banks, credit unions, and savings and loans
- Notes, loans, and seller-financed mortgages (where you are the seller)
- Income tax refunds (That's right! If the IRS pays you interest on a refund, you have to give back some of the interest in tax.)
- Bonds and debentures
- Certificates of deposit
- U.S. Treasury notes, U.S. Savings Bonds, and Series EE Bonds
- Fair-market value of incentives for opening an investment account
- Loans to individuals (including family members)

Just how low will the IRS go to account for your taxable income? Get this: If you open a savings account and the bank gives you a mere *toaster,* the value of the toaster is considered taxable interest income.

Notice that if you used TurboTax last year, the program automatically lists all the names of last year's sources of interest income for you.

Nobody sent me a 1099

"Hey!" you may say. "I didn't get any 1099 forms in the mail. Am I off the hook?"

Sorry, but the rules here are clear. It's your job to know what you earned and to put that amount on your tax return. People paying you interest and dividends are supposed to send a 1099 form if they paid you $10 or more during the year. If the payment didn't reach $10, they can send you a form if they want to, but they don't have to. But just because you don't get a form doesn't mean that you don't have to report the income.

Some interest amounts that you receive are subject to special tax treatment, such as a deferral (or even a complete waiver) of taxes. When TurboTax asks whether the interest you earned should receive special tax treatment, look on the 1099-INT form for special notations like these:

- ✔ **Interest received as a nominee**

    Nominee interest is interest that belongs to you but that generated a 1099-INT issued in someone else's name. That person knew that *you* are really supposed to pay tax on the interest, so she issued a new 1099, called a 1099-Nominee, and transferred the amount to your name (bless her meticulous heart).

- ✔ **Interest received on a mortgage that you financed**

- ✔ **Original Issue Discount interest**

    If the 1099 form is called 1099-OID, you know that you have OID interest.

- ✔ **Private Activity Bond**

    This bond includes such items as state and local municipal bonds.

- ✔ **Tax-exempt interest**

    If the interest is tax exempt, that fact should be indicated somewhere on the form.

- ✔ **Interest on Series EE Savings Bonds**

    You can buy these bonds now to pay for college for your kids later. Assuming that you actually use the bonds to pay for college costs, the interest is tax free. (If you're called upon to do so, you may have to demonstrate that you paid for tuition during the same year you cashed in the bonds.)

TurboTax expects you to enter interest on Series EE bonds along with other interest on U.S. government bonds. Then, when all interest income has been entered, TurboTax checks around to see if you reported any U.S. government interest. If you did, it asks whether some of that interest is excludable as Series EE interest. (*Note:* This question about Series EE interest is not a part of the HeadStart version of TurboTax.)

Dividend income

One of the nicest things about investing in stocks is those checks that come in the mail every three months. These payments, called *dividends,* are taxable and need to be reported. The amounts you receive, whether you get them sent to you in quarterly checks, deposited in an account, or reinvested in additional stocks, are reported to you on Form 1099-DIV.

TurboTax asks you for the name of each company that paid you dividends. Notice that if you received dividend income last year and used TurboTax, the company names carry forward to this year.

After you enter the name of the dividend-paying company, TurboTax wants to know whether the income is a nominee dividend or part of an ESOP plan. You see a little box on the 1099 for these items. If that box is checked, check the appropriate box in TurboTax.

You may include three types of income on your 1099-DIV, and TurboTax wants to know all about them. The three types are as follows:

 ✔ Ordinary Dividends

 ✔ Capital Gain Dist(ribution)

 ✔ Nontaxable Dist(ribution)

When TurboTax asks you to report your income from dividends, include the total amount that you received. Then the program gives you a chance to identify which amounts relate to which kind of dividend.

 Suppose that you used TurboTax last year. The names of companies and institutions that paid you interest or dividends are listed, but some of them are no longer applicable. How do you get these things off the form? Select the company name that didn't pay you anything this year, click Next, press the Delete key on your keyboard, and then click Next through each request for interest or dividend information until you are asked whether you have any more interest or dividends to report.

Types of dividend income

Three kinds of dividend income can appear on your 1099-DIV, and each kind gets a different tax treatment.

✔ Ordinary Dividends are your share of the earnings of the company in which you invested. They're subject to the same income tax that any other income is subject to.

✔ Capital Gain Dividends are your share of capital gains earnings of the company in which you invested. Just as if you had sold a business asset at a gain and reported the income on Schedule D (see "Selling Stocks and Other Valuable Things," later in this chapter), when the company in which you hold stock sells business assets at a gain, your share of that income is reported on Schedule D. Some

members of Congress have been trying for years to change the rate at which capital gains are taxed. As of the time this book went to press, capital gain income cannot be taxed at a rate higher than 28 percent for 1995. TurboTax recognizes any changes in this rate and calculates your tax properly.

✔ Nontaxable Dividends come from a company paying dividends out of its assets rather than out of its earnings. You do not pay income tax on these dividends. However, you need to keep track of the amount of nontaxable dividends you received. When you sell the stock in that company, your cost should be reduced by the amount of nontaxable dividends you received.

'Fess up! What about that Swiss bank account?

TurboTax and the IRS want to know whether you have any foreign investments. When you enter dividend and interest income, TurboTax asks whether any of the income is from foreign sources, whether any foreign tax was withheld on it (and, if so, how much), and in what country the income was earned. If foreign taxes were withheld on this income, TurboTax asks whether you prefer to have the taxes deducted as an *itemized deduction* or taken as a *tax credit*.

The IRS wants you to file a Form TD F 90-22.1 if you have foreign investments and if the aggregate value of those foreign accounts exceeds $10,000. You can prepare that form in TurboTax if you go to the Forms mode, click the Go to Forms button, and fill in each line of the form that applies to your foreign income situation. Note that the Form TD F 90-22.1 doesn't get filed with your income tax return. It is due on June 30 and gets mailed to this address: Department of Treasury, P.O. Box 32621, Detroit, MI 48232.

TIP

Is it interest or is it dividend?

Sometimes it's hard to tell whether you've got interest or dividends. And the people making the payments don't help. Credit unions are notorious for confusing people. On your statement, it says that you received a dividend, but really you were earning interest. Money market funds sometimes make you think that you're getting interest, when really they're giving you dividends.

Here's a test you can use to help figure it all out: If you are earning money on cash that is sitting idle

in an account, it is *interest.* Savings accounts at banks and credit unions, interest-bearing checking accounts, Christmas clubs, certificates of deposit, and similar kinds of things pay interest. If you put your money into a *fund,* the people at the fund invest your money in stocks or bonds or something else that earns income, and then the fund pays you a part of that income, you've got dividends. Mutual funds, money market funds, and investment clubs all pay *dividends.*

Your child's investment income

If your child has income from investments, you may be able to report that income on your own tax return, thus saving you the enormous amount of paperwork and headaches associated with preparing a separate return for your child — not to mention the extra postage.

You can include your child's income on your tax return if all the following requirements are met:

- ✔ The child is under 14 years old on December 31, 1995.
- ✔ The child earned more than $650 (if $650 or under, he or she doesn't have to file a return or report the income).
- ✔ The child's income did not exceed $5,000.
- ✔ The child's income is made up of only interest and dividends.
- ✔ No estimated tax payments were made by using the child's social security number, nor was any income tax withheld.
- ✔ If the child filed his or her own tax return last year, no refund was applied toward this year.

If you want to report your child's income on your tax return, answer <u>Y</u>es to the question as shown in Figure 7-7. The child's income goes on Form 8814. Again, TurboTax is way ahead of you — it already has the form ready and waiting for you to put in the numbers.

Figure 7-7:
Save
yourself the
trouble of
filling out a
tax return
for your
child by
answering
Yes here.

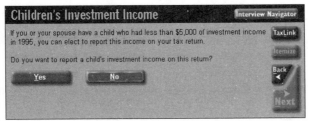

Selling Stocks and Other Valuable Things

Anytime you sell stocks, the IRS wants to know about it. Isn't that just like the IRS? If you sell stocks through a broker, the broker issues a Form 1099B, a copy of which gets sent to (you guessed it) the IRS.

Whether you make a killing, lose your shirt, or perform somewhere in between, you need to report the sale of your stock on your tax return, Schedule D. Right after you finish reporting your dividends and interest income, TurboTax quizzes you about sales of stocks and other items held for investment, which can generate taxable income or losses.

Here's the tricky part: Not only do you have to know how much money you made on the sale, but you also have to go back to your deep, dark past and dig up the original purchase date and cost of the stock. This process can get confusing if you bought a couple of shares at a time in dozens of separate purchases. After you have all the purchase information, proceed into the Stocks and Assets section of TurboTax and feed it the information it wants.

Treat sales of other things you own — car, boat, furniture, library, record collection, or whatever — just as you do sales of stock *if you sell these other items at a profit*. If you sell your private collection of *National Geographic* magazines but lose money on the deal, don't bother reporting the loss on your tax return. But if you sell your rare collection of *Rex Stout Mystery Magazines* from the 1950s and make a killing, you have to share the proceeds with the friendly folks at the IRS.

TurboTax can't distinguish between a loss on the sale of your IBM stock and a loss on the sale of your ten-speed bike, but the IRS can. Items that you bought for personal use — such as bikes, jewelry, furniture, or artwork — are taxable when sold at a *gain* but have no impact on your tax return if you sell them at a *loss*. Therefore, you should not even list personal items on your Schedule D if you lost money on the sale.

Sell Your House! Win Valuable Prizes!

If you own your home and then sell it, guess who wants to know? Gain or loss, it doesn't matter; you still have to report the sale on your tax return. Of course, you don't get any tax benefit from the loss, but selling a house at a gain has some interesting tax ramifications.

Actually, there is one situation in which you can save on your taxes if you sell your house at a loss: if you use part of your house for a business. The percentage of your house that represents an in-home office is multiplied by the loss, and you actually get to deduct that portion.

You can avoid paying taxes on the profit (gain) from the sale of your home in two ways:

- ✔ Purchase a new home within two years of selling the old home and reinvest the entire amount you received from the sale of the old home or more in the new home.

  or

- ✔ Choose to pay no tax on a gain of up to $125,000. You have this option only once in your life, and you must be at least 55 years old.

Figuring the basis and sale price on your home

The *basis* of your home starts with the cost of the house and increases by certain closing costs and the cost of permanent improvements to the house and land. Include such items as

- ✔ Fees and other costs associated with purchasing the home (title search, recording charges, abstract, attorney fees, and so on)

- ✔ Capital improvements such as room additions, a fence, trees, built-in shelving, and electrical wiring

The cost of your house must be reduced by any depreciation that you have claimed on the house in prior years.

It's in your interest to increase the basis of your home because the gain ultimately decreases if you sell the house at a profit.

The sale price of your home is the amount for which you sell the house, decreased by the following items:

- ✔ Costs of the sale, such as sales commissions and other expenses incurred at closing

- ✔ Costs of fixing up the home to ready it for sale, both inside and out (these costs must be incurred no earlier than 90 days from the date of sale).

- ✔ Advertising expense regarding the sale of the home

The lower the sale price, the smaller the gain on the sale and the lower the taxes thereon.

If neither circumstance applies, you must pay tax on the entire gain on the sale of the old house.

When figuring your gain, you need to deduct your *basis* from the sales price (I define *basis* in the sidebar "Figuring the basis and sale price on your home"). If the difference is a positive number, it's a gain. If the sales price is lower than the basis, you had a loss.

Installment sales: Sell now, get the money later

If you sell something today but agree to accept the money in installments over time, the gain also gets reported over time. TurboTax asks you to provide information such as the selling price of the item, the cost or basis of the item, the amount of depreciation on the item that you claimed over the years, and the costs of the sale.

If you sold a business asset (for example, something you used in your business on Schedule C, F, or E) at a gain on the installment method, that business asset has been depreciated; if you owned that asset for more than one year, you need to jump through awful hoops to calculate a potential recapture of depreciation expenses. This procedure is so awful that TurboTax won't even try to do it for you. Get yourself a copy of the instructions to Form 4797 and try to figure it out yourself. Or it may well be a good time to call a tax accountant. Say "Help! Form 4797! Depreciation recapture!" and he or she will know just why you called.

Trading up: Like-kind exchanges

If you have something that Joe wants and Joe has something that you want, you can trade. The problem with this system is that your something may not be worth as much as Joe's something. Someone may clean up on the deal, and someone else may get stuck with a lemon. The IRS understands. You can get favorable tax treatment on this transaction when you trade business property or property held for investment, as long as the two things are similar. In other words, if Joe gives you his FAX machine and you give him your copier, those items are similar because they are both office machines. Likewise, other similar exchanges include land for land, vehicles for vehicles, or buildings for buildings. If you give Joe a piece of land in exchange for his FAX machine, no like-kind exchange takes place. It's equivalent to a sale.

The benefit you get is this: Say that I had a $750 industrial washing machine and you had a $600 industrial clothes dryer. (Assume that those values are the *depreciated* values.) We trade. Your basis in your "new" washing machine is $600 and my basis in my "new" dryer is $750. We keep the basis of the property we give up, so record-keeping is easy. We make up for the difference in the exchange when we sell or dispose of the property. TurboTax does these computations for you, so you don't have to figure out how the process works. Seem weird? Don't worry — it all comes out in the wash.

Reporting Income from K-1 Forms

If you are a partner in a partnership, a shareholder in a small business (S) corporation, or a beneficiary of an estate or trust, then income (and losses) from that entity is passed through to you on a K-1 form.

When TurboTax asks if you have any K-1 forms, prepare to be taken line by line through your form as you give TurboTax each number that appears there. Numbers from your K-1 forms end up in all different places in your tax return. TurboTax takes all your K-1 numbers and shoots them out like meteors throughout your tax return forms.

Frequently, the numbers reported to you on your K-1 form fall into the category of passive income or loss.

The best part about reporting passive activity is that TurboTax takes care of figuring out what you can and can't deduct. Filling out these forms yourself is like walking through a minefield. Just keep your cool, answer the questions when TurboTax poses them, and let the computer get the headaches. For example, suppose you have a K-1 form reflecting a big loss from this Texas partnership, and you fill in all the amounts as TurboTax requests them. The K-1 amounts go to Form 8582, Passive Activity Losses. TurboTax figures out how much loss you can actually claim this year.

Passive income (Sleep while you make money, Part I)

Passive income is income you earn for not doing much of anything. Suppose you own a piece of a partnership that, for example, digs oil wells off the coast of Texas. Maybe you live in Maine and have never even seen Texas or an oil rig, not to mention any of the other members of the partnership, but every now and then they send you a postcard saying, "Oil any day now. Wish you were here." That's a *passive* investment — one to which you don't devote any particular time or effort, but you get a piece of the action if they strike it rich, and you foot part of the expenses if they don't.

Income from passive investments is called *passive income*. The handy thing about passive income is that if you happen to have *passive losses*, such as the expenses on the oil speculation, you can deduct them only if you have passive income to offset them. Otherwise, they just bubble and fester and wait for years until you either get yourself some passive income or give up and get out of the investment group.

Passive losses (Sleep while you make money, Part II)

Investments that generate passive losses result in heavy-duty accounting and record-keeping requirements. If you have significant passive losses, it would be wise to seek a tax professional who can help you sort out the tax ramifications.

You can deduct passive losses only to the extent that you have passive income. You cannot offset a passive loss against your W-2 income or other things on your tax return. Passive losses that cannot be deducted due to lack of passive income get carried over to future tax returns.

That amount goes over to your Schedule E and becomes part of your reportable income and expenses for this year. The rest gets carried forward to next year, when you can once again try to take a deduction for the loss.

If you did not use TurboTax to prepare your tax return last year and want to find out whether you had any passive losses to carry over, look for Form 8582 in last year's tax return. If line 3 contains a positive number, there is no carryover. If this line lists a loss, look down to line 11 (total losses allowed from all passive activities for 1994). If line 3 equals line 11, there is no carryover. If line 11 shows a loss smaller than that on line 3, compare the two and carry over the difference to 1995.

If you belong to a partnership or S-Corporation or are a beneficiary of a trust or an estate, you should receive a K-1 form. If you have not received this form and are getting antsy to finish your tax return, call the office of the organization issuing the K-1 form. You can even ask that person to read you the numbers over the phone (be sure to write down the line number they come from or the description on the line). Unlike W-2 forms, K-1s do not need to be attached to your tax return. If the person you call doesn't know the status of the form, find out who is responsible for preparing and sending out the K-1s.

How did my loss get suspended?

A passive loss that you cannot use in the current year is called a *suspended loss*. It doesn't go away; it just carries over into the future until you have passive income against which to offset it. TurboTax keeps track of your suspended passive losses and drags them out each year to see whether they can be used. If they can be used, you get the deduction. If they can't, the program just puts them away again for another year.

Is Nothing Sacred? Reporting Your Retirement Income

There's retirement income and there's retirement income, but, more importantly (at least for your purposes), there's Form 1099-R. When you get income from a retirement plan, you receive a Form 1099-R. The form tells you up front what is and is not taxable. Just follow along in TurboTax, typing exactly what you see on the form.

If federal income tax was withheld from your retirement income, Form 1099-R should say so. If that's the case, you are expected to attach a copy of that Form 1099-R to your tax return.

IRAs

If you're retired, you should report withdrawals from an IRA fund just as you report retirement income. Just follow along and fill in the blanks in TurboTax. Be aware of the fact that, because special rules govern the tax status of IRAs, you may have to withdraw money from an IRA earlier than you were supposed to. A pretty stiff penalty is involved in doing so. TurboTax goes ahead and computes the penalty for you, but that doesn't make it any nicer.

Social security benefits

Social security information comes to you on Form SSA-1099. Railroad Retirement benefits come on Form RRB-1099. These are considered the same for tax return purposes. All the information you need is in the boxes on the form. Fill in the blanks in TurboTax, and you're in business.

Getting Tax Refunds Back in the Mail

It's such a pleasure to open the mailbox and find a tax refund check waiting for you. It's like having an extra birthday. Tax refunds are probably the nicest part of filing tax returns (although some people would argue that getting a refund just means that the government holds too much of your money all year and only reluctantly gives it back, without interest, after you file a lengthy and time-consuming tax return).

Beware! If you get a tax refund from some place other than the U.S. Government, you may need to report it on your tax return. The rule is that if you deducted your state income taxes on your tax return last year (see "Have Deductions, Will Itemize" in Chapter 8) and then got back some of the income tax in the form of a refund, you should add the refund back to your income.

Make sense? No? Well, as usual, it doesn't have to. TurboTax asks you questions to determine whether you need to report your tax refund as income this year. Have last year's tax return handy when entering your tax refund.

Unemployment Compensation

You must include unemployment compensation in your income on your tax return. TurboTax asks you for this amount and plugs it into your tax return on page 1.

May I Have the Envelope, Please?

Everyone likes to win prizes. Just imagine that ubiquitous Publishers Clearinghouse truck pulling up to your front door with that oversized check for $10,000,000 made out in your name. Or lower your sights to Win-a-Car night at the local AAA ball park. Maybe you won first prize and a check for $500 at the State Fair. Whatever fun contest or raffle you win — dum-de-dum-dum (as they say on *Dragnet*) — don't forget the omnipresent IRS waiting patiently for its share.

Prize winnings, like just about every other form of income that comes into your life, are taxable. More and more, taxes are being withheld right off the top of big cash prizes. If you win a boat or a luxury vacation, however, you need to foot the tax bill yourself. If you win personal property such as a car or boat, or if you win a trip, find out the value of the prize. You should report that amount on your tax return. It goes on page 1 of Form 1040 on the line called Other Income.

When TurboTax asks you whether you had any gambling income, it doesn't refer only to the time you picked the right horse in the fifth race at Belmont. Betting on animals, card games, lotteries, slot machines, prizes, raffles — it's all the same to the IRS. You need to report all gambling income on your tax return.

It's not all bad news when it comes to reporting gambling seccesses to the IRS. Gambling winnings may be offset with gambling losses. Refer to the section "Gambling losses (deductible only to the amount of gambling winnings)" in Chapter 8.

Your Loss Is Your Gain

Check last year's tax return. You may have a *net operating loss* carrying forward to this year. A loss coming forward from last year reduces your income this year, thus reducing your income taxes.

In order for a net operating loss to be eligible to carry back to a prior year or carry forward to the next year, it must result from business expenses or from deductions that result from your position as an employee (see "Have Deductions, Will Itemize" in Chapter 8), or it must be the result of a casualty loss like a hurricane or theft (again, covered in Chapter 8). If you prepared your tax return with TurboTax last year and elected to carry forward a loss, never fear — your operating loss is here, carried over from the preceding year. If someone else prepared your tax return, chances are that a carry-forward list that shows which, if any, items should come forward to this year is somewhere in last year's papers.

Net operating losses typically get carried back before they get carried forward. A loss can be taken back three years and applied against income from those years; then whatever remains gets carried forward for up to 15 years. If you had a net operating loss on your tax return last year, a statement should be attached to the return if the loss is to be carried forward to this year.

Back Up — You Forgot Something

Time for review: Look around you on the table. You should have taken everything out of the pile of receipts and papers representing *income* and placed it in the pile representing *finished.* If something is still in the income pile, you need to incorporate it into your tax return somehow.

Through EasyStep, you can easily backtrack to an earlier part of your tax return, either to check to see whether something already has been included (and just not moved out of the pile) or to see whether something was inadvertently left out.

The Interview topics in the EasyStep system are listed on the right side of the EasyStep window and labeled Interview Topics. You can click the arrow to the right of the topic box, drop down a list, click any item in the list, and go directly to that part of the tax return. The EasyStep questions that go with that topic repeat themselves so that you can add anything that you missed.

Or, if you know where you want to go and prefer to go right to the form and enter the number yourself, click Go to Forms at the bottom of the EasyStep screen. EasyStep turns itself off, and you can click the Forms button to pick the form you want to go to.

When you're ready to return to EasyStep, click the EasyStep button; then choose Resume to go back to where you left off in the tax return process or choose Where I am now to go to EasyStep questions about the active form on-screen.

Chapter 8

In One Hand, Out the Other: Tracking Deductions in TurboTax

● ●

In This Chapter

▶ Making adjustments to income

▶ Tracking contributions to retirement plans

▶ Taking a deduction for moving expenses

▶ Understanding the difference between itemized deductions and standard deductions

▶ Finding out which items count as itemized deductions and getting them on your tax return

▶ Finding a place on your tax return for unusual deductions

▶ Summarizing your tax status thus far

● ●

*I*n their generosity and wisdom, those great minds that came up with the idea of income taxes decided to give you a fighting chance to get back some of what you so loyally report as income in the first half of your income tax return. Thus came the concepts of *adjustments* and *deductions*.

Adjustments to income are what tax accountants fondly refer to as *above-the-line* items. These reductions to your income are taken before you compute the figure called *Adjusted Gross Income* (AGI). The two big advantages to reducing income above the line are the following:

✔ Several below-the-line deductions, or *itemized deductions,* are computed based on the amount by which they exceed Adjusted Gross Income. The lower the AGI, the higher the particular type of itemized deduction — thus the lower your income tax.

✔ Most state tax returns start with Federal Adjusted Gross Income and go from there. Because the state income tax computation is based on AGI, you want to get that AGI as low as possible. Adjustments help accomplish this feat. The lower your AGI, the lower the state income tax.

The first part of this chapter deals with adjustments — above-the-line stuff. The rest of the chapter gives you details about itemizing deductions — when to do it and what kind of stuff qualifies as a deduction. Also, be sure to check out Chapters 15 and 21, which discuss ways to shift income and expenses in and out of your tax year, thus giving you some planning ability and power over your tax liability.

Adjustments: The First Step in Reducing Gross Income

AGI is *Adjusted* Gross Income. The Adjusted part of AGI lets you whittle away at your income, lowering the amount on which income tax is based. You can only adjust a few items, but a handful of specific deductions is better than nothing. Following is a list of the things that qualify as adjustments to income:

- IRA contributions
- Moving expenses
- Retirement contributions if you're self-employed
- Self-employment tax and some of your health insurance cost
- Penalty for early withdrawal from a savings account
- Alimony paid

IRA: Not the army, the investment

In the TurboTax Interview, right after the questions about your income from retirement funds, TurboTax asks you if you've made contributions to an IRA or other retirement fund. If you earn taxable income, you are eligible to set up an IRA. What's an IRA? An *Individual Retirement Account*. You can make contributions to this account while you're working, and the amounts you contribute are not subject to income tax, which encourages you to save and put aside money for your retirement rather than squander it at the local video arcade. When you retire, you'll have a nice nest egg to live on in your old age — or so the theory goes. It has kind of a fairy-tale ring to it.

The current state of IRAs is as follows: You and your spouse can each make tax-deferred contributions (you don't have to pay now, but you'll pay tax on the money when you withdraw it after age 59 $^1/_2$) to an authorized IRA account (the institution where you set up the account authorizes it) of up to $2,000 per year or the total amount of income you earned, whichever is lower. You can deduct the contribution from your income if the following statements are true:

✔ You are not covered by a retirement plan at your job.

✔ Your spouse is not covered by a retirement plan at his or her job.

If either of you is covered by a retirement plan at work, you may still be able to deduct part of your IRA contribution, depending on how much income you make. (The more you make, the less likely you are to get the deduction.)

Using TurboTax, fill in the amounts of the IRA contributions that each of you made when the program asks you to do so. TurboTax figures out how much of your contribution you can use to reduce your income.

Congress would love to make IRAs more accessible to taxpayers, including nonworking spouses. As this book went to press, there were rumblings in Congress about liberalizing the rules for IRA contributions, including a provision to allow nonworking spouses to contribute up to a full $2,000 per year. Check news coverage, the instructions that come with your tax return, or with a friendly accountant after the first of the year to find out what, if any, changes have been made in this area. Changes in this area of the law could affect your 1995 income tax return, or the changes may not be put into place until 1996.

If you're contemplating making a contribution to your IRA, run a sample contribution through your tax return with TurboTax first. Then click the Tax Summary button to see the before-and-after tax effects of your contribution. The amount you are able to deduct may have some bearing on how much you want to contribute. See Figures 8-1 and 8-2 to get a feel for how the Tax Summary looks when you do this.

Figure 8-1:
The Tax Summary gives you the bottom line. This screen shows this taxpayer's figures before he or she enters a sample contribution to an IRA.

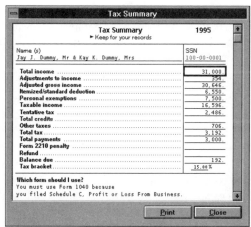

Figure 8-2:
As this Tax
Summary
shows,
making a
$4,000
contribution
to an IRA
saves this
taxpayer
$600 in the
balance
due.

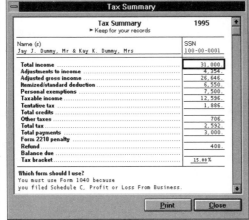

Tax Summary	**1995**
▶ Keep for your records	
Name (s)	SSN
Jay J. Dummy, Mr & Kay K. Dummy, Mrs	100-00-0001
Total income	31,000.
Adjustments to income	4,354.
Adjusted gross income	26,646.
Itemized/standard deduction	6,550.
Personal exemptions	7,500.
Taxable income	12,596.
Tentative tax	1,886.
Total credits	
Other taxes	706.
Total tax	2,592.
Total payments	3,000.
Form 2210 penalty	
Refund	408.
Balance due	
Tax bracket	15.00 %

Which form should I use?
You must use Form 1040 because
you filed Schedule C, Profit or Loss From Business.

Move it!

You can take an adjustment for some moving expenses on your tax return if your move meets certain requirements. After you've finished entering your income in the TurboTax Interview, you are asked, Do you wish to deduct any moving expenses you paid in 1995? Answer Yes if you want to deduct your moving expenses, but keep in mind that in order to qualify for any kind of adjustment to income for moving expenses, you have to meet these tests:

✔ The move has to be in connection with a job.

✔ The distance from your new home to your old place of work has to be at least 50 miles more than the distance from your old home to your old place of work.

If your employer pays for or reimburses you for any of your moving expenses, the employer is required to include that amount on your W-2 form. You automatically report this amount as income on your tax return, so you should have great incentive to offset as much of that as possible with the actual moving expenses.

You are allowed to take an adjustment to your income for the following types of moving expenses:

✔ The cost of moving household goods and personal effects

✔ The cost of travel (if you drive your own car, include gas, oil, and repairs relating to the trip, or a standard rate of 9 cents per mile) and lodging along the way (not including meals) for you and your family while relocating from your old location to the new location

Deductions for all the old moving stuff in years gone by — pre-move househunting trips, costs of selling your old place, costs of purchasing the new home, and costs of breaking a lease — have gone by the wayside. Some of the costs of selling and acquiring a home get applied to the cost of the home. See Chapter 7 for more information about selling a home.

Health care for the self-employed

Congress had a hard time making up its collective mind about whether or not self-employed people should get to deduct part of their health insurance as an adjustment. The deduction is not allowed on Schedule C, where it really belongs. You can now deduct 25 percent of your health insurance as an adjustment. Health insurance costs that can't be deducted as an adjustment get lumped with other medical expenses on Schedule A, Itemized Deductions.

TurboTax will quiz you about health insurance for self-employed individuals while you are filling out your Schedule C for business income (as described in Chapter 7).

Retirement contributions

Contributions to Keogh plans and SEP plans are allowed as adjustments to income. A *Keogh* (pronounced *key-oh*) is a retirement plan for self-employed individuals; employers create *SEP plans* (Simplified Employee Plans) for their employees. Contributions to both Keoghs and SEP plans are tax deferred. You pay tax on the money when you eventually take it out of the plan (ideally, when you retire and your tax rate is lower than it is now).

Providers of these plans inform the plan participants of the contributions made during the year by sending year-end statements. TurboTax asks for the amount that you contributed.

There are limits to how much you can contribute to these plans (see the following IRS Stuff). TurboTax, however, is a trusting computer program. Tell it that you contributed $2,000,000, and, hey, what does it know? TurboTax will go ahead and let you deduct any amount you like. Check the rules outlined in the following section to make sure that your contribution is within acceptable limits.

Deductions for contributions to SEP plans are limited to 15 percent of your annual wages, not to exceed a deduction of $30,000. The contribution can be made by you, your employer, or a combination of both, but the limit of the total contribution deduction is the same in either case. Keogh plans also limit the amounts that can be deducted. The limits are a function of the income of the plan participant as well as the type of plan it is. Check your plan documentation or check with the plan administrator to find out which limits apply to you.

Early withdrawal penalty

You may find yourself in a situation where you've just got to get at that money in your savings account, even if the account has a timer on it. CDs, for example (not the musical kind — the certificates of deposit you buy from the bank), typically come with a maturation date; you're not supposed to take back your money until that date. If you pull the money out before the CD matures, you owe the bank a penalty. The IRS no doubt feels some sense of responsibility toward the people who have to pay this penalty, probably because the early withdrawals are usually made by people trying to scrounge up enough money to pay their taxes.

Therefore, if you suffer a penalty at the bank for early withdrawal of funds that were in some sort of savings plan, you can report that penalty as an adjustment on your tax return. The amount of the penalty appears on your 1099-INT or 1099-OID form.

In the EasyStep Interview, TurboTax asks whether you paid a penalty on early withdrawal from a time savings account (like a bank CD). If you did, say Yes and enter the amount of the penalty in the blank.

Alimony

Regular payments of alimony (as opposed to a lump sum) under the auspices of a divorce decree, support arrangement, or some sort of official judicial order are allowed as adjustments to income for the person making the payments. TurboTax asks you to enter the alimony that either you or your spouse paid.

Have Deductions, Will Itemize

Schedule A, the schedule of itemized deductions, is the breeding ground for most of the special-interest lobbying groups that flourish in this country today. You can tell the strongest groups by the types of deductions that are still allowed: home mortgage deductions and charitable contributions are the main ones left. Credit card interest has gone by the wayside, and the deduction for medical expenses has been greatly reduced. Even the deduction for the cost of a CPA to prepare your tax return has been subjected to a Miscellaneous Deductions limitation (guess we CPAs need to improve our lobbying efforts).

For those people who don't have enough of the types of expenses that qualify as itemized deductions, the IRS offers the standard deduction, one final hit at reducing your income before the tax rates are applied. You don't, however, get both a standard deduction and itemized deductions — you get to take whichever one is bigger as a reduction to your income on your tax return. But wait! Even if you know that your itemized deductions won't exceed the standard deduction, there are a couple of good reasons to go ahead and enter information into your tax return's itemized deductions section.

✔ Anything you enter as an itemized deduction that may apply next year (such as the names of charities to which you contributed) gets carried forward to your 1996 tax return. Entering deductions now will save you time next year if it turns out that you will be able to itemize then.

✔ You may surprise yourself. As you begin entering itemized deductions and TurboTax quizzes you about the types of expenditures you had during 1995, you may find that you have more deductions than you realized. You may be able to itemize after all!

The standard deduction is your *minimum* deduction. If you can come up with more in itemized deductions than the standard deduction amount, go for it!

The standard deduction amounts appear in Table 8-1.

Table 8-1	Standard Deductions for 1995
Filing Status	*Standard Deduction*
Single	$3,900
Married filing joint return	$6,550
Qualifying widow(er) with dependent child (a qualifying widow(er) is one who has been a widow for no more than two full tax years since the spouse died)	$6,550
Married filing separate return	$3,275
Head of household	$5,750

When you get to the section on itemizing deductions, TurboTax asks if you want to itemize your deductions on Schedule A. This question seems totally unfair, as if you're expected to calculate the exact amount of your itemized deductions and figure out which would benefit you more, itemized deductions or the standard deduction. Never fear! If you think you can beat the standard deduction, go ahead and pick Itemized Deductions and give it a try. If your itemized deductions fail to exceed the standard deduction, TurboTax tells you that you're better off with the standard deduction and will use the appropriate number from Table 8-1 in your tax return.

Even if you're not sure that you can do better with itemized deductions than with the standard deduction, you should enter your itemized deductions in TurboTax for two reasons. First, if you come close to the standard deduction and then find another expense you can deduct, you can just go back into the itemized deductions part of your tax return and enter that new expense. If it's enough to put you over the standard deduction, TurboTax goes ahead and changes your tax return to use the itemized deductions. Second, entering your itemized deductions this year means that many of those items will already be in place for next year's tax return and won't have to be re-entered.

Meanwhile, you can still greatly reduce your tax bite in the remaining ripe areas on Schedule A. The following sections give you the scoop on reporting your itemized deductions.

Medical deductions

When TurboTax asks you to enter your total medical and dental expenses for Schedule A, you see a portion of the Schedule A form for itemized deductions, and on it you can see the amount of medical expenses you need to beat in order to make this deduction worthwhile. TurboTax calculates 7.5 percent of your Adjusted Gross Income to get this medical expense limitation. You can look on the Schedule A form and see how much you need to have spent for medical purposes in order to make the cut for this deduction. If your medical expenses do not come close to exceeding 7.5 percent of your Adjusted Gross Income (as shown on line 3 of Schedule A), don't bother with this section. If you know that your medical expenses are higher than 7.5 percent, or if you think that you've got a fighting chance, go ahead and summarize your medical expenses.

When entering deductions (as well as other information in TurboTax) you can create *itemization* statements that provide more detail than the tax form allows. Access the itemization feature by clicking the Itemize button at the top of the EasyStep screen or the Itemize button on the toolbar in Forms mode. For example, if you are entering doctor expenses and want to prepare a doctor-by-doctor list so you'll have a record of exactly where you spent all that money, you can make an itemization for doctor expenses.

When you ask to itemize an amount, TurboTax gives you an itemization box in which you enter the detail of the particular expense you want to itemize. When entering information in an itemization box, use the Enter key to move from one line to another. Click the Close button to close the itemization schedule and carry the total to the tax return line in TurboTax.

You can use Table 8-2 to summarize your medical expenses on paper before entering them in TurboTax. Go ahead, write in the book. Really — it's okay. You'll want a new one next year, anyway.

Table 8-2 Itemized Deductions for Medical and Dental Expenses

Item	Amount
Prescription medicine	
Medical insurance premiums	
Doctors	
Dentists	
Other medical professionals	
Hospitals	
Clinics and other medical care facilities	
Lab and X-ray fees	
Eyeglasses and contact lenses	
Medical supplies and equipment	
Miles driven for medical purposes multiplied by 9 cents	
Other medical transportation (taxis, ambulance, and so on)	
Lodging at or near medical facilities	
Medical improvements to home	
Other medical stuff that doesn't seem to fit above	
Total	

Okay, so you have nice little blanks to fill in. Now you need to know what all these things mean.

- ✔ **Doctors, dentists, and other medical professionals:** The amounts you pay for care and advice to someone who has been trained in a special field of medicine. This category includes psychologists and psychiatrists, chiropractors, nurses, ophthalmologists, and so on. (You know, all those folks who drive fancy cars.)

- ✔ **Hospitals, clinics, and other medical care facilities:** If you have to go someplace to get your medical care and that place charges you for being there, you incur a medical expense. This category includes treatment centers for controlled substances.

- ✔ **Miles and other transportation:** Keep track of the miles (on your own car, that is) that you spend driving yourself and your dependents to and from the doctor's office, hospital, or even the drugstore (assuming that you took the trip to pick up medicine, not to get toothpaste).

✔ **Health insurance:** If you pay for health insurance yourself, list it here. If your employer pays for your health insurance, you don't get the deduction — your employer does. If you purchase health insurance through a cafeteria plan at your place of employment, you can't claim a deduction.

A *cafeteria plan* is a benefit wherein you get to purchase perks such as health insurance with before-tax dollars. The gross wages amount on your W-2 form does not include the cost of your health insurance, so you are not paying income tax on that part of your income — thus you do not get to deduct the health insurance cost. In effect, that cost has already been deducted because it isn't in your income in the first place.

If you receive a reimbursement of health insurance in 1995 for medical expenses you paid in 1995, you can't deduct the expenses, even though the reimbursement isn't income to you. If you receive a reimbursement in 1995 for medical expenses you deducted on your 1994 tax return, you should report the reimbursement as income this year. It goes in Other Income on page 1 of your 1040. If you have such a reimbursement, be sure to look at last year's tax return and make sure that you actually got the benefit of that medical deduction. If your medical expenses from last year didn't exceed 7.5 percent of your Adjusted Gross Income, don't worry about adding back any insurance reimbursements.

✔ **Medical supplies and equipment:** This category includes crutches, bandages, antiseptic, contraceptives (when prescribed by a physician), cold and allergy medicine (again, if prescribed), eyeglasses and contact lenses and their supplies, walkers, oxygen, hearing aids, seeing-eye and hearing-ear pets, and wheelchairs.

✔ **Prescription drugs:** Medicine that requires a prescription. Insulin counts, too.

✔ **Lab and X-ray fees:** All the extra expenses for things they do at hospitals and medical care facilities — the stuff that always surprises you when it shows up on your bill.

✔ **Lodging at or near medical facilities:** Lodging at a medical facility where you or one of your dependents is receiving treatment. If you pay to stay near (rather than at) such a medical facility, put the cost of the facility here. The IRS puts a cap on this expense: $50 per day per person maximum. You can count the person in need of medical care and one other person, if that second person is there to provide assistance to the one needing care.

✔ **Medical improvements to home:** Ramps, stair elevators, special hand rails, and other things that are expressly for the purpose of providing medical care or making the house accessible to someone in need of medical care — these expenses go in this category. If the improvements have uses other than medical care, you're expected to prorate the cost between a deductible medical portion and a nondeductible personal portion.

✔ **Other stuff that doesn't seem to fit in any of the previous categories:** Schools for physically or mentally disabled people, telephone devices for the deaf, and other things that serve some medical purpose apply here.

✔ **Grand total:** Put it all together and what have you got? Enough to exceed 7.5 percent of your Adjusted Gross Income, or this exercise was all for naught.

Tax deductions

You can reduce your income (that is, increase your itemized deductions) according to how much you pay in certain taxes, the theory being that you shouldn't end up paying taxes on taxes, or something like that. Not every kind of tax you pay qualifies as an itemized deduction. Look out for the following:

✔ **Federal estimated taxes:** No, this isn't an itemized deduction on your Schedule A, but since your entering your other taxes here, TurboTax has chosen this place in the Interview to let you enter the estimated taxes you paid the IRS for 1995. Enter the dates and amounts you paid quarterly estimated taxes, and TurboTax carries those amounts to their proper places on the 1040.

✔ **State estimated taxes:** If you paid estimates for your state income taxes, enter them on Schedule A. TurboTax prompts you with questions about when and how much you paid. One especially neat thing about this feature is that if you're using TurboTax to prepare your state tax return, the state estimated tax information you enter here transfers to your state return.

✔ **Overpayment of prior-year taxes:** If you qualify for a refund on your state tax return from last year and elect to let the state hold on to it, that's the same as if you got the money, deposited it in your checking account, and then turned around and wrote a check back to the state. Because the process is the same as making a tax payment, leaving the tax with the state on your tax return counts as an itemized deduction.

✔ **State payments by trust:** If you are the beneficiary of a trust (if you don't know what this means, then you're probably not), and if that trust pays state taxes for you, you will get a statement from the trust to that effect. Record the amount of state taxes that the trust paid for you when TurboTax asks for this number.

✔ **State extension for 1995:** Has April 15 come and gone? Did you extend your state tax return when it was due in the spring? Did you pay some tax with that state extension? If your answer to all these questions is yes, then enter the amount that you paid with your state extension.

✔ **Local estimated taxes:** If you happen to be lucky enough to live in a place that charges not only federal and state but also local taxes, count your lucky stars. And enter the amounts you paid for local taxes when TurboTax requests them.

- ✔ **Real estate taxes:** Any real estate taxes that you paid are deductible on Schedule A, unless they were paid on business property (over on Schedule C, F, or E, for example). If you had office-in-the-home expenses on Schedule C (or some other place in your tax return) and listed real estate taxes there, TurboTax automatically carries the taxes that don't go on Schedule C over to Schedule A.

- ✔ **Property taxes:** If you pay taxes on personal property such as automobiles, the tax is deductible. To see whether you pay personal property taxes on your automobile, check the registration or the receipt you got from the license bureau when you bought your license plate tags. Somewhere on there is a references to taxes. *That amount* is what you can deduct — not the entire cost of the plates. Only certain types of tax qualify: property tax, excise tax, and car tax are acceptable, but sales tax, hotel tax, and pet license fees *are not.*

Interest (ing) deductions

You can deduct two kinds of interest without having to make big explanations. One is interest on home mortgages and the other is investment interest. Both, of course, have exceptions — you wouldn't need books like this one if rules had no exceptions.

Mortgage interest expense

When TurboTax asks you whether you paid home mortgage interest in 1995, it doesn't want to know the total amount you paid on your mortgage for the year, but rather the portion of the total amount that represents interest. If you're like most people, that means that only about 99.9 percent of your payment is deductible interest; the remaining smidgen goes toward reducing the huge principal balance on your house.

If you bought your house this year and paid those funny things called *points,* or some other things called *loan origination fees* (sometimes you may be tempted to call these little payments *kickbacks* to the bank that did you the favor of issuing the loan, but of course that wouldn't be very polite . . .), you can deduct them as well. Alternatively, if you *refinanced* rather than bought your house this year, any points paid must be deducted ratably over the life of the loan.

Don't add up all the interest and points into one bundle; TurboTax asks you for each amount individually.

You can deduct mortgage interest on only two homes. So if you are paying on a mortgage on your main house and then have three vacation cottages on which you are also carrying mortgages, you can take your mortgage interest deduction only on the main house and one of the vacation homes.

Banks that hold mortgages issue statements around the end of each year to tell you how much you paid. If you look closely in all the corners of this statement, you should find the number 1098, the official bank mortgage statement number. The IRS gets a copy of this statement, too.

Sometimes you pay mortgages to people instead of to banks. TurboTax knows this, so don't worry; it asks you for all the information it needs about the person to whom you pay your mortgage.

Investment interest expense

The other type of interest you can deduct on Schedule A is investment interest expense, which is the interest you pay on money that you borrowed in order to invest. To make the interest deductible, what you invest in must be income-producing — stocks, bonds, and oil wells, for example.

If you borrow some money and only part of it goes toward an income-producing investment, you must keep track of how much of the interest on the loan is investment-related interest. The rest is not deductible.

Interest expense paid on money borrowed in order to purchase *tax exempt* stuff, such as Puerto Rican road repair bonds or funds that turn around and invest in state governments and schools, cannot be deducted. In other words, the investment that generates this deduction must itself be of the taxable-income variety.

Entering investment interest expense

You might have investment interest expense reported to you on a Schedule K-1. The invested interest expense from your Schedule K-1 will be entered at the place where you enter other Schedule K-1 information (see Chapter 7). Be careful not to duplicate that expense by entering it again on Schedule A.

Investment interest expense that you can't deduct this year gets carried over to your 1996 tax return. Likewise, you can use as a deduction on your 1995 return any investment interest expense you had in 1994 that you couldn't deduct last year. If you used TurboTax to prepare your income tax return for 1994, that carryover amount should already be in place on your 1995 Schedule A. If this is your first year using TurboTax, enter your unused investment interest expense from 1994 here on your 1995 tax return. TurboTax asks you for this amount when it starts summarizing your investment income. Be patient — you'll soon see a screen for Investment Interest Expense Carryover.

You may have to attach Form 4952 (Investment Interest Expense) to your tax return to help compute your investment interest expense deduction. Give thanks to the TurboTax gremlins who figure out whether you need this form and then fill it out for you if you do.

Contribution deductions

A charitable donation, be it cash, a household item, or investment property, can be claimed as an itemized deduction. Naturally, this isn't as easy to figure out as it sounds.

The organization to which you donate things must be recognized by the IRS as an acceptable place for receiving charitable contributions in order for you to get the deduction. Generally, you get a receipt for your contribution, and the receipt will designate whether your donation is tax deductible.

If you don't have a receipt acknowledging your tax-deductible contribution, contact the organization to which you donated. Someone there ought to know whether the charity is recognized. You can check the list of which types of organizations are recognized in TurboTax by clicking the underlined words *cash contributions* in the TurboTax Interview and then clicking *most charities* on the Tax Help screen.

Your deduction depends on the type of donation:

- ✔ If you give cash, the amount of cash you give equals the amount of deduction you take.

- ✔ If you drive your vehicle for charity, you can take a deduction for mileage. Enter the number of miles when TurboTax asks for it; the program multiplies your number by 12 cents to figure your deduction.

- ✔ If you give *things* instead of cash, be prepared to list the name and address of the organization that received your stuff, the date on which you made the donation, and your estimate of the value of the item(s) you contributed.

If you donate used personal belongings such as clothing and household items, you need to come up with a value. Check out resale stores — run by Goodwill, the Salvation Army, and so on — to estimate prices.

Keep detailed lists of the items you give to charity. Consider taking photos of the items you donate. Be sure to get a signed receipt from the charity when it accepts your donation.

Note: The law now states that you must have a signed receipt from the charity that accepts your donation if you value the item(s) at $250 or more.

Casualty and theft deductions

Note: I've included information about casualties and thefts here because this is where it falls on the tax return. TurboTax, however, has other ideas about where you should enter this casualty and theft stuff. At the place where you enter capital gains and losses (see Chapter 7), you have an opportunity to enter gains and losses from casualties and thefts.

When life's little tragedies (not to mention the big ones) become reality, the IRS may not be the savior you expect to hear knocking at the door. Nevertheless, tax savings are sometimes available for people who have suffered tragedies.

A *casualty,* for tax return purposes, is a sudden, unpredictable, devastating event, an unexpected catastrophe that results in damage or loss to personal property. Fires, floods, hailstorms, tornadoes — these types of things qualify as potential casualty-makers. Damage resulting from such events can be costly. Usually, insurance takes care of reimbursing you for destruction from Mother Nature's wrath. Sometimes, however, you're not insured or you have to pay a large deductible portion.

Theft is what you think it is: Somebody steals something from you. The stolen item has to be some kind of personal property (stealing your hubcaps counts, but stealing your thunder doesn't). If someone ransacks your house and gets away with dozens of items, all the items together count as one loss from theft (one big loss is better from a tax deduction standpoint than many little losses — see IRS Stuff coming up).

You need to do some figuring here: how much the damaged property was worth before the calamity and how much (if anything) it's worth afterward. TurboTax gets you through all this by asking questions to determine the amount of the deductible loss.

As much as you might think that an army of termites eating away at your bedroom walls ought to qualify as a casualty, the IRS doesn't agree. Things that take a long time to happen, like bugs in the walls or rust under your car, don't pass muster on the casualty meter. The event must be swift and sudden in order to count.

Figuring out the amount of your deduction is only the first step. The IRS, like your insurance company, has its own deductible portion. The first $100 of your loss is not allowed as a deduction. If you have two or more casualty or theft losses during the year, $100 is taken off each of them. That's not all: After reducing your loss by $100, you have to reduce it again by 2 percent of your Adjusted Gross Income.

You need to attach Form 4684 to take a claim for casualty and theft losses. TurboTax asks you some questions to prepare this form. Expect to be asked things such as the following:

- ✔ Date of loss.
- ✔ Type of loss (earthquake, tornado, robbery, and so on). Then select Property A if this is the first loss your are reporting, Property B for the second loss, and so on.
- ✔ What did you lose (brief one- or two-word description)?
- ✔ When did you acquire the item(s)?
- ✔ How much did it cost?
- ✔ How much insurance reimbursement did you get (or how much do you think you'll get)?
- ✔ How much was the damaged (or stolen) item worth before the casualty or theft?
- ✔ How much is it worth now (in other words, how much would someone pay you for the item in the state it's in now)?

Stolen items have no current worth, so answer *none* to the last question.

Miscellaneous deductions

Some deductions just don't fit nicely into any particular category. Rather than say you can't have them, the IRS kindly set aside a special group called Miscellaneous Deductions. This classification includes the following:

- ✔ Business expenses for which you did not get reimbursed
- ✔ Job search expenses
- ✔ Education expenses

- Professional dues and subscriptions
- Work clothing and uniforms
- Investment fees
- Safe-deposit box rent
- Tax preparation fees
- Gambling losses (you can only deduct losses from gambling as an offset to gambling winnings — if your losses exceed your winnings, you get no deduction for the excess)

Taking these deductions isn't as easy as it may seem. The miscellaneous expense deduction has a stringent limit: you can deduct these items only to the extent that they exceed 2 percent of your Adjusted Gross Income (oh, *that* again . . .). See line 32 of your 1040 for your AGI — or better yet, don't worry about it. TurboTax knows where to find this number. As you enter your miscellaneous deductions, TurboTax compares them to the 2 percent AGI limit. Once you surpass that threshold, the deductions become viable.

Herewith is a description of common miscellaneous expense deductions:

Employee business expenses

If you have to spend money to do your job — money you wouldn't otherwise spend — chances are that you can deduct that expense as an itemized deduction. TurboTax asks you whether you had business expenses that were *not* reimbursed by an employer. Click Yes if you spent your own money and didn't get any of it back from your boss. Click No if you spent your own money but your boss returned at least some of it to you.

If your employer reimbursed you for some of your miscellaneous business expenses, you have to file a Form 2106 with your tax return. Should you care? Nope. That's why you have TurboTax.

Some of the business-related things on which you may have spent your money include the following:

- **Automobile and other local transportation expenses:** You can report auto expenses either by keeping track of your mileage or by calculating actual expenses of operating your car (see "The high cost of driving" in Chapter 7 to figure out how to report automobile expenses)
- **Air/Train/Bus fare:** Actual amount, no limit
- **Meals:** Limited to 50 percent of amount actually spent on business-related meals
- **Parking fees and tolls:** Actual amount, no limit

✔ **Business gifts:** Limited to $25 per recipient per year

✔ **Professional or trade licenses and fees**

✔ **Business-related books and subscriptions**

✔ **Medical examinations required for your employment**

✔ **Telephone expenses specifically related to your job**

List each item individually as TurboTax asks you for your expenses in the itemized deduction section of the Interview. After you've listed everything, TurboTax goes to work figuring out if you can actually deduct this stuff, based on the 2-percent-of-AGI limit.

Job search expenses

This is actually a pretty cool thing that the IRS does. You can take a deduction for the expenses you incur looking for a job: resumés, travel to interviews, postage for answering ads, and employment agency fees, for example. The catch is that you must have already had a job in that profession; this can't be your first job out of school, nor can it be a switch to a job in a new profession.

You get only one line on which to describe each expense; meaning that you can only enter **Job Search Expenses** on that line and not the various *types* of job search expenses. If you want to include with your tax return a list of just exactly what kinds of job search expenses you had, go ahead and type **Job Search Expenses** when asked for the type of expense, and then click the Itemize button on the toolbar when it's time to fill in the amount of your expense. You can then list all the specific job search expenses you incurred.

Education expenses

Somewhere, sometime, when you least expect it, you may find yourself back in school, carrying home books and doing your homework. As with job search expenses, TurboTax doesn't give you any guidance in this area. You have to know whether you qualify for this deduction.

Herewith, the picky rules for qualifying to take the education expense deduction. You need to meet one of two requirements:

✔ The education must be a requirement for you to keep your current job or your current salary, *or*

✔ The education must maintain or improve job skills that you already possess and that you use in your current job.

But note the following exceptions to the rule. Even if you meet one of the preceding requirements, you still may not be able to deduct education expenses if one of the following is true:

- ✔ The education is required and merely meets the minimum educational needs of your present job, *or*
- ✔ The education is preparing you for a new trade or business, even if you have no intention of pursuing that new trade or business.

If you pass, go ahead and enter your education expense when TurboTax asks whether you had any other miscellaneous itemized deductions.

Education expenses consist of tuition, books, supplies, lab fees, travel to and from wherever it is you're getting educated, meals you buy while at the educational institution taking classes (subject to the 50 percent limitation that all meal expenses are hit with), and odds and ends such as paying to have your term paper typed.

Dues and subscriptions

You can deduct dues to professional societies (assuming that the organization is somehow related to your occupation) as well as subscriptions to professional journals and magazines that relate to your occupation. You can also deduct union dues. These things go in the miscellaneous deductions part. TurboTax prompts you for a description of whatever it is you are trying to deduct and then asks you for an amount.

Work clothing and uniforms

If you have to pay for uniforms that are required for your job, you can deduct their cost as well as the cost of caring for (that is, cleaning and repairing) them as a miscellaneous deduction. This area is a little sticky. Many people wear things to work that feel like uniforms but really aren't, at least not as far as the IRS is concerned.

The uniform rule is as follows: If you wear the clothes outside your workplace and people who see you don't recognize what you're wearing as a uniform, then what you're wearing isn't a uniform. You may wear a three-piece suit to work and not wear it anyplace else in your life, but if you put it on and walk into a department store, strangers won't look at you and think that you're wearing a uniform.

Investment fees

The category of miscellaneous deductions also includes payments to institutions such as banks, mutual fund companies, and stock brokerage firms for the purpose of keeping track of your money and your investments or collecting your interest or dividends. Also, the costs of keeping up with your investments, such as subscriptions to magazines that report trends or newsworthy items about the things in which you have invested, qualify as miscellaneous deductions.

Fees paid to brokers for the purpose of purchasing stocks are not deductible here. Instead, these costs get added to the cost of the investment and presumably are recouped at some time in the future when you sell the stock.

Safe-deposit box rent

You can treat the cost of your safe-deposit box rental as a miscellaneous deduction, provided that you use the safe-deposit box for something that is income-related. So put stock certificates, deeds to your rental property, savings bonds, and other boring but income-related stuff in the box.

Tax preparation fees

Finally, you've reached the most important part of your tax return: where you get to deduct the cost of this book. That's right! You paid hard cash in order to get all this invaluable help with the preparation of your income tax return, and now you get a payback.

Other tax preparation costs include fees to tax preparers, the cost of your TurboTax software, long distance phone calls to gather information for your tax return, and the cost of filing your return electronically.

You're supposed to deduct costs in the year in which you paid them, not the year to which they apply. Therefore, if you spend money this spring to help you prepare your 1995 tax return, the costs will be deductible on your 1996 tax return.

Gambling losses (deductible only to the amount of gambling winnings)

Money that you spent gambling can be deducted as a miscellaneous deduction. Wow! Las Vegas, here I come! Actually, it's not as slick as it sounds. The amount you deduct as gambling expenses cannot be higher than the amount you declare as gambling winnings (which you already reported under Miscellaneous Income — see "May I Have the Envelope, Please?" in Chapter 7). Sooooo, it's kind of a wash. You report the gambling income and you can deduct gambling losses up to that amount.

Gambling losses are not subject to the 2 percent AGI limit. Wait patiently until you've waded through all your other miscellaneous deductions, at which point TurboTax asks specifically if you have gambling losses to report.

The IRS expects you to keep some kind of record of your gambling in order to support this deduction. Keep a little journal listing every time you gamble: what you played, where it was, how much you spent, and how much you won. Hang on to any receipts or tickets you get that support your costs.

TurboTax is right on top of things when it comes to this gambling business. If you try to deduct gambling losses in excess of your winnings, you get bombarded with error messages and a loud alarm, and uniformed men start knocking at your door. Just quietly say, "I'm sorry," fix the amount that you deducted (or increase the amount that you put down as gambling winnings), and everything will quiet down.

The Deduction Finder

TurboTax has a really nice little feature called the Deduction Finder that looks through your entire tax return and asks you questions about all the areas where you may have overlooked taking a deduction. Right now — right after you enter your deductions — would be an appropriate time to use the Deduction Finder, but TurboTax doesn't agree with me on that. Instead, the Deduction Finder is part of the TurboTax Final Review, the final look-at-the-whole-picture process that is performed after you have finished (or think that you've finished) your entire tax return.

So be patient; you have a little ways yet to go. If you get antsy to see this Final Review, skip ahead to Chapter 12 and check out the section about the review process.

How you're doing: Instant summary

If you're curious about what your tax looks like at any point in the game, click the Summary button at the right side of the EasyStep screen.

After you've finished cheering (or agonizing) — and remember, this isn't final yet — close the Summary by clicking the Close button in the Summary window. The Summary vanishes, and you're back in action.

"I'M PAYING $28,000 DOLLARS A YEAR TO AN IVY LEAGUE UNIVERSITY SO THAT YOU CAN BECOME AN EXPERT IN ARTIFICIAL INTELLIGENCE?"

Chapter 9

Help! Error Messages and Problem Solving

In This Chapter

▶ Recognizing things that might go wrong

▶ Knowing what to do when you have an error

▶ Finding out whether you have any errors

▶ Getting on-screen help

▶ Cross-referencing numbers in your tax return

▶ Dial-a-problem: Using TurboTax's technical support line

▶ Commiserating with other tax preparers on online forums

*S*o there you are, working diligently on your tax return, munching a little pizza on the side and trying not to get tomato sauce on your keyboard, when suddenly, seemingly without warning, a red flag goes out. You find yourself in the tax return penalty zone, not knowing where to go next.

Fear not! You can pick your way deftly through TurboTax error messages with a few simple keystrokes, find answers to complex questions right on-screen, and even get human help when you need it.

Common TurboTax Error Messages

TurboTax is fairly nonchalant about a lot of errors that can occur while you enter your data. Errors and omissions are calmly noted, logged, and stored away. TurboTax plans to discuss these items with you before you finalize your tax return. Before you print your return, when you put yourself through the Final Review process, the program gives you the opportunity to sort through all the errors that it has noted and make restitution.

Some of the things that may end up on your error list include pieces of information that you inadvertently left off your forms. For example, you may have skipped over the zip code part of your address, or maybe you didn't fill in your occupation. Some forms contain questions that need to be answered; perhaps you overlooked a question at the time TurboTax asked it, or maybe you weren't sure of the answer, thought that you would come back to it, and then forgot. You might have entered negative numbers as positive or entered expenses with a minus sign. The IRS is extremely precise about the way in which you enter information if you plan to file electronically, so you may get nailed with an error message if you type too many digits in entering your social security number on your W-2 form.

Whatever the error, TurboTax keeps a nice list for you and lets you work your way through the list at your leisure before you finalize your tax return.

To check whether you have errors from EasyStep, click the Review tab, make sure that Errors is checked, and then click Start Review. If other items on the Review tab are also checked, you may not get to the error section right away. When you do get to the error section, you'll know it: TurboTax displays a red bar across the top of the screen that contains the emphatic message, You Must Fix This Error. The error itself is described, the offending form is displayed on the lower half of the screen, and you are given an opportunity to either Fix This Problem or Skip This Problem, as shown in Figure 9-1.

TurboTax takes you by the hand and, one by one, leads you to each form that contains an error or omission, telling you what the problem is, showing you the error on the form below, and giving you an opportunity to fix the problem. Choose Fix This Problem, and TurboTax asks you for information that it needs to know to correct the problem. Choose Skip This Problem, and TurboTax saves the error, allowing you to return to this process later if you want to confront the error at another time.

Using the Forms method, view a list of errors by clicking the exclamation point button, the one described as Display a list of errors in your return (see Figure 9-2). Click this button, and the list of errors appears at the top of your screen (see Figure 9-3). You can double-click an error or click an error and click the Go to Error button to display the error on-screen and get the opportunity to examine and correct the error.

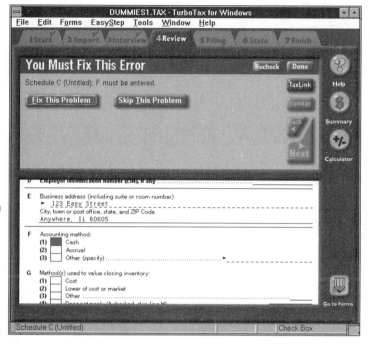

Figure 9-1:
In EasyStep, you choose whether you want to fix or skip the problem.

Figure 9-2:
Click me for instant help.

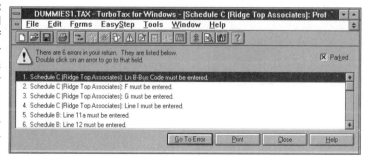

Figure 9-3:
Aaargh! All sorts of error messages appear when you click the Error Summary button.

If you view errors from the Forms method (click the Go to Forms button in EasyStep), you can view the entire list of problems and then choose the ones that you want to deal with in any order you please. Attacking errors in EasyStep is a little more structured — you get the errors in the order TurboTax wants to present them. You decide, one at a time, which ones you want to deal with.

How Do I Get This Thing Off My Screen?

There are spring showers, and then there are gale-force hurricanes that rip off the sides of buildings and carry them halfway across town. Likewise, there are mild-mannered error messages that you can retrieve at your leisure, and then there are critical error messages that leap onto the screen, leer at you, interrupt your concentration, and won't go away until you pat them on the head or feed them a couple of fat laboratory rats.

Critical error messages demand your attention. An example of a critical message appears in Figure 9-4. It throws itself on-screen in the form of a box labeled `Error Alert` and kicks and screams until you acknowledge its presence. The Error Alert box includes a description of the error and explains what you should do to rectify the situation. The type of error that causes this much commotion thoroughly disrupts the tax computation on your tax return. You won't see many of these errors (with luck, none at all), but if you do encounter one, read what the message says, note what it says to do (write it down if necessary), click the OK button that the box provides, and then do what TurboTax asks of you. If you don't, the error message will continue to pop out at you and refuse to leave you alone.

Figure 9-4:
Don't ignore these messages; they'll stick around and haunt you until you fix the problem.

You do have the power, however, to put this error alert in its place. If you click the little Hide further error warnings box that appears at the bottom of the error message box, you can keep these messages from pestering you. Doing so, however, prevents you from seeing that you have done something that is really causing a problem with your tax return. I don't recommend turning off the display of critical error alerts.

So you've turned off the error alert display and now you're feeling remorseful? Don't worry. You can bring those pesky errors back to life by opening the Edit menu, choosing Options, and then choosing Show Error Alerts.

I can't tell you what error messages *you* might see — the messages are a direct result of information you enter and I, of course, can't predict what that will be. What I can tell you is this: Read what the message says and try to do what TurboTax asks. Critical error messages mean critical problems. If you can't find a reference in this book to the topic generating the error message, bring in the big guns at TurboTax — call Technical Support (see "TurboTax Telephone Support," later in this chapter).

I Can't Believe My Computer Ate the Whole Thing!

Your tax file is gone?! Oh, no! Well, some problems may occur that have nothing to do with TurboTax. Your tax file may get lost on the vast continent that is your hard drive, or it may disappear altogether through no fault of your own. This is not in any way meant to confirm the frequently bandied-about rumor that malicious gremlins live inside our computers, waiting until we are completely trusting and unsuspecting and then eating our files at will. Instead, this section attempts to guide you in figuring out what has become of a missing file and restoring it to its past glory.

If you suspect that your tax file is among the missing (clues: you start up TurboTax and your familiar tax file doesn't immediately join you on the TurboTax screen, or while in TurboTax you choose File⇨Open and — alas! — your file is not on the list), follow these Windows 3.x steps to recovery (or, at least, confirmation that the file is actually lost):

1. **Return to the Program Manager. (Press Ctrl+Esc; in the Task List, select Program Manager, and then click Switch To.)**

2. **Open the File Manager (double-click the little yellow filing cabinet in the Main group window).**

3. **Choose File⇨Search from the menu.**

4. **In the Search For box, type *.TAX. Then press the Tab key.**

5. **In the Start From box, type C:\.**

   (If your TurboTax program is not on your C drive, type a different drive letter in place of the *C*.) If Search All Subdirectories isn't checked, click the box to check it.

6. **Click OK.**

After a few seconds, you see a window on your screen labeled `Search Re-sults:`. Inside this box, you should see the names and locations of all tax return files on your selected drive. Make a note of what you see, and then choose File➪Exit to leave File Manager. If the search results indicate that `No matching files were found`, you should repeat the preceding steps using a different drive letter if an alternative drive exists on your computer.

If you use Windows 95, follow these steps to search for your missing file:

1. **Click the Start button.**

2. **Click Find.**

3. **Choose Files or Folders.**

4. **In the Find: All Files window that opens, type *.tax in the Named: section.**

   The Look In: section should contain the drive on which you want to search. Be sure that the Include subfolders box is checked.

5. **Click the Find Now button to begin the search.**

The list of search results appears at the bottom of the Find: All Files window, as displayed in Figure 9-5. You can perform the search over again, trying a different drive, if the first search fails to bring up any tax files.

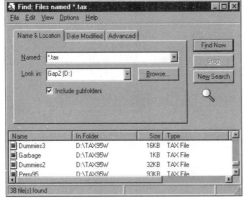

Figure 9-5:
Here are the results of my search in Windows 95.

If you have exhausted the possible search locations and still have not found your tax return file(s), get out the disk onto which you should have backed up your tax return. (See "Save This Year's Tax Return on a Disk" in Chapter 21.) Put your backup disk in your disk drive and start TurboTax again. Choose File➪Open from the menu. Where you are asked for a filename, type **A:** (or **B:** if the floppy drive you are using is your B drive) and then click OK. Select your tax return filename from the list of files that appears under the File Name area and then click OK. Your tax return is now back in action on-screen. Before doing anything else, choose File⇨Save As from the TurboTax menu, type **C:\TAX95W** (replace **C** with the letter for whatever drive on which you want to save TurboTax), and then type a backslash and the name of your tax file in the place for a filename and click OK. Doing so places your tax return file back on your hard drive. Also, it ensures that the tax return you continue to work on will be the one on your hard drive instead of the one on the disk.

If you were unable to find your tax return file and you had not previously copied it onto a floppy disk, I'm afraid that you're stuck with having to re-create the whole thing. From here on, be sure to make a disk copy and save it in a secure place.

Second-Guessing TurboTax

Sometimes, trying to figure out what's causing an error is a chore akin to building the pyramids or trying to find a purple button on a neighborhood scavenger hunt. TurboTax does its best to give you guidance and information that helps you through the tangle of errorland. Occasionally, however, that's not enough. Herewith, some additional hints for digging up the cause of error messages:

✓ **Cross-Reference:** While using the Forms method, you have the capability to find the source numbers that have been planted on your tax forms. See "Where the Heck Did This Number Come From?" later in this chapter for more detail about the Cross-Reference feature.

✓ **Interview Navigator:** Using EasyStep, click the Interview Navigator button. At the My Tax Data tab, you can see all the pieces of information you have entered into your tax return thus far. Click any item, and then click Interview to go to the part of the Interview where you entered that item. Click Go to Form to go directly to the form, where you can see what you've done and make changes.

✓ **Interview Navigator, take two:** Still in EasyStep, still in the Interview Navigator, click the Topics tab and view a list of all the major topics of your tax return. Choose a topic by clicking it, click Interview to go to the Interview for that topic, and then click Go to Form to fly over to the form for that topic.

✓ **Back track:** In EasyStep, you can go back one screen at a time, reliving the data entry process that you previously endured. Just click the Back button whenever it is not dimmed, and you get to see the questions you just answered. This approach to moving back in time can sometimes help you figure out how you got to where you are now, which, in turn, can help you solve irritating problems.

> ✔ **Check this valuable and comprehensive guide:** Try the index and table of contents of *TurboTax For Windows For Dummies,* 2nd Edition and search for the topic that's giving you headaches. Also, check out Appendix B, a 1040 cross-reference that guides you to where in this book you can find information about a particular line on your tax return.

Tax Help Straight from the IRS

If you're using the HeadStart version of TurboTax, you've probably already stopped to scratch your head a couple of times, wondering where this much-ballyhooed IRS tax help is hiding. Well, give up searching (and scratching) — the IRS help is hiding in the TurboTax Final version. On-screen instructions straight from the horse's mouth, as it were, are at your fingertips when you click the Help button in the EasyStep mode (see Figure 9-6). After Help opens, you can choose the IRS Instructions tab which (in the Final Version) displays real instructions from the IRS. Click the Tax Help button on the toolbar in the Forms method (see Figure 9-7) to get the same help window.

Figure 9-6: Help! Click here from EasyStep.

Figure 9-7: Click here from the Forms method for more Help.

Help with the Forms

Wondering what goes on a particular line or in a particular box on your tax form? Clicking the Help button that appears on the side of the screen in EasyStep (refer to Figure 9-6) or at the top of the screen in the Forms method

(back in Figure 9-7) returns you to basic information about what goes on your form. Here you'll find a wealth of information:

- ✔ Tax Help includes general information about what you are expected to enter on your tax return and technical terms that have been underlined — click the underlined term for a definition and examples.

- ✔ IRS Instructions takes you to the heavy-duty technical stuff.

- ✔ Cross-Reference shows you which form or schedule the number you are currently working with comes from.

- ✔ Program Help provides you with sage advice about the inner workings of TurboTax.

Clicking the Print button in the Help box gives you the opportunity to print the help topic if you want a hard copy to keep as a reference.

Where the Heck Did This Number Come From?

TurboTax does a lot of calculating and carrying numbers here and there, placing things on lines long before you get there. Sometimes you can look at a form and find that it's been completely filled out for you. How did this happen?

You can trust TurboTax to know what goes where, but if you're still curious, flip over to the Forms method and click any number on any tax form. At the bottom of the screen, you should see a message like QuickZoom, Calculated Value, Date Field, Checkbox, Numeric Input Field, or Text Input Field. The message changes depending on which line you're on, and each message tells you where the number came from. When you see QuickZoom, that means the number you are pointing at comes from another form. Click the Help button at the top of the Forms screen (back in Figure 9-7) and a box appears, telling you the source of that number. You can clear the cross-reference box by clicking Close.

To actually visit the source of a number on one of your tax forms, click twice on the number. You are *QuickZoomed* to its form of origin.

You've Got the Whole World in Your Hands

Well, maybe not the whole world. . . . But you do have a source book, this one, in your hands, and it is a good place to start when you are trying to solve problems. The mouse in your hand is another friend when you find that you have a problem. Go to Help, use the on-screen IRS instructions, and check the TurboTax manual that came with your program. You have several sources right at your fingertips for solving the problems that you may encounter in this computer program.

Sometimes, however, even all this stuff isn't enough. That's when you can pick up the phone. . . .

TurboTax Telephone Support

Dial in to TurboTax technical support for your choice of tape-recorded messages or a real person. For help of the tape-recorded variety, call 800-685-7369. You can get answers to the questions that TurboTax has determined are those most frequently asked.

You must have a touch-tone phone to receive tape-recorded support. If you call from a phone without a touch-tone feature, you are simply disconnected. You don't even get a nice message apologizing for the inconvenience.

Most of the information on the automated support line is about installation and printing. If you have technical tax questions, call the regular technical support and talk to a real person. The real people are at 520-295-3090. Prepare to stay on hold, longer and longer as the spring progresses. The closer April 15 gets, the more desperate people there are out there.

There are alternatives to telephone hold limbo, though. See the next section.

Party Lines for TurboTax Geeks

Wait a minute, you say? This can't be the right place for you? Don't be so sure. The computer geeks who eat programs like TurboTax for breakfast may be just the ticket to solving your problems. If you have a modem, you can get online not just with technical support representatives from TurboTax but with real users of the program, who relish the opportunity to solve other people's problems.

The technical support forums on the various major networks like CompuServe, GEnie, America Online, and Prodigy are populated with people who (1) probably have encountered a problem like yours already and (2) will find great enjoyment in helping you solve it.

Call up these forums and browse through lists of questions that have come before yours. Chances are that your question is already there, complete with its answer. If not, add yours to the list and someone will respond to you (frequently, several people will respond with alternative suggestions and stories of how they were so smart to figure out the answer).

In order to use any of these networks, you have to purchase a membership. Frequently, membership drives are held and you can join for little or no initial cost. You can find out about joining CompuServe by calling 800-524-3388 (ask for Operator 145 for information about a free introductory membership that includes a usage credit). Contact GEnie at 800-638-9636. American Online can be reached at 800-827-6364, and Prodigy is at 800-776-3449. The back of your TurboTax manual, just before the index, contains information about signing on and joining these forums. If you've been contemplating joining anyway, this may be a good excuse to do so.

Part III
You Owe
How Much Tax?!?

"I just don't know where the money's going."

In this part...

Tax is a funny thing. It gets sucked out of everybody's paychecks all year long and hardly anyone complains, but having to write a check for even a few dollars come April 15 is somehow very galling.

The back page of your tax return skips back and forth between taxes and credits, as does TurboTax's Interview process. To make things easier for you, and for the sake of my own sanity (I believe I still have some), I've grouped all the taxes in one chapter and the credits in another. Look up the specific tax or credit that intrigues you and read about it instead of trying to work through this section from start to finish.

In this part, you can discover what's lurking on the bottom line of your tax return, remove the last elements of mystery, uncover the last available deductions, check to see that everything is in order, and hold your breath, hoping that a big refund (or at least a very small payment) awaits.

Chapter 10

The Tax Calculations

*T*he old days of adding up your income, subtracting your expenses, and multiplying the difference by 1 percent (the original income tax rate, established in 1913) are so far buried in the past that you'd be hard pressed to find anyone who even remembers that kind of taxation. Now you have to pay not only income tax (at a rate slightly higher than 1 percent) but all kinds of other taxes as well.

This chapter attempts to shed some light on the whole tax computation business. Computing taxes in TurboTax is almost akin to the calm after a summer storm: It's so straightforward compared to your hard work in entering all your income and expenses. You're finished gathering up 1099s, W-2s, medical expenses and related insurance statements, business expenses, and receipts for contributions. Now it's time to sit back and answer some questions so that TurboTax can figure out how much tax you owe.

Don't get totally discouraged if your tax liability grows as you go through this section. TurboTax computes taxes first; the section on tax *credits* — those little wonders that may lower your tax liability — comes later.

The Tax Table versus the Tax Rate Schedule

Some sort of great mystery seems to center on whether income tax should be computed by using the Tax Table or by using the Tax Rate Schedules. The answer is one of those secrets that tax accountants have kept to themselves for years. Are you ready? *There is no difference between the Tax Table and the Tax Rate Schedules!* In fact, in the good old days before computerized tax return preparation, CPAs used to figure out income taxes by using the Tax Table and then double-check their accuracy by figuring out the tax on the same income by using the Tax Rate Schedules. Now, don't you feel smug?

Of course, you don't have to worry about which method to use to calculate your income tax because TurboTax does it for you. In fact, TurboTax doesn't even give you a chance to discuss the choice — it just goes ahead and computes the tax. But in case you're curious, Figures 10-1 and 10-2 show you what these forms look like.

Figure 10-1:
The Tax Table looks like this.

Section 5.

1995 Tax Table

Use if your taxable income is less than $100,000. If $100,000 or more, use the Tax Rate Schedules.

Example. Mr. and Mrs. Brown are filing a joint return. Their taxable income on line 37 of Form 1040 is $25,300. First, they find the $25,300–25,350 income line. Next, they find the column for married filing jointly and read down the column. The amount shown where the income line and filing status column meet is $3,799. This is the tax amount they must enter on line 38 of their Form 1040.

Sample

At least	But less than
25,200	25,
25,250	25,3
25,300	25,7
25,350	2

If line 37 (taxable income) is—		And you are—				If line 37 (taxable income) is—		And you are—				If line 37 (taxable income) is—	
At least	But less than	Single	Married filing jointly *	Married filing separately *	Head of a household	At least	But less than	Single	Married filing jointly *	Married filing separately *	Head of a household	At least	But less than
		Your tax is—						Your tax is—					
0	5	0	0	0	0	1,300	1,325	197	197	197	197	2,700	2,725
5	15	2	2	2	2	1,325	1,350	201	201	201	201	2,725	2,7
15	25	3	3	3	3	1,350	1,375	204	204	204	204	2,750	2,7
25	50	6	6	6	6	1,375	1,400	208	208	208	208	2,775	2,800
50	75	9	9	9	9	1,400	1,425	212	212	212	212	2,800	2,82
75	100	13	13	13	13	1,425	1,450	216	216	216	216	2,825	2,8
100	125	17	17	17	17	1,450	1,475	219	219	219	219	2,850	2,87
125	150	21	21	21	21	1,475	1,500	223	223	223	223	2,875	2,9
150	1	2				1,	1,5	22	22				

Where Tax Tables and Tax Rate Schedules differ

Actually, there is one big difference between the Tax Table and the Tax Rate Schedule. The Tax Table figures tax only on income up to $100,000 — the people who have to type those pages after pages and columns after columns of tiny numbers don't get paid enough to keep on going after they get to $100,000. So if your taxable income crosses the $100,000 threshold, you're stuck figuring your tax with the Tax Rate Schedules, which takes only slightly more effort than finding your income on the Tax Table and moving your finger across the column until you find the correct tax number.

IRS STUFF
1040

SCHEDULE Y-1:		Married Individuals Filing Jointly and Qualifying Widow(er)s 1995		
Taxable Income				**of the amount**
Over	**But Not Over**	**Pay**	**+ % on Excess**	**over —**
$ 0-	$ 39,000	$ 0	15	$ 0
39,000-	94,250	58,500	28	39,000
94,250-	143,600	21,320	31	94,250
143,600-	256,500	36,618.50	36	143,600
256,500-	....	77,262.50	39.6	256,500

Figure 10-2:
A sample
Tax Rate
Schedule.

Self-Employment Tax for People Who Don't Have "Real" Jobs

Employees get paychecks, and payroll taxes, including federal income tax, state income tax, social security (FICA), and Medicare, are withheld from their pay. Those who employ themselves — the Schedule C people (not to mention the Schedule F people and some of the Schedule E people) — have to worry about paying all those taxes themselves. One of the most difficult taxes for the self-employed to swallow is the self-employment tax.

Self-employed people pay no more self-employment tax than employed people, but it seems like they are paying twice as much. How does this happen? Employed people have only *half* their social security and Medicare payments withheld from their paychecks. They never see the other half because their employer sends it off to the government without telling them about it. On the other hand, self-employed people don't have employers to sneakily send off half their social security and Medicare tax, so they pay both halves of that tax at one time come April.

The self-employment tax section appears in TurboTax after you enter information for Schedules C and F (see Chapter 7). Since this is a tax, however, and it falls in line with the other taxes on the tax return, I've included the information you need to know in this chapter with the other taxes. Here are the questions that you need to be able to answer in order to get through the self-employment tax section in TurboTax (you won't see these questions if you are not subject to self-employment tax):

✔ **Would you like to use the *non-farm optional method* to calculate self-employment tax?** TurboTax asks you this question only if it determines that you qualify. This optional method allows you to pay *more tax than you actually owe* — just in case you didn't think that you were paying enough. To find out why you'd want to do something like that, see the upcoming IRS Stuff.

✔ **Did you receive income as the employee of a church that claims a special exemption from the employer's portion of social security (FICA) tax?** If you did, you can apply for an exemption from self-employment tax.

The non-farm optional method of figuring your self-employment tax is for people who have limited income from self-employment, not because of the low amount of their receipts but because of the high amount of expenses with which they must offset the income. The optional method permits self-employed individuals to pay a higher self-employment tax and thus (presumably) receive additional social security benefits when they retire.

If you want to use the non-farm optional method for computing self-employment tax, or if you are an employee of a church claiming the special FICA exemption, click the Adjustments button at the start of the self-employment tax section and answer the ensuing questions appropriately.

More Tax? What's This AMT?

The Alternative Minimum Tax, otherwise known as the AMT, is one of those taxes that nobody really understands. What's more, nobody *wants* to understand it. The people who made it up don't even want to hear about it.

The Alternative Minimum Tax caught on back in the halcyon days of tax shelters, in an era when taxpayers at relatively high income levels were investing in bizarre limited partnerships that somehow managed to generate year after year of mega tax deductions for minimal investments. In an effort to curb the tax savings that these arrangements were creating, the tax authorities came up with this tax, which attempts to ensure that everyone pays a fair share. In a way, the AMT made sense because some of those investments were pretty shady. Now, however, the tax has somehow managed to creep into the lives of the regular tax-paying public.

The theory is that you can pay this *alternative* tax, which is a little higher than your regular income tax, just in case your income tax isn't high enough.

TurboTax puts you through the AMT grinder even if there isn't a chance in the world that you have to pay this tax, so be prepared to answer the following types of questions:

✔ **Did you try to deduct too much investment interest expense on your tax return?** Shame on you. Go to the Forms method and take a look at Form 4952. A Form 4952 worksheet accompanies this form, so open that up, too. Look at the worksheet on-screen, or print out a copy to have by your side, and add up the amounts on lines 21, 22, and 23 of the worksheet. Now flip back to the Interview and enter the sum of those lines in the section that asks you to adjust investment interest.

✔ **Did you exercise an incentive stock option (a stock option that you acquired from your employer)?** If you got the option in 1995 and exercised it in 1995, skip this question. If you received an option in an earlier year and exercised it this year, you must report the difference between what the option was worth when you got it and what you actually paid for it when you exercised it.

✔ **Did you have any passive activities?** If so, you may need to make some AMT adjustments to the gain or loss you are reporting from these activities. This stuff is nauseatingly complex. Call an accountant.

✔ **Did you have research-and-development expenditures? Intangible drilling costs? Depletion? Circulation expenditures?** (You know, you were at a party and you started circulating, you had to purchase a few drinks, and. . . .) *Pleeease!* This is ridiculous. If you think that any of this stuff affects you, you've probably already called an accountant.

Yes, there's more. Mining exploration, tax shelter farms, pollution control facilities . . . give me a break! This form is totally out of control, and you shouldn't be expected to know any of this. TurboTax provides detailed instructions for computing the AMT implications of all this stuff. Does anyone understand them? Not even the people who wrote them. Actually, people didn't write these rules; those monkeys at typewriters who don't get fed until they've typed something coherent wrote this stuff. Once again, go get an accountant if you're in this much trouble.

✔ **Did you purchase and take a tax credit for alcohol fuel?** (You don't have to say what you did with it.) If so, enter the amount of the credit you claimed this year.

✔ **Do you have any related adjustments?** I particularly like this option: a crystal-clear description of what you need to report. If you got this far, take a deep sigh of relief, click the Next button, and get out of here.

✔ **Did you have a net operating loss on your Alternative Minimum Tax form last year?** If you had no AMT form last year, the answer is obviously an emphatic *no.* If you had such a form in last year's tax return, look on line 21 and report any number that appears there.

End of Alternative Minimum Tax. Take a much-deserved break.

Kiddie Tax, or the Family That Earns Together Pays Together

If you have a child who is under age 14 and has dividend or interest income from investments in excess of $650 but not greater than $5,000, then celebrate! You have someone from whom you can borrow when you're in a bind.

If the child's investment income is $650 or less, you don't need to file a tax return for the child because the income isn't taxable.

If the child's investment income is greater than $650 but less than $1,200, or if it's greater than $5,000, you must fill out a separate form with separate tax computations for that income for the child. Tax on the investment portion of the income (dividends and interest) is computed at the parent's highest rate. Ouch!

If the child's investment income is between $1,200 and $5,000 *and* the child had no other type of income *and* no estimated payments were made using the child's social security number, you may choose one of two ways in which to report this child's income and pay the tax:

- ✔ Using Form 8814, add this child's income to your own and file only one tax return for parent(s) and child.

- ✔ File a separate tax return for the child, but compute the tax on the child's investment income by using your tax rates.

TurboTax introduces this subject in the Investments topic, right after you report your own interest and dividend income. If you choose to report your child's investment income on your own tax return, you report it after your interest and dividends. It appears on page 1 of your tax return on the Other Income line.

When filing a separate tax return for a child who will be taxed at the parents' tax rate, finish preparing the parents' tax return first and have it nearby. In order to compute the child's tax, you must report some amounts from the parents' tax return on the child's return.

You may not think that there would be much difference, but think about it for a minute. If you add the child's income to yours, your Adjusted Gross Income increases, and if you itemize your deductions on Schedule A, your potential medical, investment interest, and miscellaneous deductions (the deductions that are limited by a percentage of your AGI) are reduced. You may also suffer a reduction of available IRA contributions or child and dependent care credit.

If the child has other income besides dividend and interest income, you have no choice; you must file a separate tax return for the child.

So when would you want to report the child's income on your tax return? Use just one form (if you're not required to use a separate one for the child) in the following circumstances:

- ✔ You have no itemized deductions.
- ✔ The child has no itemized deductions (investment expense, charitable contributions, and so on).
- ✔ You're not deducting a contribution to an IRA.
- ✔ You don't have a child and dependent care credit.

Generally speaking, in a situation in which the child had between $650 and $5,000 of unearned income (such as interest or dividends or a distribution from a trust), there is no advantage to adding the child's income to that of the parent and filing one return for everyone. You will probably be money ahead if you file separately for the child, even though the child's tax is computed at the parent's rate.

Penalty Taxes on IRAs

If you receive a distribution from an Individual Retirement Account (IRA) during the year, the amount you receive may be subject to both income tax and a special 10 percent, leave-that-money-alone penalty. When you pulled that money out of your IRA, you probably didn't realize that you were going to have to give almost half of it back in taxes.

First you have to pay income tax, which may be as high as 39.6 percent, depending on how high your taxable income is. Don't forget state income tax and maybe even city or county income tax, depending on where you live. Then on top of all the income tax is a 10 percent penalty. Ouch!

So when TurboTax starts nosing around and asks whether you rolled over your IRA withdrawal into a new fund, the program is trying to figure out whether you deserve to be hit with the penalty.

Recapture Taxes

In some special situations, you actually have to add taxes to your tax return because you took too much credit in a prior year. As nasty as this sounds, it's true. Fortunately, it hardly every happens anymore (about 15 years ago, it was pretty common). Nevertheless, if you happened to take a credit on a prior year's tax return for Investment Tax Credit, Low Income Housing Credit, or Federal Mortgage Subsidy Credit (you know who you are) and didn't meet all the requirements necessary to earn that credit, you have to give back the part to which you weren't entitled. TurboTax asks you what it needs to know about this stuff. If you think that this recapture business applies to you but are not sure, you may want to check in with your neighborhood tax professional.

Miscellaneous Taxes

For those annoying odds-and-ends taxes that don't deserve a section all to themselves, TurboTax has a catch-all "Other Miscellaneous Taxes" topic that puts the burden on you. The program asks, Do you expect to owe any additional taxes that have not yet been mentioned? It's certainly easy enough to say No to this question and be done with it. Just in case, however, you should check under mattresses and seat cushions to see whether any taxes are lying about that you might owe.

I'm talking about pretty obscure things here, like miscellaneous penalties and taxes on some types of benefits that you weren't really supposed to receive. If you think you owe something that you haven't reported anywhere else on your tax return, this might be the catch-all place you're looking for.

Once again, when you get into these confusing little areas, call for help. You don't have to spring for an island vacation for your favorite accountant; just call with a question or two, and the fee should be minimal.

The Defense Rests

That's it — the jury is out on taxes. All your tax computations are completed. Clicking the Summary button in either EasyStep or the Forms method should give you a pretty fair idea of your bottom line. You have just a few more items to tackle — some credits that may cut your tax liability a bit more. Read Chapter 11 to find out how to find those credits.

Chapter 11

Cutting the Tax Down to Size

*A*fter you reduce your income, and thus your tax, by claiming all the deductions you can find, tax credits are last chance chunks of tax that you can pull off and throw away. A deduction reduces your income, and then the tax rate is applied. So if your tax rate is 20 percent, you benefit by 20 percent of your tax deductions. Unlike deductions that reduce your income before the tax is computed, tax credits reduce your tax *dollar for dollar.* That's right — every dollar of tax credit reduces your income tax by a dollar. There aren't many of these things, but if you can get them, they are sweet.

The Babysitter's Club: Form 2441

You may be able to claim a credit for expenses paid to a caregiver, a day care center, or even a day camp if it meets certain requirements. In order to claim the child and dependent care credit, you (and your spouse, if you're married and are filing a joint return) must have paid for care while you worked, looked for work, or went to school. The care must have been for one or more of the following people:

> ✔ Your child, if that child was under 13 years old while receiving the care (apparently, the IRS feels that 13-year-olds don't need child care — or maybe they do need the care, but the IRS isn't willing to foot the bill once they reach this age)

Note the strange and seemingly contradictory fact that you can't take this credit if the child receiving dependent care is age 13 or older, which seems to imply that children 13 and older are responsible enough to care for themselves, yet you can't hire your own child if he or she is age 13 to 18 to provide care worthy of a credit.

- ✔ Your spouse who is physically or mentally unable to care for himself or herself

- ✔ Anyone who qualifies as your dependent if that person is physically or mentally incapable of self-care

Your expenses are prorated if the person received the care for only part of the year or if that person met the preceding qualifications for only part of the year.

Alert: If you pay one of your children to provide the care, the child has to be at least 19 years old. TurboTax checks that out and passes you to the next step if the child meets the 19-year-old requirement. However, in addition to being at least 19 years old, the child providing the care must not be your dependent. You can still claim a 19-year-old who is still in school as your dependent. TurboTax doesn't address this issue, but it assumes that a child who is at least 19 years old is not your dependent. Therefore, it's up to you to recognize whether or not a 19+-year-old caregiver who is your child qualifies you for this credit.

When you are ready to enter information about the child and dependent care credit, TurboTax asks for the number of dependents for whom you are claiming this credit. Whether you enter one or two dependents makes a difference in the amount of your credit. Having three or more, however, is the same as having two as far as the credit you can claim is concerned, so don't labor too long over how many qualifying dependents you may or may not have.

The amount of dependent care credit to which you are entitled is twice as much for two dependents as for one, but the credit does not increase beyond that amount if you have more than two qualifying dependents.

If you withhold tax from your caregiver's pay, you now have the option to remit that tax with your federal income tax return. The new Schedule H, Household Employment Taxes (fondly referred to as the "Nanny Tax"), has been added this year. A discussion of this form is up front in Chapter 2 with the other stuff that's new for 1995.

Expenses that qualify you for the credit

The amount that you can claim in dependent care expenses is based on the amount that you spent during the year for the care of your dependent(s) and the amount of your earned income (a discussion of earned income follows in the next section). This amount includes expenses for the following:

✔ Fees paid to a caregiver or babysitter, either in your home or away from home, including day care centers

✔ Payments for household services such as housekeeping and cooking, if those services include the care of a dependent

✔ Costs of day camp (overnight camp does not count, however, even in part)

✔ Costs of nursery school (attending children must not yet have entered first grade)

If the costs of nursery school includes actual schooling as opposed to just child care services, and if that schooling cost is identifiable and separable from the total cost, then only the child care cost qualifies as a tax credit.

If your dependent child was born in 1995, you may be better off taking the extra credit portion of the earned income credit than taking a child care credit for the costs of caring for this child. (That's right — you can use a child for only one of these credits.) TurboTax figures both credits for you, and you can select the one that's greater. (See "Earned Income Credit," later in this chapter.)

TurboTax doesn't realize that you may calculate both the child care credit and the extra credit portion of the earned income credit based on the same child. If you calculate both credits in order to determine which is better, be sure to go back into TurboTax via the Forms option on the toolbar (stop the Interview and click the Forms button at the top of the screen) and delete the information on the form for one of the credits before filing your return. It's a good idea to remove your own mistakes instead of letting the IRS remove things for you.

You need to provide the name, address, and social security number of each care provider in order to take the credit for payments to that person. I can't emphasize this point enough. If your babysitter or care provider won't give you a social security number, you don't get to claim a credit.

Figuring earned income

In order to compute the child and dependent care credit, you must place your *earned income* on the form. Earned income is income that you work for as opposed to income that you receive from investments. TurboTax can find the amounts that qualify as earned income from all the other forms in your tax return, so you don't need to pick apart your tax return line by line, trying to discern earned income.

You *do* need to do one thing, however, in order to solidify this earned income figure. If either you or your spouse was a full-time student or was physically or mentally unable to perform basic care services, you can increase your earned income amount by $200 per month for each month of education or impairment.

Generally, the higher a spouse's earned income, the higher the credit. This rule isn't *always* true, but it applies often enough that it's worth your time to figure this $200-per-month amount and have TurboTax add it to your earned income. Just for the record, if you increase a spouse's earned income on this credit form by using the $200-a-month method described in the preceding paragraph, you don't pay tax on it. This is just your little secret with the dependent care credit form; TurboTax doesn't go blabbing this amount to the other forms as if it were something that should be added to your taxable income.

Credit for the Elderly and the Disabled: Schedule R

Life is full of little treats for the elderly: lower ticket prices at movie theaters, senior citizen night at the Waffle House, aches and pains that mere midlifers can only imagine, and a special tax credit, the credit for the elderly or the disabled.

To qualify for this credit, you must be either of the following:

✔ Age 65 or older by the end of the year

✔ Retired on permanent and total disability

Basically, the credit works as follows: If you meet one of the preceding criteria and your income is under $17,500 if you are single, $20,000 if you are married filing jointly and only one spouse is eligible for the credit, or $25,000 if you are married filing jointly and both spouses qualify, then you may be able to get at least a partial credit. The maximum credit allowed for 1995 is $1,125 ($750 if you're single).

You have to have a very low income to qualify for this credit, so most people don't get to utilize it. Trust TurboTax to figure out whether you qualify; it knows all about this credit, so you don't have to do any calculating yourself.

Credit for Paying Taxes to Foreign Places: Form 1116

It's really only fair, when you think about it: If you earn income in another country, you should pay to support the government programs in that country. But then to come back here and pay taxes again on the same income — well, with all these taxes, you may reach a point where your income vanishes into the thin air of the IRS office (and foreign equivalents).

Therefore, if you earn income abroad and pay tax on it in that country, you still have to include the income with your other income on your U.S. tax return, but you can take a credit for the taxes you paid to the other country. The theory is that you avoid being taxed twice on the same income.

Foreign tax issues are actually addressed by TurboTax in the income part of your tax return, just after questions about social security benefits and retirement contributions. If you need to go back to this section to re-address the foreign tax credit issue, click the Interview Navigator button, click the Topics tab in the Navigator, and scroll up (or down) until you find the topic called Foreign Tax Issues. Click this topic and then click the Interview button, and TurboTax deluges you with questions about your foreign income. Based on the answers you provide to these questions, TurboTax figures your foreign tax credit for you.

Untaxes

The *Alternative Minimum Tax,* or AMT, is a silly, irritating little tax, seemingly designed just to steal credibility from the most weathered tax accountants. This section is not about the AMT (see "More Tax? What's This AMT?" in Chapter 10) but instead is about the *Minimum Tax Credit.* The Minimum Tax Credit is actually a reversal (of sorts) of the AMT — the Un-Alternative Minimum Tax, if you will.

What happens when you get stuck paying the Alternative Minimum Tax is that, in addition to nailing you with a higher tax, the IRS takes away some of the tax credits you just worked so hard to create. You can carry *some* of those credits forward to the next year so that you don't completely lose them. Thus the creation of this Un-Tax, an attempt to give you a chance this year to use up the credits that were stripped away from you last year.

You must have your Form 6251 (Alternative Minimum Tax) from last year handy in order to clear the record of those credits that this credit-gobbling tax scarfed away from you. Just follow along with TurboTax, entering the numbers that it requests as it attempts to recover items that you lost last year.

Earned Income Credit

Congress keeps finding ways to make earned income credit more universally available. Someday, everyone may just file for the earned income credit and not worry about the rest of the tax return.

What is this thing?

The earned income credit is a *refundable credit.* Refundable credits are the coolest kind because you get to claim them even if you don't owe any taxes. Usually, if your tax is low or zero, you can't reduce it below zero, and if your other credits exceed the amount of tax you owe for the year, you don't get to request a refund. But the earned income credit is different. Its presence sends shudders down the spines of all those check-writers in Washington, because no matter how little your tax liability is and no matter how big your earned income credit is, you get the benefit of the credit.

How do I get this credit?

The credit is computed on Form EIC. TurboTax knows how to prepare this form.

To qualify for the earned income credit, all the following circumstances must be true:

✔ You or your spouse must have one child who is under age 19 (age 24 if a full-time student) and who lived with you as your dependent for at least six months during the past year, *or* you must be at least 25, under 65, and can't have been claimed as a dependent on someone else's tax return.

✔ You must be working.

✔ You must have earned income of under $24,396 if you have one qualifying child or $26,673 if you have more than one qualifying child, or under $9,000 if you have no qualifying children. (***Note:*** That $9,000 figure was still in IRS limbo at the time this book was written. If you think that you qualify for this credit, check the instructions that come with your Schedule EIC in your income tax return booklet to verify the amount of income for child-less credit-claimers.)

TurboTax does a pretty good job of figuring out your earned income for the year, but you may have to give it a little help. If you had earned income that was not taxable, you must feed this amount to your computer so that TurboTax can close in on an exact amount for earned income. TurboTax gives you an opportunity to enter nontaxable income that you may have earned (fellowships, for example), or you can leave the Interview, go to the Forms method by clicking the Go to Forms button at the bottom of the EasyStep screen, select the worksheet W-EIC Adjustments, and enter amounts directly on that page.

Beyond that, TurboTax figures out what it needs to know and computes this credit if you're entitled to it.

Because this credit is refundable, you can still file a tax return and get this credit refunded to you even if you don't owe any tax.

Chapter 12

Odds and Ends

- -

In This Chapter

▶ Playing with your completed tax return

▶ Printing your tax return

▶ Paying your taxes

▶ Mailing your tax return

▶ Forgetting to mail your tax return

▶ Amending your tax return

▶ Preparing and filing your state tax return

- -

*I*n this chapter, I'll pick up all the little bits and bytes of things that I didn't trip over in previous chapters, including some nifty shortcuts and tricks that make fooling around with your tax return actually seem like fun!

Don't get too carried away, though. Before you know it, you'll have to pop your return into the mail, and I'll talk about how to do that, too. And although I can't possibly cover the ins and outs of every state income tax return here, I can speak in generalities that should help when you're ready to prepare yours.

So get ready to wrap things up and reward yourself for a job well done.

Hey, Look Me Over!

It may seem like it's time to print this puppy and take a look at it, but wait! Before wasting all that paper, you can view your tax return on-screen in several different ways. Get a feel for how it all fits together, let TurboTax point out potential problem areas, make last-minute corrections, and brace yourself for that bottom-line amount — and hope for a refund!

After you finish your tax return, you may feel friendly enough with TurboTax to poke around in some of the areas that went into the completion of your return, as well as some of the features that are new. Nifty places you can explore in TurboTax (once you're free of EasyStep) include the following:

✔ Tax Summary

✔ Specific forms that are in your tax return

✔ Other forms that didn't make the cut into your tax return

✔ Error Summary

✔ File Cabinet

Leave EasyStep whenever you want to by clicking the Go to Forms button in the lower-right corner of the EasyStep screen. (See the Go to Forms button in Figure 12-1.) In Forms mode, you have free access to your tax return forms in whatever order you want to see them, to the buttons on the toolbar, and to the menu choices.

Figure 12-1:
Click here while in EasyStep and you'll sidestep over to the Forms method.

The Tax Summary

Go ahead — get it over with and look at the bottom line. In EasyStep, click the Summary button on the right side of the screen — it looks like a big dollar sign (see Figure 12-2). If you are in the Forms mode, Summary is up on top on the toolbar (see Figure 12-3). Clicking the Summary button shows you a quick analysis of your income, adjustments, deductions, exemptions, taxes, credits, payments, and, of course, the bottom line: Refund or Balance due. Figure 12-4 shows a summary that I reproduced.

TurboTax updates this summary every time you make a change to your tax return, so whenever you feel the urge to see your current tax situation, just go over to the Summary button and click away.

Figure 12-2:
Click here to pop that Summary onto your screen in EasyStep mode.

Figure 12-3:
Click here to pop up that summary in, you guessed it, Forms mode.

Figure 12-4:
A summary of income and expenses based on the financial information that this taxpayer has entered so far.

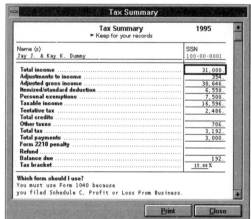

To close the Tax Summary, just click the Close button. If you prefer to use the keyboard method, press Alt+C.

Viewing specific forms in your tax return

In Forms mode, move to any form by clicking the Forms button at the top of the screen (see Figure 12-5 — it's the button that looks like a messy pile of papers). Doing so pops up a list of *all* the forms TurboTax has to offer, not just the ones that you are using in your tax return. You can click the Show My Return button to see just the forms in your tax return (see Figure 12-6). If you're in EasyStep and want to see a particular form, click the Go to Forms button to switch over to Forms mode. From the list of forms, you can click any form you want, whether or not it applies in your case. Sometimes it's fun to peek at the other forms. (Tax Nerd check: Am I the only one who feels this way?)

Figure 12-5:
Click this
Forms
button to
open up a
list of forms
from which
you can
choose.

┌ Click here to show just the forms in your tax return

Figure 12-6:
Choose
a form
from this list,
click Open,
and —
presto
chango—
the form
appears on
your screen!

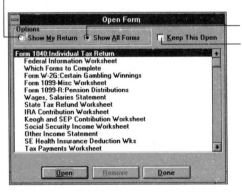

Click here to show all the forms in the world

Click here to leave this window on-screen

When viewing the list of just the forms in your tax return, pay special attention to the forms with the message [NOT DONE] next to their names. These forms are supposed to be in your tax return, but TurboTax feels that they are incomplete. Actually, you probably ought to go here first. If TurboTax indicates that any form is unfinished, double-click the form name (or click the form name and then click OK) to open the form.

Here's a neat trick for figuring out what's missing on one of those unfinished forms. After you open it by double-clicking it, by selecting it and clicking OK, or by selecting it and pressing Enter, press the F7 key. Press it again. Each time you press F7, TurboTax toggles through all the areas of the particular form where something is incomplete. (There may only be one incomplete area, in which case there will be no toggle to a new line.) Go ahead and fill in what's missing in the incomplete lines. Duh! After you complete all the unfinished spots, pressing F7 provides you with the message No Missing or Incomplete Items....

Other forms that didn't make the cut into your tax return

If you're interested in visiting forms that won't be joining your tax return this year, you can get to them in a variety of ways.

- ✔ In the Forms method, click the Forms button at the top of the screen and choose the form you want to see.

- ✔ Choose File Cabinet from the Window menu and select the topics that lead to the forms you want to see.

- ✔ Double-click the box to the right of the line number of the 1040 tax return that reflects the number generated by that particular form. For example, if you want to see a Schedule F (Farm Income), go to page 1 of the 1040 and double-click to the right of line 18 (Farm Income or Loss). Doing so pulls up a box from which you can select the farm form you want to view. Double-click the name of the form you want and see your Schedule F.

Error Summary

You can access the Error Summary while in Forms mode by clicking the Error Summary button on the toolbar (see Figure 12-7). In the Error Summary window that appears atop your screen is a list of all the forms that contain potential problems. TurboTax takes you right to the scene of the error when you double-click any item in the error list. You don't necessarily need to change these problems — check them out and see whether they're important. You can also locate errors from EasyStep by clicking the Review tab at the top of the Interview screen.

Figure 12-7:
Click me to
see a list of
your errors!

For details about what to expect from the Error Summary and how to deal with error messages, see Chapter 9.

The File Cabinet

To access the File Cabinet, click the little yellow file cabinet icon on the toolbar in Forms mode. The File Cabinet is an alphabetical listing of tax topics. Choosing a topic from this list and then clicking the <u>S</u>elect button pops up the form on which that particular tax item should appear. Use the File Cabinet to add information to your tax return that you left out during the regular preparation process — either information that surfaced after you completed the EasyStep process or information that didn't seem to fit neatly into any particular category while you were going through EasyStep.

For example, say you looked down on the floor and found a receipt for a case of dog biscuits that you donated to the local Humane Society but forgot to deduct when you were entering your charitable contributions. Open the File Cabinet and scroll down the list until you find *contributions*. (You can look for dog biscuits, but you won't find anything — sometimes you have to hunt around in the File Cabinet until you hit the right word to describe what you've done.) After you find contributions, click <u>S</u>elect. TurboTax opens the form that you need and also slaps some general instructions onto the screen so that you can figure out how to enter information on that form.

Whenever help-type instructions clutter your screen and you don't need them anymore, click the <u>C</u>lose button at the bottom of the help window, and the window will go away.

Wow! Graphing Your Results

"Wow" hardly does justice to my feelings about this special TurboTax feature. Believe me when I say that the idea of seeing a graphical image of just how much of my money is going toward income tax, presented in three-dimensional color, is not just slightly depressing; it really spoils my day. But if you're a visual sort of person and find colorful graphs a cool way to look at your finances, click the Graph button while in Forms mode (or choose <u>W</u>indow⇨Tax<u>G</u>raphs from the menu bar) and choose from the following graphs:

✔ **Income Sources:** A pictorial summary of where all your income comes from (see Figure 12-8).

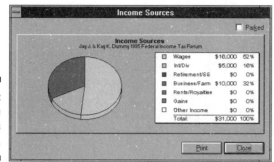

Figure 12-8:
The Income
Sources
graph.

✔ **Deductions:** A summary of your expense deductions (see Figure 12-9).

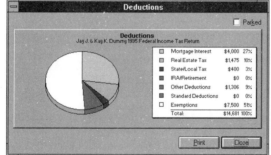

Figure 12-9:
The
Deductions
graph.

✔ **Where Your Money Goes:** In one door and out the other. Here's what the government does with your hard-earned dollars (see Figure 12-10).

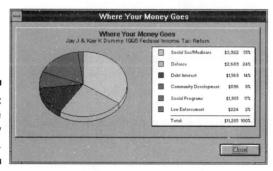

Figure 12-10:
The Where
Your Money
Goes graph.

✔ **Tax Analysis:** A different way of graphing — tubes instead of pie pieces. Hmmm. Here's a breakdown of the various taxes you paid (see Figure 12-11).

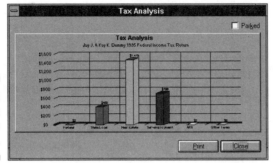

Figure 12-11:
The Tax
Analysis
graph.

You can print TurboTax graphs — sort of. The graphs look nice when printed on a color printer, but on a black-and-white printer, they come out, well, all black and white. If you want to give it a try, display on-screen the graph that you want to print and then click the Print button at the bottom of the graph window.

See It in Print

And speaking of printing . . . If you have checked everything out on-screen and are ready to print a hard copy of your return, choose File⇨Print from the menu. You can also press Ctrl+P. Both methods get you to the same place, the Printing dialog box, which is illustrated in Figure 12-12.

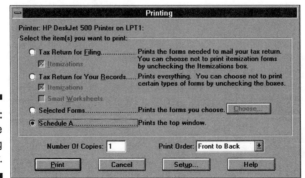

Figure 12-12:
Choose
something
to print.

Indicate which form or group of forms you want to print. The Schedule A form is selected by default in Figure 12-12 because it was on top of my TurboTax screen when I fled to the Print menu.

When you select the Print option, TurboTax assumes that you want to print the topmost form, schedule, or graph that is currently displayed on-screen. If that's okay with you, click Print, and that's what you'll get.

To select from the entire list of forms that are available to print, choose Selected Forms and then click Choose. Up pops a list of all the forms that are currently associated with your tax return. Choose the one you want to print by clicking the name of the form. You can choose more than one form at a time by holding down the Ctrl key while clicking the various forms you want to print. When you have selected the item(s) you want to print, click OK.

Getting Rid of a Form You Don't Need

There comes a time in almost every TurboTax user's life when you just can't resist futzing around with the forms that have no place in your tax return. You get into the Forms menu and just can't help yourself. Before you know it, you have half a dozen forms running around in your tax return that have no business being there.

You may be playing with all the strange forms for fun, you may have selected a form accidentally, or you may have legitimate concerns about how a certain form may play in your return if that particular income or expense event takes place in a future year. Whatever your excuse, there's no reason not to fool around with new forms — as long as you know how to get rid of them after you're finished.

You have to be using the Forms method to remove a form from your tax return. Go to the form that you no longer need and make sure that it appears on top of all the other forms on-screen. Choose Forms⇨Remove (Form Name) from the menu, and the form *on top* of your screen disappears.

How Am I Going to Pay for All This?

Sometimes, figuring out the tax on your tax return is the easiest part. The hard part comes when you owe money, particularly if you had counted on getting a refund. Here are some suggestions for circumventing that problem.

With(or without)holding

Withholding is perhaps the easiest way to pay tax — a steady, predictable amount of taxes is withheld from each of your paychecks and sent off to the IRS by your employer. But what happens when the withholding is not enough?

You have the right to have extra tax withheld from your paycheck. You can ask your employer for a Form W-4, the tax form that you fill out when you first start your job. Use this form to request *additional income tax withholding* or request *fewer exemptions*. The number of exemptions that you put on this form usually coincides with the number of exemptions that you claim on your income tax return. You can lower the number of exemptions on your W-4 form, thus increasing your withholding. If you like, you can print a W-4 form from TurboTax. Just fill in the blanks and take it to your employer.

Claiming fewer exemptions on your W-4 form at work affects only your withholding, not the number of exemptions that you claim on your income tax return.

Obviously, either method of increasing your withholding results in more tax paid to the IRS but *less* cash for you on a week-to-week basis. Make sure that you can afford to reduce your paychecks in this fashion. Of course, if you have too much tax withheld, the IRS will return it to you in the form of a refund after you file your income tax return.

MasterCard or VISA? Paying the piper

Alas, the IRS hasn't yet moved into the paying-with-plastic age. Make your payments with checks or money orders payable to Internal Revenue Service. For some reason, the IRS says that it doesn't want payments made out to IRS, but something tells me that it will still cash the check. In fact, I've heard stories about people who make out their checks to Uncle Sam and, miraculously, the IRS finds it in its heart to cash the check.

You just bought a new car, your mom's in the hospital, and other good reasons for not paying your taxes

Hey, it happens. Sometimes that April tax bill comes as a total blow to your budget and you just don't have the money. In recent years, the IRS has made great strides toward being understanding, but you have to play by its rules. When you prepare your tax return and find out how much you owe only to discover that the old checking account isn't quite going to cover it, the IRS wants you to (choose one):

(a) Write a bad check.

(b) File the tax return without any payment.

(c) Fill out and attach Form 9465, Installment Agreement Request, asking the good folks at the IRS to let you pay your taxes in installments.

If you guessed (a), you're absolutely right! Just kidding — the correct answer is (c). Request Form 9465 from the Forms mode, fill in the blanks, and beg for mercy.

Estimated payments (or guess your tax)

If you owe more than $500 on your 1995 income tax return, it's possible that you should have made estimated payments during the year. Tsk, tsk. Estimated payments are the IRS's way of letting you pay as you go when withholding doesn't quite cut it. For people who don't have taxes withheld at all (*independent contractors* is the fancy term), using this method is the only way to get taxes paid during the year. See "Pay as You Go: Quarterly Estimated Taxes" in Chapter 15 for more information about paying on a quarterly basis.

Paying quarterly estimated taxes isn't just a convenient way to avoid having to take out a second mortgage on the house come April. It is a *required* method of payment for those whose tax liability is not covered by withholding: independent contractors, people with high investment income, and people who have few deductions. If you haven't paid taxes throughout the year and you owe more than $500, chances are good that you will be hit with an underpayment penalty in April.

Calculating the underpayment penalty

TurboTax automatically computes an underpayment penalty for you. If it thinks that the penalty applies, the program asks you a few questions to determine how much penalty you have to pay.

The underpayment penalty is typically based on the assumption that you earned all your income and incurred all your deductible expenses evenly throughout the year. If, instead, your cash flow was sporadic, you may elect to *annualize* your income for purposes of computing the underpayment penalty. Using this process, you divide your taxable income and deduction activity into chunks: the amount received and spent from January 1 – March 31, from January 1 – May 31, and from January 1 – August 31. TurboTax then computes what your tax would be if you had earned your income at the same rate all year as you earned it during each chunk and figures the penalty based on that amount. This is pretty heady stuff — fortunately, it's just the kind of thing that TurboTax likes sinking its computer chip into. Just follow along, answer questions as precisely as you can, and let TurboTax figure out the lowest possible penalty for you.

Making estimated payments

If you owe an underpayment penalty this year, you may be a good candidate for making estimated payments of 1996 income tax. TurboTax gladly computes these payments for you in the Final version. Estimates for 1996 are computed in the Finish section of the Interview.

TurboTax computes estimated payments precisely, with no rounding. This calculation method often results in amounts such as $247 or $1,563 — amounts that end in numbers that aren't nicely rounded with zeros at the end. Personally, I prefer to round my payments to the nearest multiple of $10 or $25, so these amounts would become $250 and $1,575. Always round *up!* If you choose to round your payments, go into the Forms mode. Choose Forms⇨Show <u>A</u>ll Forms, and then select 1040ES Worksheet from the bottom of the list by double-clicking it (don't give up—it's down there). Then choose a number higher than the one TurboTax estimates for you. The TurboTax amounts are minimum amounts that you should pay in order to avoid a penalty next year. If you round them down, you may end up owing an underpayment penalty.

Sometimes it's wise to round your estimated payments up substantially, such as to the nearest $100 instead of the nearest $10. If you are uncertain about what your income will be next year, rounding up higher than you need to gives you a good cushion of paid-in taxes. You can always revise your estimates toward the end of the year if you calculate your income and find that you're paying too much.

If you choose to revise your estimated payments and change the amounts that TurboTax calculates for you, click the amount you want to change and then choose <u>E</u>dit⇨<u>O</u>verride from the menu at the top of the screen. Type the number that you want to use for the quarterly payment and then press Enter. Your number appears with a little *o* after it, designating an overridden amount.

Filling out this 1040ES-W worksheet automatically sends the tax payment amounts to quarterly voucher forms, 1040ES Vouchers 1, 2, 3, and 4. Be sure to print these vouchers when printing your tax return (see the section "See It in Print," earlier in this chapter).

Be aware that estimated payments *do not get mailed to the same address as your income tax return.* Check Table 12-1 for mailing addresses for estimated payments. Mailing addresses for income tax returns can be found in Table 12-2.

Table 12-1 Where to Mail Quarterly Estimated Tax Payments

If You Live in This State	Mail Your Estimated Payment to:
Florida, Georgia, South Carolina	Internal Revenue Service Center P.O. Box 970004 St. Louis, MO 63197-0004
New Jersey, New York, New York Counties[1]	Internal Revenue Service Center P.O. Box 162 Newark, NJ 07101-0162
New York Counties [2], Connecticut, Maine, Massachusetts, New Hampshire, Rhode Island, Vermont	Internal Revenue Service Center P.O. Box 371999 Pittsburgh, PA 15250-7999
Illinois, Iowa, Minnesota, Missouri, Wisconsin	Internal Revenue Service Center P.O. Box 6413 Chicago, IL 60680-6413
Delaware, District of Columbia, Maryland, Pennsylvania, Virginia	Internal Revenue Service Center P.O. Box 839 Newark, NJ 07101-0839
Indiana, Kentucky, Michigan, Ohio, West Virginia	Internal Revenue Service Center P.O. Box 7422 Chicago, IL 60680-7422
Kansas, New Mexico, Oklahoma, Texas	Internal Revenue Service Center P.O. Box 970001 St. Louis, MO 63197-0001
Alaska, Arizona, California, California Counties[3], Colorado, Idaho, Montana, Nebraska, Nevada, North Dakota, Oregon, South Dakota, Utah, Washington, Wyoming	Internal Revenue Service Center P.O. Box 510000 San Francisco, CA 94141-5100
California Counties[4]	Internal Revenue Service Center P.O. Box 54030 Los Angeles, CA 90054-0030
Alabama, Arkansas, Louisiana, Mississippi, North Carolina, Tennessee	Internal Revenue Service Center P.O. Box 371300M Pittsburgh, PA 15250-7300

[1]Nassau, Rockland, Suffolk, Westchester
[2]All New York counties not listed in (1)
[3]Alpine, Amador, Butte, Calaveras, Colusa, Contra Costa, Del Norte, El Dorado,
Glenn, Humboldt, Lake, Lassen, Marin, Mendocino, Modoc, Napa, Nevada,
Placer, Plumas, Sacramento, San Joaquin, Shasta, Sierra, Siskiyou, Solano,
Sonoma, Sutter, Tehama, Trinity, Yolo, and Yuba
[4]All California counties not listed in (3)

Pay now, file later

You may just not have enough information to prepare your tax return on a timely basis. You may have other reasons for not filing on time, such as a death in the family or a major calamity in your life. Whatever the reason, the IRS doesn't really want to hear about it. That doesn't mean that it won't give you a break in the event of a true crisis, but it would really prefer that you file your tax return on time. Short of that, the IRS will love it if you prepare an estimate of your income and file for an extension of time for filing your return.

Form 4868, Application for Automatic Extension of Time to File U.S. Individual Income Tax Return, was designed for just this purpose. The way it works is this: You ballpark what you think your taxable income will be, figure out how much the tax will be on that taxable income, put that amount on the form, put down how much you've already paid in through withholding and estimated payments, and pay the difference.

As long as it has your money, the IRS is perfectly willing to wait four months without complaining for you to get around to filing your tax return.

The Final version of TurboTax gladly prepares Form 4868 for you, but it doesn't do so as part of the regular Interview process. Leave the Interview by clicking the Go to Forms button, click the Forms button on the toolbar, and scroll down until you find Form 4868. Tax liability, based on the amounts of income and deductions that you have already entered into TurboTax, carries to this form. You can override this number with your own better estimate of your actual tax merely by clicking the amount already on the form and changing it.

Payments that you've made during the year, both in the form of withholding and in the form of quarterly estimates, are automatically carried to this form. If you have not yet entered all this information on the regular input forms in TurboTax, you can enter an amount directly on this form.

Double-check the amounts that TurboTax carries to Form 4868. If you are filing an application for an extension, chances are good that the information you have entered on the regular tax forms is not yet complete. It's best to overestimate your income and underestimate your payments in order to avoid a potential penalty for underpayment. If you overpay your taxes on the extension, you can get a refund when you finally file your real tax return.

Filing Form 4868 without making a payment doesn't work. When the IRS gets wind of people who haven't paid their tax by April 15, the folks there get very upset. The extension form is available for people who, for one reason or another, can't get their income tax return filed on time. It is *not* a vehicle for tax avoidance. You still must pay your taxes by April 15!

It's April 15: Does the IRS Know Where Your Tax Return Is?

Finishing your tax return by April 15 is one thing; getting it out the door and into the hands of the IRS is another thing altogether. Uncle Sam doesn't have any way of knowing whether you prepared your tax return on time if it sits on your desk looking pretty while you catch your breath after all your hard work.

In order for the tax return to be considered timely filed, it must be postmarked by midnight on April 15 (remember that the 15th is sometimes the 16th or the 17th if the real 15th falls on a weekend). Your tax return doesn't actually have to be at the IRS office as long as it has the postmark on it. Many post offices, especially those in large cities, accommodate this last-minute deadline by staying open until midnight, their little postmark stamps poised and ready to keep you legal, as streams of cars wind their way through the maze of the post office parking lot. Even if you manage to file your tax return several weeks early, you ought to go to the post office late on the 15th just to see the show.

Be sure to put the correct postage on your tax return envelope! If the IRS has to send it back to you with postage due, it considers your return late.

Putting the Package Together

Okay, so you printed out your entire tax return and then you dropped it on the floor and the forms went in a zillion directions. Does it matter how you put things back together? Well, of course it does! This is the IRS you're dealing with, one of the biggest bureaucracies in the western hemisphere — you don't think it wants to see things in a particular order?

Tax forms, like all paperwork that comes out of our government, are numbered. I don't mean the big numbers, like Form 4562 for Depreciation Expense or Form 2441 for a Child and Dependent Care Credit. No, I mean the little *secret* numbers, the ones just under the big form numbers that are labeled Attachment Sequence Number. These little numbers give you the pecking order for assembling your tax return.

So Where Do I Send This Thing?

The easiest way to send in your tax return if you're not filing electronically (see Chapter 13) is to use the envelope that comes in the Forms and Instructions packet sent to you by your friends at the IRS. Sometimes, however, that method just won't work due to one or more of the following problems:

- ✔ You didn't get a Forms and Instructions packet.

- ✔ You got a packet, but the envelope is missing.

- ✔ You've moved and your forms need to be mailed to an address different from that on the envelope.

- ✔ Your tax return is too fat to fit in the envelope.

- ✔ Your dog ate the envelope.

Fear not. The envelope is there for your convenience, but you don't have to use it. Use whatever envelope you like. Missing the address? Check Table 12-2 for the IRS address that fits your state.

Table 12-2   Where to Mail Your Income Tax Return

If You Live in This State	Mail Your Tax Return to:
Florida, Georgia, South Carolina	Internal Revenue Service Center Atlanta, GA 39901
New Jersey, New York Counties[1]	Internal Revenue Service Center Holtsville, NY 00501
New York Counties[2], Connecticut, Maine, Massachusetts, New Hampshire, Rhode Island, Vermont	Internal Revenue Service Center Andover, MA 05501
Illinois, Iowa, Minnesota, Missouri, Wisconsin	Internal Revenue Service Center Kansas City, MO 64999
Delaware, District of Columbia, Maryland, Pennsylvania, Virginia	Internal Revenue Service Center Philadelphia, PA 19255
Indiana, Kentucky, Michigan, Ohio, West Virginia	Internal Revenue Service Center Cincinnati, OH 45999
Kansas, New Mexico, Oklahoma, Texas	Internal Revenue Service Center Austin, TX 73301
Alaska, Arizona, California, California Counties[3], Colorado, Idaho, Montana, Nebraska, Nevada, North Dakota, Oregon, South Dakota, Utah, Washington, Wyoming	Internal Revenue Service Center Ogden, UT 84201

If You Live in This State	Mail Your Tax Return to:
California Counties[4]	Internal Revenue Service Center Fresno, CA 93888
Alabama, Arkansas, Louisiana, Mississippi, North Carolina, Tennessee	Internal Revenue Service Center Memphis, TN 37501

[1]Nassau, Rockland, Suffolk, Westchester
[2]All New York counties not listed in (1)
[3]Alpine, Amador, Butte, Calaveras, Colusa, Contra Costa, Del Norte, El Dorado, Glenn, Humboldt, Lake, Lassen, Marin, Mendocino, Modoc, Napa, Nevada, Placer, Plumas, Sacramento, San Joaquin, Shasta, Sierra, Siskiyou, Solano, Sonoma, Sutter, Tehama, Trinity, Yolo, and Yuba
[4]All California counties not listed in (3)

Filing a Late Tax Return (Legally)

There's a right way and a wrong way to do almost anything, and filing a late tax return is certainly no exception. The IRS provides you with the mechanism for procrastinating without getting into trouble.

The first step in filing a late tax return is to file the extension form, Form 4868 (see the section, "Pay now, file later," earlier in this chapter). Doing so buys you four months to postpone the inevitable. Now your tax return is officially due on August 15.

Four months isn't quite enough time, you say? You can try for another two months' extension by filing Form 2688, Application for Additional Extension of Time to File U.S. Individual Income Tax Return. TurboTax prepares this form for you if you request it from the Forms menu in the Final version. This application isn't automatically accepted like Form 4868 is. You need a good excuse for being late, and you need to put that excuse right on the form. (Generally speaking, "I forgot" doesn't get you too far with the IRS.) Don't wait until August 15 to file this form because the IRS has the right to reject it. If you get your rejection late in August, you're already too late to file your return on time.

Filing your tax return on August 15 (or October 15, if you manage to slip in an additional extension) is just as easy (cough) as filing it on April 15. There is no difference except that you ought to attach Form 4868 to your tax return when you file it in August, just to avoid a lot of unnecessary questions. Prepare your tax return by using TurboTax just as you would prepare it in April. In the tax payment section, TurboTax asks whether you requested an extension of time to file this tax return. Answering Yes prods TurboTax to ask you how much, if anything, you paid with this extension. That amount gets recorded on your tax return.

The Cost of Filing Late

Penalty . . . interest . . . letters from the IRS . . . all those things that you don't want to happen to you. That's your change (as my children would say) if you don't file your tax return on time.

The penalty for filing a late tax return is 5 percent of the amount of tax still owing. You get hit with another 5 percent for each month you file late, and it adds up quickly: 5 months late = 25 percent penalty. This nonsense stops after five months, though, so 25 percent is as high as this particular penalty gets.

There's also a penalty for *paying* your tax late, which seems a lot like the penalty for late *filing*, but the percentage is different. This penalty is $1/2$ percent per month (6 percent per year) of the unpaid tax. Once again, this penalty stops when it hits 25 percent of the unpaid tax, which means that this penalty can pile up for years.

On top of the penalty for filing late and the penalty for not paying your tax is interest on the tax not paid. There's also interest on the penalty for filing late. The IRS did a good job of making all these layers of penalties and interest so confusing that figuring it out without one of those fancy calculators with dozens of buttons with funny symbols on them is pretty much impossible. The IRS must feel that if you get to this point of lots of penalties and interest and penalties on the interest and interest on the penalties, you'll just trust it to figure out the right amount and send you a bill. Of course, much like the national debt, it increases every hour. . . .

Changing Your Tax Return After You File It

Hard as it is to believe, sometimes people make mistakes. Fortunately, the IRS knows this and provides you with the opportunity to change your tax return after you file it. I think it would be really nice and cooperative of the IRS if it would just let people phone in changes: "Excuse me, is this the IRS? Well, this is Gail Helsel, and I just wanted to let you know that I forgot to list my daughter as a dependent. Yes, that's right. She sort of slipped through the cracks, so to speak. So if you could just make that little adjustment and send me a refund . . . thanks so much!"

Alas. Instead, you are relegated to the task of preparing and filing what is known as the 1040X, Amended U.S. Individual Income Tax Return.

Be sure to have a hard copy of the original tax return in front of you before amending. If you can't find a copy of the return as you originally filed it, print a new copy. After you amend your tax return, the numbers change and you won't be able to go back and print a copy of the original return (unless you saved it in a separate file by choosing File⇨Save As from the menu and giving it a new name — not a bad idea).

The Final version of TurboTax has Form 1040X. It works like this: Say you are revising your 1995 tax return, having already filed an incorrect copy with the IRS. Go to the forms that are changing on your 1995 tax return: Either select the specific forms by clicking the Forms button at the top of the screen and choosing each form that is changing, one at a time, or start up the Interview again, go to the topic you need, and let TurboTax ask you questions about the amounts you're changing.

After you change all the appropriate forms so that your tax return in TurboTax now reflects the correct numbers, open Form 1040X (leave the Interview if you are using that feature) by clicking the Forms button and double-clicking Form 1040X. After the form is in view, press the F7 key to get to the top of the form where it asks you what year you are amending. Type **95** and press Enter. Whoa! The form magically fills itself out, all except for the first column. In the first column, you need to fill in the numbers from your original tax return — the one you already filed with the IRS, which you should have in your hot little hands.

After TurboTax calculates the amounts on page one (make sure that the tax calculation agrees with the change in tax you are expecting), scroll down to page two. Banging on the F7 key won't get you there; you need to go to page two on your own. Fill in the appropriate sections:

- ✔ Part I is for calculating the change in your exemption deduction if the number of dependents in your family changed. Skip this part completely if your exemptions are remaining the same.

- ✔ Part II is required. Here you explain why you are amending the tax return. Type the line numbers that changed on page one, and then explain why you are making a change (for example, "I received another 1099 form after I filed my tax return").

- ✔ Part III is for taxpayers who feel a pang of remorse about the way in which they originally chose to answer the Presidential Election Campaign Fund question. Be sure to give this part all the time and consideration it deserves.

Pressing F7 on Form 1040X does not move you to page two of the form. You are required to fill in page two, giving reasons for your change, so you have to scroll down there yourself in order to type in the reasons.

Print the 1040X along with each form that changed from your original to the revised return. Better yet, to be on the safe side, just print the entire revised tax return. Attach everything together with the 1040X on the front, and be sure to sign the bottom of the 1040X. If you owe additional tax, attach a check. Mail the 1040X to the same address where you mailed the *original* tax return, even if you have since moved to a new filing district.

State Tax Preparation

TurboTax for Windows has finally come of age when it comes to state income tax return preparation. As of 1995, all states that have income tax are available in software form from Intuit (the company that makes TurboTax).

State income tax software is *not* part of the TurboTax federal income tax return software. You must purchase the state program separately. If you have purchased and installed state software on your computer, preparing your state income tax return is as simple as clicking the State tab at the top of the EasyStep menu and jumping through a few simple hoops. Or click the File menu and choose Go to State if you are in the Forms method.

When you choose to create a state tax return, TurboTax adds the state tax return to your federal return in the same file, pulls in information from the federal return, and gives you a state return based on the federal information.

Saving Time with Baby Icons

If you plan on moving in and out of your tax return frequently, save yourself a few steps by adding an icon for your tax return to your Windows Program Manager or desktop. Follow these steps for Windows Version 3.1:

1. **From the Windows Program Manager screen, click the TurboTax top hat icon once and then choose Copy from the File menu.**

2. **Select TurboTax for Windows from the list of available group windows and then click OK.**

   A new top hat icon appears in the TurboTax group window.

3. **Click the new icon and then choose Properties from the File menu.**

4. **In the Properties dialog box, click right after the TTAX94.EXE filename (see Figure 12-13), type one space, and then type the filename of your tax return file (for example, MYFED.TAX). While you're there, change the description from** `TurboTax for Windows` **to the name of your tax return (see Figure 12-14). Then click OK.**

   This title appears under the icon on your Program Manager screen. See the end results in Figure 12-15.

You now have an icon for your tax return on the Program Manager screen. In the future, when you want to open your tax return in TurboTax, just double-click this new icon. The TurboTax program opens and your tax return appears on-screen, ready for you to work on it.

Figure 12-13:
Add your tax
return name
to the
command
to start up
TurboTax
here.

Figure 12-14:
The name
of your tax
file has
been added,
and you've
made the
description
meaningful
for this icon.

Figure 12-15:
Here it is:
your new
baby icon.

Follow these steps in Windows 95:

1. **Click Start.**
2. **Click Settings.**
3. **Click Taskbar.**
4. **Click the Start Menu Programs tab.**
5. **Click Add.**
6. **Click Browse.**

7. **Change the Files of type to read All Files.**

8. **Change the Look in (if necessary) so that it displays the drive on which your TurboTax program resides.**

9. **Double-click the TAX95W folder.**

10. **Click the file that contains your tax return data.**

11. **Click Open.**

12. **Click the Next> button.**

13. **Click the Next> button again.**

14. **Type a friendly name for your tax return, like** Uncle Sam isn't any uncle of mine **or** My Tax Return.

15. **Click the Finish button.**

Whew! That's a lot of steps. But to start TurboTax and open up your tax return in Windows 95 from now on, just click the Start button, click Programs, and click the friendly name you gave your tax return (see Figure 12-16).

Figure 12-16: Click here and watch your tax return magically open on your screen.

Chapter 13

Zap! Whoosh! Electronic Filing

· ·

In This Chapter

▶ Getting the scoop on electronic filing

▶ Determining which forms you need

▶ Understanding the advantages and disadvantages of electronic filing

▶ Filing not-so-electronically with the 1040PC

▶ Filing by phone: dial-a-tax return

· ·

*I*f you expect to *owe* tax instead of getting a refund, skip this chapter. You have no need to file electronically unless you are trying to speed the receipt of your refund. Likewise, if your refund is relatively small, filing electronically may not be cost effective because you have to pay a fee for this electronic filing service. TurboTax charges $14.95 to do the job. You may be able to shop around and get a better deal, but the places that I've seen advertised charge more than TurboTax.

The IRS is doing its best to stay on top of modern technology, which is no mean feat for an organization that is hopelessly lost in the dark ages when it comes to being nice. So why does the IRS want to do you this big favor and let you file your tax returns quickly and easily?

Here's the secret behind the IRS's apparent generosity. It's easier for the IRS if its computer can do the talking instead of having to process tax returns by using humans from the ripping-open-the-envelope stage all the way to the mail-a-refund-check stage. The processing of your tax return electronically can go much faster than it does when humans are keying numbers into a computer, and there's less chance for error. In fact, if you request that your refund be deposited directly into your bank account, the entire process can be executed electronically, save for the single-page paper form that you must sign and mail to the IRS.

Filing your tax return electronically, however, is not as simple and easy as it may seem. You may have a modem for your computer and you may have prepared your tax return by using TurboTax, but that's not enough. In fact, much as you might like to, you can't just dial up the IRS and shoot your tax return out over the phone lines. Unfortunately, you must jump through some hoops in order to file your return this "quick-and-easy" way.

The Electronic Filing Process: How Do They Do That?

Filing electronically by using TurboTax is a process involving several steps:

1. **Early in the TurboTax Interview process, the program asks whether you want to file your return electronically. Answer this question Yes.**

   If you originally answered No and want to change your mind, click the Interview Navigator button. Scroll through the My Tax Data list until you find Taxpayer Date of Birth (`Info Wks, TP Date/Birth` in TurboTax lingo). Click that Date/Birth item, and then click the Interview button. Doing so puts you very close to the Electronic Filing part of the Interview. You have to re-answer a few questions that you've already come across about being legally blind and sending money to the Presidential Campaign Fund, and then you arrive at the question about whether you want to file the return electronically. Answering Yes to this question causes TurboTax to prepare a Form 8453, U.S. Individual Income Tax Declaration for Electronic Filing.

2. **Finish preparing your tax return and use the Final Review option to make sure that you haven't left out anything important.**

   See "Hey, Look Me Over!" in Chapter 12 for more information.

3. **Click the File menu and choose Electronic Filing.**

   TurboTax checks over your tax return to make sure that it meets the IRS requirements for electronic filing and creates a transmission form and a transmission file.

4. **Exit TurboTax.**

   Choose File⇨Exit. Be sure to say Yes when TurboTax asks whether you want to save the tax return.

5. **Back at the Program Manager, click twice on the Electronic Filing icon in your TurboTax for Windows group window (see Figure 13-1).**

Figure 13-1:
Click here
to file
electronically.

When prompted for a tax return, look at the file number of the return that TurboTax has chosen for electronic transmission. That number should match the social security number on the tax return that you are filing. If it doesn't, press N for No and select the proper tax return ID number from the list that TurboTax provides.

6. **Select your transmission of choice: Modem (you have to have a functioning modem to choose this one), Disk (have a floppy disk ready if you pick this option), or Paper.**

Whichever method you pick, TurboTax gets busy and prepares what it needs to file your return electronically. See the following Technical Stuff sections for descriptions of all these choices.

Modem transmission

Press M for modem. Modem transmission is arguably a bit easier than packaging up and mailing a disk. However, you still have to mail the transmission forms and your check, so you really don't save any time by filing by modem. If you have a modem, however, sending in your return this way gives you something to do with it. . . .

After you select the modem option by pressing M, TurboTax asks you a few perfunctory questions about your modem. Then it dials up the TurboTax electronic filing department and sends your tax return there. You still have to send your signed Form 8453 (see step 1 on the preceding page) as well as the Federal copies (copy B) of your W-2 forms and any other papers you are required to attach to your tax return. In addition, you have to send a check or money order for $14.95 payable to TurboTax Electronic Filing. Alas, nothing is free.

If you want your refund deposited directly in your bank account, send along a voided check or a copy of your bank statement showing your account number and the bank's name and secret coded numbers. You also need to send a TurboTax Electronic Filing Order Form. When the people at TurboTax get all this stuff, they deposit your check, shoot your tax return out into space, and send your signed forms and W-2 stuff on to the IRS.

Disk transmission

Press D for disk. This procedure copies the electronic stuff from your tax return onto a floppy disk. (Be sure to have a disk formatted and in the proper drive. To avoid confusion, use a fresh disk or one that doesn't have letters to your girlfriend on it.) You have to send the disk to TurboTax, along with the fee and the forms mentioned in the "Modem transmission" section.

Paper transmission

Press P for paper. Choosing this option doesn't really do anything. Some technical stuff happens on your disk drive so that TurboTax can keep track of the fact that you've been here and indicated that you want a paper return, but that's about it. If you want to use this option, go back into the regular TurboTax program and print out the entire tax return. Then bundle up your W-2 forms and sign the tax return and that Form 8453 (all the stuff mentioned in the "Modem transmission" section). Send everything off to TurboTax (or, for that matter, take it to some other electronic tax filing service), and they will input your data to the IRS.

Lots of tax return services are authorized to dispatch returns electronically to the IRS. You can check the Yellow Pages or newspaper ads or check with your bank. You can even call the IRS office nearest you and ask for names of authorized services.

Lost in Space

Just what happens when your tax return gets beamed into the IRS netherworld? Nothing at first. The IRS receives your transmission and then patiently waits for the hard paper stuff to arrive — your W-2, other attachments that indicate tax withholding, and the signed Form 8453, on which you verify that you are who you say you are and that the total income and tax computations agree with the numbers on your real tax return. (This form is also signed by an ERO. Although this acronym probably really stands for *Erratic Return Operator,* the IRS thinks that it means *Electronic Return Originator.*)

After all your stuff arrives at the IRS, the numbers from your tax return, as flown across the fiber-optic superhighway, are entered into the rather large IRS computer, chewed up, and regurgitated in the form of a refund check that is supposedly mailed to you within three weeks. If you choose to have your refund deposited directly into your bank account, the money may arrive faster.

Special Rules for the Electronic Tax Return

Some forms disqualify your tax return for electronic filing. If you use either of the following forms in your tax return, you are not a candidate for the jet set:

✔ Form 4868, Extension for Filing U.S. Individual Income Tax Return

✔ Form 4684, Casualties and Thefts (you can file one of these forms electronically, but attempting to file more than one disqualifies you)

A few other, more obscure forms can kick you out of e-mail contention, but don't worry. TurboTax knows whether you have one of these offending forms and lets you know if you can't file by using this method.

Partial High-Tech with the 1040PC

The 1040PC, kind of a quasi-electronic return, gives you the opportunity to try for a quicker-than-usual refund without the added cost of the true, electronically filed tax return. You can also save scads of paper and printing time by using this format. A 30-page tax return that I tested printed out in five pages in 1040PC format.

The 1040PC is a form that you can generate through TurboTax. To use this format, follow these steps:

1. **Save your tax return.**

2. **Choose <u>P</u>rint from the <u>F</u>ile menu and click the 1040PC Format for Filing option.**

3. **Click the <u>P</u>rint button.**

   TurboTax checks your tax return for potential 1040PC filing problems or missing items. If it finds a problem, it tells you about it. You can then return to the regular TurboTax program, fix the problem(s), and return to step 1.

The 1040PC takes the place of your regular tax forms. Sign the 1040PC at the bottom of page 1, attach your W-2 forms as you normally would, and mail the 1040PC to the same address that you would use for a regular 1040.

Phone-in Filing: Dial-a-Tax Return

The IRS has expanded its successful phone-in tax return filing program for 1995 for filers of Form 1040EZ. If you do not receive Tele-File information in the mail, you are probably not eligible to use this service. To use the Tele-File system, call the number in your tax forms packet on a Touch-Tone phone, and press phone keys to answer the questions you are asked.

You will still need to send your W-2 form(s) to the IRS. The form to which you attach your W-2 is in the tax forms packet you receive in the mail.

Part IV
The Land Beyond 1040

The 5th Wave
By Rich Tennant

"ALL THIS STUFF? IT'S PART OF A TAX PREPARATION PROGRAM DESIGNED TO HELP UNCLUTTER YOUR LIFE."

In this part...

This is the after-the-tax return part. You're finished preparing your tax return; it's out in the mail, winging its way to the IRS. That's it for this year, right? Well, no, not if you want to avoid repeating this headache next year. You can do lots of things now to get yourself ready for the next tax return — get organized so that you won't race around frantically next April looking for missing receipts, and start thinking about your finances from a tax point of view.

In this part, you can also get help in figuring out whether you should be paying quarterly estimated tax payments rather than relying on withholding at your job or waiting until the tax return is due to make a big tax payment.

I also look at the dreaded Tax Return Audit: what it is, how the IRS picks returns to audit, and what to do if you're one of the lucky few.

Use this part as a catch-your-breath section. Read it at your leisure, after you're no longer under the gun to get your tax return out by the due date. Refer to it during the year and remind yourself of ways in which you can improve your methods of getting ready for tax time.

Chapter 14

Every Taxpayer's Nightmare: The IRS Audit

In This Chapter

▶ What happens to your tax return after you put it in your mailbox

▶ How to use TurboTax's Review feature to take an IRS-guided tour through your return

▶ What the IRS thinks of taxpayers like you; or how you measure up according to the IRS

▶ What to do if your tax return gets audited

*T*he IRS office is a mystical place. Few people really know what goes on there, yet everyone has some sort of image of what it must be like. My personal image calls up stories of the medieval dungeons of yore where social outcasts were locked up and never heard from again. However, in the halls of IRS office buildings, I've witnessed bright lights, windows, and pictures of family members on the desks of IRS employees. (I've always wondered, though, about what goes on in the basement. . . .)

What Happens After You Send in Your Return?

You mail your tax return to one of the Service Centers. These buildings are filled with employees throughout the spring, temporary workers whose job is to enter the numbers from tax returns into a computer that checks to see that everything adds up properly. A machine opens your envelope and somehow removes the check, and then the tax return moves on to one of the Service Center employees — the first stopping-off point. Chances are that your tax return will sail through this point with flying colors because you prepared it by using TurboTax, a computer program known for its capability to add 2 + 2 and get 4.

After this initial check, your tax return numbers are dispatched to the great IRS computer at the National Computer Center in West Virginia. There, your tax return is analyzed, turned inside out, stretched out of proportion, examined with a magnifying glass, and generally given the once-over (in about a hundred different ways). Your tax return is compared to national averages to determine whether or not the amounts fall within standard ranges. Tax returns harboring amounts that fall out of the average ranges get pulled for audits, but this criterion alone doesn't mean that you will have the pleasure of being audited. Only a small, randomly selected percentage of those chosen in this process actually get audited.

The Review: TurboTax's Guided Tour of Your Tax Return

Let TurboTax take you on a tour of the things that the IRS looks at when it gets out that giant magnifying glass and pores over your tax return. After you go through the Interview and finish entering all your income, expenses, and other vital statistics, the Review kicks in. TurboTax's Review feature gives you a summary of the following types of things in your tax return:

- Errors and things that don't make sense
- Information that you may have left out
- Suggestions of ways in which you might reduce your tax liability
- Entries that might trigger an audit
- A reminder of places in the tax return where you have chosen to override the TurboTax calculations
- Typical types of deductions that people take on tax returns similar to yours

You can pick and choose from the selected Review topics by clicking Pick Reviews, but the preferred method is to choose All Reviews. Let TurboTax show you all its Review features, and take a careful look at the things TurboTax has to say about your tax return. You may find some useful hints that can save you some income tax.

Read through the information in this Review. Turbo Tax is bound to have suggestions that trigger ideas for you. Even if the points that TurboTax makes don't apply to your tax return this year, read them with next year in mind. You may find that you can structure your personal financial situation in such a way as to take advantage of some of the ideas presented here. The more complex your tax return, the more ideas TurboTax has to offer.

The error summary section of the Review is the most important. You can clear the errors as TurboTax presents them to you. TurboTax points out actual errors and also considers the things that don't make sense. Chances are that if they don't make sense to TurboTax, they won't make sense to the IRS, either. See Chapter 9 for more information about dealing with errors in TurboTax.

The Interview process in TurboTax eventually leads you to the Final Review, but you can get there whenever you want to by clicking the Review tab. If you are using the Forms method to complete your tax return, I strongly recommend that you pop over to EasyStep before wrapping up your tax return and run through the Review process. Just click the Review tab and pick All Reviews.

Fan Mail from the IRS

Uh-oh. An envelope in the mail that says Internal Revenue Service in the upper-left corner. And if that envelope happened to arrive via *certified mail,* well, shouldn't you just head for the hills, shouting to the mail carrier, "Return to sender!" as you bolt out the back door?

The IRS counts on its ability to intimidate the average taxpaying citizen, and so far the gamble has been successful. If it weren't for intimidating IRS agents, people everywhere would just throw up their hands and say, "This is too hard. I can't do it!" and that would be the end of taxation as we know it.

Now what? Step one is *don't panic.* If your tax return has been chosen for an audit, keep in mind that an audit is merely a complete stranger sitting across a desk from you, asking you questions about the numbers on the tax forms that you (or in this case, TurboTax) supplied. The agents are doing their jobs. They didn't ask to see you; some computer did. And the agents aren't making up the questions as they go along. They have a list of things that they are supposed to ask you.

Meeting the IRS Agent

Your job in an audit is to answer the questions as clearly and concisely as possible. The *concise* part is important. More people trip up by spilling their guts to IRS agents than you may think. The agent doesn't want any information beyond what he or she asks you, but if you offer something, the agent is obliged to record it. So when you are asked whether the dependent receiving child care who enables you to take a child care credit is your own child, just answer yes or no. Don't start talking about how the child spent two months at Aunt Nell's house while you and your husband tried to work out your marital problems, which resulted in a separation and a convoluted custody arrangement whereby you get the child every Monday through Thursday except in months that start with *J* and . . . do you get my drift? Opening up such stories can only lead the agent to ask you more questions about your life that may or may not impact your tax return but that, at the very least, will keep you sitting in the office of an IRS agent for a much longer time than is necessary.

The IRS isn't going to hurt you. They didn't single you out because you're a bad person. Chances are, you're not in any kind of trouble. But you may feel that none of that matters. Getting the letter from the IRS that asks you to provide more information about your tax return in the form of an audit is one of the scariest things that can happen in the world today. While the shivers are still climbing up and down your spine, try to remember this: A computer picked your name. Computers aren't human. (Some IRS agents may not be, either, but that's neither here nor there.) Just give them what they want, no more, and get it over with.

If it turns out that you made a mistake on your tax return, just chalk it up to another Life Experience. Don't forget, however, that mistakes work both ways. If, since you filed your tax return, you think of some expense that you forgot to deduct, the audit is a perfect place to bring up the item. As long as your tax return is open for examination, you can make changes to it, and those changes can be in your favor. It's possible that you could walk away from an audit with the IRS owing *you* money.

If you are called in for an audit, go through your tax return, refamiliarizing yourself with every part of it. As you gather the documentation that the IRS requested in order to support the items under examination, think about other things that you may have left off the tax return that could sway things in your favor.

In an audit, the IRS examiner can ask you questions *only* about the items listed in the letter you received. He or she cannot bring in new subjects while you're sitting in the office. *However,* if you introduce a new topic, the agent has the right to quiz you about it, so *keep your mouth shut!* Answer only the questions that you are asked and only if they pertain to the items being examined as set out in the letter you received.

Deductions You May Have Forgotten

As you prepare for an audit, you may want to consider the following areas in an attempt to bring more last-minute deductions into your audit:

✔ **Investment expenses**

If you have dividend or interest income and you incur expenses associated with earning or tracking that income, those expenses are deductible as miscellaneous expenses on Schedule A, Itemized Deductions. If you pay interest on money borrowed for the purpose of investing, that interest is deductible as Investment Interest in the interest expense section of Schedule A.

✔ **Business expenses**

If you own your own business, look long and hard at your activities during the year to see what can be considered a business expense. Review the "Business deductions for people who run their own businesses" list in Chapter 7 and try to find some new things that might qualify. If you have a separate checkbook for your business expenses, take a few minutes to look through your personal checkbook to see whether you wrote some personal checks for things that are really business related.

✔ **Auto mileage**

You drive your car for so many things: charitable organization events, trips to the doctor, or running errands for your boss. Even if you don't have a formal record of specific mileage for these things, go back through your personal calendar for the past year and note times when you used your car for these types of things. Estimate your mileage and use your calendar to collaborate the use of your automobile.

✔ **Long distance phone calls**

Just as with the auto mileage, if you have been using your telephone for making long distance calls regarding charitable purposes or for your business, their cost is deductible.

The main point to keep in mind as you face an audit, whether it is occurring now or may occur down the road, is the importance of good record-keeping. It does you no good to spend hours entering numbers from receipts into your tax return if you turn around and lose those receipts a week later. In an audit, you have the burden of proof. Save the papers that support the numbers on your tax return. And find a nice organized way to store them in the future (see Chapter 16 for record-keeping advice).

Chapter 15

Using TurboTax to Plan for Next Year

*N*ow that you're promising never to go through a last-minute rush again, you can use this chapter to help you start getting ready for next year's tax return. Let TurboTax do a rough estimate of next year's income tax, and then you can spend the year whittling away at that amount. Read about tricks for moving things in and out of tax years — that is, shifting income or expenses from one year to the next, depending on concerns such as in which year you generate a higher tax rate because of higher income or tax law changes and in which year you expect to have more deductions and thus a lower tax rate.

While you're here, take a peek at what's on the TurboTax planning board for next year's program.

Tax Saving Suggestions

You can cut your taxes in two ways: report less income or spend more on deductible items. The first method, reporting less income, doesn't necessarily mean the same as *earning* less income. And it doesn't mean just neglecting to report the income you earned. The IRS tends to frown on behavior like that. Instead, read on to discover ways in which you can report less income *legally*.

Reduce taxable income

There are some fairly common ways in which you can earn income and save tax dollars at the same time. For example, consider these suggestions:

- ✔ If you are paying tax on earnings from an investment, such as a savings account or a mutual fund, you may want to consider tax-free investing. Tax-free investments generally pay a lower rate of return than their taxable counterparts, but the fact that there is no tax on the income can more than make up for the difference.

- ✔ If your employer provides a *cafeteria plan* — a plan to which you make contributions for particular benefits such as medical expenses, child care expenses, legal assistance, or eye care — the amount you withhold from your income to pay for these benefits is not taxable. So if you would purchase these items anyway, consider paying for them with tax-free dollars.

- ✔ A different approach to reporting less income is to control the year in which you pay tax on the income. You may not be able to control when an employer issues your paycheck, but you may be able to control when you receive income from other sources. If you send bills that generate revenue, consider sending your December bills a bit late, thus ensuring that the revenue will be pushed to the next year. Alternatively, if you expect your income to be higher next year and wish that you could report some of next year's income this year, try doing a bit of January's work in December and bill for it early enough that you will be paid in December.

Increase tax deductions

The more frequently used method of saving tax dollars involves taking deductions against your income for the things you spend your money on. Take a look at Chapter 8 for lots of ideas about expenses that can reduce your income.

What follows is a short, simple list of miscellaneous items that you can think about during the year — potential ongoing deductions that you may not be taking advantage of now.

- ✔ **Mileage:** Try keeping an auto mileage log in your car for a while. A little notebook or pad of paper will do. You may find that you drive your car for tax-deductible purposes a great deal more than you realize. Jot down the date and how many miles you drove for income-producing meetings, business-related trips, medical visits, and charitable business; these can include the following:

- Visits to the doctor's office

- Trips to the office supply store or the post office for your boss

- Trips to charitable organizations to make a donation

- Hauling Girl Scouts around town to sell cookies (that is, driving charitable miles)

- Trips to the drug store to pick up prescriptions

- Trips relating to your own business

- Trips to oversee rental property

- Travel while volunteering your time to church activities

Read the appropriate sections in this book to find out how to claim this mileage on your tax return: "The high cost of driving" in Chapter 7 and "Medical deductions" and "Contribution deductions" in Chapter 8.

✓ **Charitable giving:** Charitable giving doesn't have to take the form of cash, although you should certainly keep track of all cash that you give to charity. The next time you clean out a closet, a cabinet, or the garage, think in terms of charity. There may be things that you no longer need — clothes or shoes that don't fit you or seem out of style, books that you won't read again, toys that your children have outgrown, tools that you no longer use, and wedding presents that you've never used. Don't just throw them away. Consider donating your items to one of the many service organizations that provide clothing and household goods to the needy or that sell your items and use the proceeds to support needy people. Chapter 8 includes information about taking itemized deductions for donating your possessions to charities.

Recognize that timing is everything

Just as you can do with a certain portion of your income, you can exert control over the timing of your tax deductions, particularly at the end of the year. If you are trying to lower this year's tax liability, try to pull expenses that will occur next January back into this year. For example, if you plan on making a donation to charity in January, make it in December. Rent and mortgage payments for January can be made in December, and to the extent that portions of these payments are deductible, the deduction gets pulled back into the current year.

Also, think about adjusting the timing of deductions to which limitations apply, such as medical expenses and miscellaneous deductions. The medical expense deduction is limited to the amount by which your expenses exceed 7.5 percent of your Adjusted Gross Income (see "Medical deductions" in Chapter 8 for more information). If you have a lot of medical bills to pay around the end of one tax year and the beginning of the next, consider trying to pay them all in one year, thus increasing your chance for getting a tax benefit from the payments.

There are many smart ways to manage your finances in order to save yourself tax dollars; this section addresses some of the more common and obvious methods. Think about scheduling a consultation with a professional tax advisor to set up a long-range tax plan that can reduce your taxes over an extended period of time.

Calculate Next Year's Taxes Now

Don't wait until this time next year to figure out what you're going to owe. It's easy to estimate your taxes for the next year by using TurboTax's *Plan Mode* feature. With Plan Mode, TurboTax takes your income and expenses, taxes withheld, number of dependents, filing status, and all the other information you entered for this year's tax return and pretends that you'll have those same amounts next year. Then it applies next year's tax rates, next year's exemption rates, and next year's standard deduction and gives you a tax calculation.

Don't attempt to use Plan Mode without carefully reading the following directions. Plan Mode can write over your current tax return file with next year's estimates before you have a chance to say, "Hey, wait a minute!" thus changing amounts on your tax return. Before using Plan Mode, you need to make a copy of your tax return file and give it a new name, leaving one copy intact as the 1995 return and giving you the peace of mind to let TurboTax have its way with the other file, knowing that no 1995 calculations will be harmed.

Here's how to use Plan Mode to estimate next year's tax liability:

1. **Save your tax return file by choosing File⇨Save.**

2. **If you are not already in Forms mode, switch over to it (leave EasyStep) by clicking the big pencil at the bottom-right corner of the screen.**

3. **Save your tax return file under a new name by choosing File⇨Save As and typing a new filename. This is the file that you'll be working with in Plan Mode.**

4. **Choose Plan Mode from the Tools menu.**

This action has the effect of recalculating your tax forms to consider the tax rates, personal exemptions, and other known changes in the 1996 tax laws. It's important to keep in mind that the estimate of tax you get in Plan Mode is based on the *1996 income tax laws as of what's known about those laws on December 31, 1995.* Any tax law changes that are enacted by Congress during 1996 will not be included in this estimate.

It's also important to remember that you are using income and expense figures from *1995.* Your income and deductions may change during 1996. If the change is not drastic, then the estimate may be fairly close to the target. If you anticipate significant changes in your income or different types of deductions in 1996, go ahead and change the numbers on the tax forms before using Plan Mode.

This method has some imperfections! You probably don't know what your exact income and deductions will be for 1996, so your numbers are estimates. Also, TurboTax doesn't know what changes are in store for the tax laws, so the tax computation may not turn out to be particularly accurate.

Don't Forget Your State!

Alas, the TurboTax state income tax programs do not offer Plan Mode. But that doesn't mean that you can't experiment!

If you are using a TurboTax state tax return package, you can generate a state tax return based on the tax return that you create in Plan Mode. See "State Tax Preparation" in Chapter 12 for more information about preparing a state tax return.

Pay as You Go: Quarterly Estimated Taxes

If you have tax withheld from your paychecks, the withholding may be enough to cover the income taxes as calculated on your federal and state tax returns. If you don't have withholding, or if you still owe income tax when you prepare your tax returns — withholding is insufficient by IRS standards if you still owe $500 or more on your federal income tax return even after considering withholding — you probably should be filing quarterly estimated tax vouchers. (*Note:* States have varying limits for requiring quarterly estimated tax payments. Check the estimated payment rules in your particular state.)

Quarterly estimated tax vouchers accompany payment of taxes when withholding isn't enough. These forms get mailed to the IRS four times a year, thus the term *quarterly.* Estimates are filed on a pay-as-you-earn basis; in other words, you pay the taxes as you earn the money. So, during 1996, you send in estimates for 1996 taxes. That way, come April 1997, you presumably will have paid in enough so that you won't owe a whole bunch of money when you file your 1996 tax return.

Quarterly Estimated Tax payments aren't just a feature that the IRS developed for your convenience. If you owe more than $500 on your tax return, you can find yourself hit with a penalty for underpayment of your tax. See "Estimated payments (or guess your tax)" in Chapter 12 for information about this underpayment penalty.

You can produce these Quarterly Estimated Tax forms in TurboTax by following these steps:

1. **Open your 1995 tax return.**

   If you are looking at the Plan Mode tax return or some tax return other than your own 1995 return, go to the File menu and choose Open. TurboTax asks whether you want to save the tax return that the program will be closing. After you save the other return (or not, if you don't want to), select your 1995 tax return from the list by double-clicking it or by clicking it once and clicking OK.

2. **Get into Forms mode to make estimated tax vouchers.**

   If you are in EasyStep, click the big pencil at the bottom of the screen. Click Forms at the top of the screen and then select Form 1040-ES Worksheet.

   The worksheet that appears shows a sample of projected 1996 income based on the income for 1995.

3. **If you know of any amounts that will change for 1996, go ahead and type over amounts that show up on this form.**

4. **At the bottom of the form are four check boxes. Check the one (check only one) for the first payment you plan to make.**

   The total estimated tax amount will be subdivided so that it fits in the right number of vouchers.

5. **View the actual tax vouchers by selecting Form 1040-ES: Vouchers 1 & 2 or Form 1040-ES: Vouchers 3 & 4.**

   These vouchers must be printed and one voucher should accompany each payment that you make. You can print them all at once and save the vouchers to file each quarter. Or, if slips of paper tend to get buried and never get recovered in your house, keep TurboTax on your computer and come back each quarter to print a voucher. For the address for making payments (estimated payments don't go to the same place as tax returns), see "So Where Do I Send This Thing?" in Chapter 12.

Due dates for filing these 1996 Quarterly Estimated Tax Voucher forms are as follows:

Quarter	Due Date
1st Quarter	April 15, 1996
2nd Quarter	June 17, 1996
3rd Quarter	September 16, 1996
4th Quarter	January 13, 1997

Notice that if the 15th of the month falls on a weekend or a holiday, the due date moves forward to the first available regular weekday.

The main thing to remember about quarterly estimated payments is that they keep you current with your tax payments so that you don't owe a big amount at tax return filing time. If you need to make quarterly payments, make them on time. The IRS prods you to remember to make these payments by sticking you with an underpayment penalty if you fail to make them on a timely basis.

See Table 12-1, "Where to Mail Quarterly Estimated Tax Payments" in Chapter 12 for mailing addresses. Quarterly payments do not go to the same address as your income tax return.

Chapter 16
Get Organized!

· ·

In This Chapter
▶ Why you should care about being organized
▶ What to use for storing things
▶ What kinds of stuff you should save
▶ How to keep good records
▶ When can you get rid of this stuff

· ·

*T*hink of how nice it would be to curl up in front of the fireplace, read a good book, and relax on April 14 instead of frantically running around searching for the mortgage statement that the bank sent you.

Some people are natural organizers. For others, getting organized takes practice, perseverance, and a good game plan.

This chapter spills the beans about the secrets of great organizers.

Why Bother to Be Organized?

You could spend hours, which add up to days, weeks, and months — incalculable lost time — wondering about, searching for, and rearranging the existence of scraps of paper that float into your life. Looking behind drawers and under sofa cushions and sifting through ever-mounting piles of papers in search of an important receipt is about the least productive way in which you can use your time.

If you live in a world of clutter, you understand that of which I speak. And beware: The disorganized tax preparer is the person the IRS dreams about finding in its random audit selection. (See Chapters 14 and 22 for more information about having your tax return audited.)

TIP

Ten advantages to getting your paperwork organized

1. Gain vast amounts of free time.

2. Save yourself embarrassment when someone calls and asks for a piece of information.

3. Make the annual TurboTax preparation of your tax return a smooth business.

4. Feel proud of yourself.

5. Gain vast amounts of free time.

6. Reduce overall clutter level in your household.

7. Remove fire hazards from your home.

8. Be able to find things at a moment's notice.

9. Long after your tax return is completed and mailed, have something to show for purchasing this book.

10. Gain vast amounts of free time.

You may tell yourself that you don't have time to set up any sort of effective filing system or method for tracking papers that enter your home. I say, you don't have the time *not* to do it. With a really small investment in financial planning software and the time spent searching for one missing slip of paper, you can set up a system that will serve you for life. You can give back to yourself all the future episodes of wasted time just waiting to happen. Take a look at the two sidebars in this chapter if you don't believe me.

Find a New Shoebox

You need a place in which to put all the papers and documents that relate to your tax life. This chapter — and this book, for that matter — is concerned with helping you prepare your tax return. Therefore, the methods that I discuss here are specifically appropriate to saving and being able to retrieve information pertinent to your tax return. But you don't have to stop there! These suggestions can apply to other record-keeping areas of your life, such as keeping track of household expenses, record-keeping for volunteer activities, and storing mementos.

You can use lots of different types of receptacles for storing your records. Choose something from this list that fits your lifestyle (or what is *soon to be* your lifestyle), or use whatever you have handy.

TIP

Ten *dis*advantages to getting your paperwork organized

1. You won't get to experience that thrilling adrenaline rush as you scramble to finish your tax return and get it in the mail by midnight on April 15.

2. Your children will get weak and flabby when their main form of exercise — climbing over your piles — is gone.

3. You'll discover that you have more floor space that has to be vacuumed.

4. Acquaintances who liked you because all your clutter made their messy homes look like palaces may start to snub you.

5. You won't have anything to put in the bottom of the bird cage.

6. You'll have to buy new clothes to fill the empty space in your closet.

7. Stray animals will stop following you home.

8. People will start pestering you to give them advice about keeping track of their records.

9. Friends will whisper behind your back. ("You know her — she's the one who's *so organized*!")

10. You'll lose your best excuse for filing your tax return late.

You see? There's just no down-side.

- ✓ **File folders:** You don't need a filing cabinet to use file folders — get a box that will hold them and put the box on a shelf; it works just as well.

- ✓ **Three-ring binder with some dividers:** Use tape or a stapler to attach small receipts to notebook paper that fits in the binder.

- ✓ **Large mailing envelopes:** Cut your investment down to nothing by recycling big envelopes that come in the mail.

- ✓ **Boxes:** Use shoeboxes, boxes from department stores, empty cereal boxes — whatever.

Basically, anything that you can compartmentalize will do the job.

Decide which type of container you want to use for storing your receipts and then label your sections — one section for each type of receipt you expect to have. Also, label the sections of your filing system with the appropriate year (for example: Medical Expenses, 1996). The types of receipts depend on your personal tax situation, but generally speaking, you'll want to have a separate folder, envelope, notebook section, or whatever for each type of income you expect to earn (job-related income, investment income, fees for contract services that you have performed) and one for each type of expense that may be deductible on your tax return (medical expenses, taxes, child care expenses, and so on).

Find a place to store your filing system. That location should be convenient and readily accessible. You don't want to make filing a chore — instead, it should be easier than stuffing receipts in drawers or wherever you put them now. And make it fun! Let your kids decorate the folders or boxes that you use, label folders with brightly colored markers, or use neon-colored paper in your notebook.

The most important aspect of using a filing system is *using* the filing system. After you've got the shell of the system and have placed it in a convenient location so that you don't have to climb over boxes in the garage or burrow into the basement to reach it, you need to make yourself use it. Whenever you open the mail or pay the bills, look at the receipts with a tax eye. Analyze them for their applicability to your tax return. If you think that something *might* be useful, take it to your file system and file it. Don't worry if it turns out that you don't need it when you actually start preparing your tax return.

When it's time to prepare your tax return, it's better to have too much information. Sort through receipts at tax time and discard those that you don't need rather than finding yourself missing receipts and not knowing where they are.

Popsicle Sticks and Band-Aid Wrappers: Which Information You Should Save

Most of the time, figuring out what you should save to support information that you plan to report on your tax return is not hard.

If you pay for something that is potentially tax deductible, keep the receipt. If you don't get a receipt, ask for one. If there is no receipt to be had, make sure that you save your canceled check. If you pay in cash and get no receipt, make your own: Write down pertinent information such as the date, amount, and name of the organization receiving your cash and the reason for the payment.

Whenever income enters your life, make a record of it. Save the paperwork that accompanies the income, save the check stub if one is included, save your receipt from depositing the money in the bank, and note the source of the deposit on the receipt or save your checkbook register and keep notes in the register about what you deposited.

For the scoop on what types of income are taxable, see Chapter 7. To delve into deductions, flip back to Chapter 8.

As a rule of thumb, it's a good idea to save your canceled checks and checkbook registers, along with all other tax-related receipts.

Don't let record-keeping get out of hand, though. One receipt is usually sufficient. If you donated popsicles to the school picnic, the sales receipt is ample support for your expenditure. Don't feel that you need to save the popsicle sticks as evidence of your donation. Likewise, getting photographic evidence of you presenting the Little League with a new first aid kit is going a bit overboard. Videotaping yourself paying the mortgage won't interest the IRS, either. Your record-keeping should be concise.

On the other hand, there may be times when you need more than a piece of paper. Suppose a tree fell over and wiped out your backyard fence. Depending on your insurance coverage, this disaster may or may not qualify you for a casualty loss deduction. But even if it does, a receipt for fence repairs may not be sufficient — the receipt alone doesn't support the tax-deductible event. Get out the camera and take some pictures of the fence with the tree lying across it.

As a basic rule, keep receipts or canceled checks to show how much you paid. Get additional supporting evidence if the expenditure could also be for a non-deductible event.

Basically, you want paper support for the items that you report on your tax return. This support generally comes in the form of paper receipts that acknowledge your payment or acquisition of income. Canceled checks with the payee's endorsement on the back make good receipts. If a standard receipt isn't available, you may need to get a little creative. Consider typing your own receipt and have someone from the organization in question sign it.

Try to pay by check when making a potentially tax-deductible payment. Doing so guarantees you a paper receipt.

And You Thought Bookkeeping Was Just for Nerds

Yes, you too can create meaningful records from the morass of receipts that you have so shrewdly begun to organize. One way to summarize your financial information is to invest in a personal financial planning computer program. There are several on the market, and they are not terribly expensive.

Some of the more well-known personal financial planning programs include

- Quicken and QuickBooks (both made by Intuit, the makers of TurboTax)
- Kiplinger's CA-Simply Money
- Microsoft Money
- BestBooks
- DacEasy Instant Accounting
- M.Y.O.B.

In these and other personal financial planning programs, you enter your checkbook transactions just as if your check register is on-screen. The program then summarizes your transactions and produces various financial statements based on that information.

Most financial planning computer programs create files that can be transferred directly into TurboTax. See "Quicken and Other Transferable Programs" in Chapter 5 for more information about how this process works.

You can accomplish much the same thing with ledger paper and a pencil. Ledger paper is extra-wide paper with lots of columns and rows forming a grid. Label each column with a category of income or expense and then list your transactions down the rows on the left side of the paper. Add up the numbers in each column to come up with a total for that category. Spreadsheet computer programs, such as Microsoft's Excel (which I used for this example) and Lotus 1-2-3, give you the same type of ledger sheet. Figure 16-1 shows one way in which you can set up this type of information on a computer spreadsheet.

Figure 16-1:
Summarize
your income
and
expenses
on a
spreadsheet.

	A	B	C	D	E	F	G	H
1	Date	Payee	Total	Paycheck	Misc Income	Mortgage	Utilities	Auto
2	Balance from prior page			21,000.00	42.00	3,450.00	1,050.00	1229.66
3	10-Jun	1st National Bank	196.61					196.61
4	12-Jun	Parkington Township	39.30				39.30	
5		Consumers Power	54.84				54.84	
6	15-Jun	1st National Bank	575.00			575.00		
7		The Company	500.00	500.00				
8								
87								
88	31-Dec	Sam's Car Wash	6.50					6.50
89	Totals			42,000.00	775.00	6,900.00	2,018.77	2,887.32

After you have totals for each type of income and expense that you received or incurred during the year, you can create your own financial statements just like accountants do. First, list income items like this:

Salary (before taxes)	42,000.00
Interest income	775.00
Total income	**42,775.00**

Then list your expense items as shown here:

Mortgage	6,900.00
Utilities	2,018.77
Auto expenses	2,887.32
Total expenses	**11,806.09**

Subtract expenses from income to see how much money you actually earned:

Net Income (before taxes)	**30,968.91**

In the Year 2525 . . . : Saving Stuff

Just how long do you need to save this stuff? The IRS says at least three years from the date on which your tax return is due, including extensions of time for filing. (So if you file for a four-month extension and file your tax return on August 15, 1996, you should keep your records until at least August 15, 1999.) But then, nothing is written in stone.

The three-year rule stems from the time period that the IRS has to begin an audit of your tax return. Generally speaking, for three years from the time you file your tax return (or the time it was due, whichever is later), your return is fair game to the IRS examiners. Applying this principle, a 1995 income tax return filed on March 15, 1996, is open to IRS scrutiny until April 15, 1999 — three years after the due date of the return. Be aware that you also have the right to amend your tax return during this same interval of years should you find an error or omission in the original forms. (For more insights into amending tax returns, see "Changing Your Tax Return After You File It" in Chapter 12.)

The three-year guideline works in most cases, and at the end of that time you can usually feel safe in tossing W-2s, 1099s, canceled checks, receipts for payments, brokers' statements, and the other trappings of your tax return entourage.

There are, however, some exceptions to this three-year term, which include the following:

- **Carrybacks of unused net operating losses:** If you operated a business that generated a loss, and that loss is carried back to an earlier year (see "Your Loss Is Your Gain" in Chapter 6 for the particulars on how this actually happens), that earlier year remains *open,* or available to the IRS for examination, for as long as the current year's return (the one that generated the loss) is open.

- **Failure to report gobs of income:** If you forget to report income and the IRS finds out about it, the IRS can keep your tax return open for six years rather than the standard three. This six-year rule comes into play only if the income you omit is greater than 25 percent of the income you report. In other words, if you reported $40,000 in income on your tax return and the IRS finds a W-2 form for $12,000 that you forgot to include (25 percent of $40,000 = $10,000, and $12,000 is greater than $10,000), then the IRS has the right to spend *six* years poring over your tax return.

- **Lying under oath:** If the IRS determines that you intentionally misstated or misrepresented information on your income tax return, there is no statute of limitations on the amount of time it has to scrutinize your return. The IRS can examine that return now, 25 years from now, 100 years from now, or whenever it wants. You are at its mercy.

Although you can usually begin to weed out your tax records after three years, it still makes sense to hold on to the tax returns themselves. Set aside a small file or box in an out-of-the-way place and put your old tax returns in it. Someday, you may need to refer to an old return. If nothing else, it makes for interesting memory-surfing.

Part V
The Part of Tens

"THE SHORT ANSWER TO YOUR REQUEST FOR A RAISE IS 'NO.' THE LONG ANSWER IS 'NO, AND GET OUT OF MY OFFICE.'"

In this part...

*I*f you've only got ten minutes to spare before you have to put this book down, this part is a good place to come for some quick insights. Ten minutes can buy you a lot of good advice back here at the end of the book.

This part is full of lists: lists to live by, lists to improve your life, and lists to copy and send to your friends.

These chapters are fun because they're quick and easy. Looking for some nice deductions? Want to hear about quick ways in which to maneuver around in TurboTax? How about some advice that will help you get ready for next year's tax return? All that and more is here. Tens of this, tens of that, tens (more or less) of important stuff that you'll be glad you took the time to read.

Chapter 17

Ten Things to Do Before You Start Preparing Your Tax Return

● ●

In This Chapter

▶ Registering your program

▶ Installing your program

▶ Gathering the important papers

▶ Dealing with state tax returns

▶ Forming the proper tax preparation state of mind

● ●

*I*t's hard to prepare a tax return with TurboTax if you just sit down at your computer and expect all the stuff to come to you like a spirit at a seance. Plan for a little start-up time, get yourself organized at the front end, and the rest of the job should fall into place like soldiers marching in cadence.

Sign Up with TurboTax

Whether you bought the HeadStart version of this program or waited for the real thing, the Final version, you need to send in the registration card that came in the box. This card tells the folks at Intuit (the makers of TurboTax) who you are and, more importantly, that it's okay for them to talk to you if you call them with questions.

Perhaps more importantly, filling in and mailing the registration card puts you on Intuit's mailing list. The company doesn't send you birthday cards or anything neat like that, but if you're on the list, Intuit sends you coupons, newsletters, and stuff about new products. Some of it is pretty interesting, especially when they throw in tips about how to use your program. If you're on Intuit's mailing list, you'll be notified next fall of the release of the TurboTax program for your 1996 tax return, and you'll get a form with which you can order the program by mail.

If you bought the HeadStart version and want TurboTax to send you the Final version (which they'll do at no charge), you have to tell them who you are and where you live — how else do you expect to get the program? *Returning the registration card is a must if you want the Final version.*

If you've already managed to lose your registration card (not a good sign), then click the Go to Forms button to get yourself to the Forms method. Click the Forms button on the toolbar and choose Registration from the bottom of the list. Up pops a substitute registration form! Fill in this form, print it, and mail it post-haste.

Load TurboTax

Okay, so you bought the program and you're ready to use it. Unfortunately, your computer won't absorb TurboTax by osmosis. You need to take the disks out of the box and install the program on your computer. Check out Appendix A for the particulars on getting this thing up and running on your computer.

Should you run into any problems with the installation, by all means get some help and get it soon. If you plan on relying on TurboTax's phone-in technical support for assistance, the earlier in the spring you call, the faster turn-around time you will get. If you're still having trouble installing your program on April 14, check out some of the ideas in Chapter 9 for last-minute help.

Find Last Year's Tax Return

Stop right here. Put down that bag of potato chips and don't do another thing until you get your hands on last year's tax return. This form is the single best resource for preparing this year's return. Lose it and you get to reinvent the wheel, as they say in more elite circles.

Last year's tax return is the key to nearly everything that goes on in your financial life. Most people don't change drastically from year to year in terms of deductible lifestyle. By looking at last year's tax return and, if you're lucky enough to find them, the supporting receipts and papers, you can remind yourself of such things as the following, which will probably apply again this year:

- ✔ Who paid you dividends and interest
- ✔ What kinds of business expenses you deducted
- ✔ What kinds of tax deductions you took
- ✔ Which business assets you have been depreciating
- ✔ Who paid you miscellaneous income
- ✔ Whom you paid for child care services (and what their social security numbers are)
- ✔ Which forms and attachments you used

It really is important to have last year's tax return with you when you work on your current tax return. If you just plain can't find it, you can call the IRS and request a copy of your tax return from last year or, for that matter, a previous year. (There's a limit here — the IRS keeps copies of your tax returns for about six years. Prior to that, you can still get information about what was on your tax returns, but actual copies are hard to get.) Call 800-829-1040 to connect with your tax past.

If you want a real copy of each page of your prior tax return, you need to request Form 4506, fill it out, and send it to the Service Center for your state. (Send Form 4506 to the same address to which you mail your tax return. These addresses are listed in Chapter 12.) The IRS charges $14 for each prior tax return you request and takes six to eight weeks to process your request. If you want to get a copy on the cheap, the IRS can provide you with a *transcript* of your tax return — a computer printout with a line-by-line summary of what was on your tax return — at no charge and much more quickly. Request the transcript by calling the number listed in the preceding paragraph. The transcript is all you need for entering information from last year's return into TurboTax.

Gather Your Paperwork

Don't start production on your tax return without first rummaging around the house and unearthing all the little receipts and other evidence of your tax deductions, as well as the forms that came in the mail telling you how much you earned. Table 17-1 provides a handy checklist to help you put together the pieces.

Table 17-1	Tax Stuff Scavenger Hunt
Things to Find	**Check Here**
W-2 forms	❒
1099 forms	❒
Statements from banks and other places that have your money	❒
K-1 forms	❒
House closing statements if you bought or sold a home	❒
Checkbook registers (both personal and business)	❒
Last year's federal income tax return	❒
Mortgage statements	❒
Prescription drug receipts	❒
Statements from doctors, dentists, and hospitals	❒
Records of charitable contributions	❒
Last year's state income tax return	❒
Anything else you can think of that may be helpful	❒

Don't Forget Your State!

Unless you live in a state that doesn't require you to file a state income tax return, you probably need to deal with your state income tax return in addition to your federal income tax return. TurboTax can prepare income tax returns for all states this year.

To use TurboTax to prepare your state tax return, you need to buy the state software separately. The same stores that sell the federal program should also sell the state program.

If you no longer live in the state in which you must file a tax return, you may have a hard time finding the TurboTax program for the state that you moved *from* in the state that you moved *to.* You can order TurboTax state tax return software by calling the TurboTax sales department at 520-295-3110.

If you don't use TurboTax to prepare your state tax return, you need to get yourself some forms. Your state probably sent you a packet in the mail. If the packet is missing, mutilated, or otherwise out of commission, the post office and the library are good places to look for state tax return forms. You can also find the phone number of your state's Department of Revenue in the telephone book. Call them, ask nicely, and they'll send you the forms you need.

Find "Free" Time

This step is really important. Set aside time and dedicate it solely to preparing your income tax returns. If you try to squeeze in the preparation over a period of several days or even weeks, you will be frustrated at the inefficiency of that method. Also, you'll probably get in trouble with other members of your household if you hog up a space with your tax stuff for a long time.

It may be a misnomer to refer to this time as *free* time, because filling out income tax returns is probably the single most *un*free act that American citizens perform. But call it what you will (and you can probably come up with some pretty creative names), you need to dedicate a chunk of time for taxes, taxes, and nuthin' but taxes.

Clear Off the Table (or Desk)

Cleaning off the table follows right along with finding free time. Don't try to fit the tax return in between the dinner dishes or your kids' homework papers. Make a space, call it your tax space (or whatever clever name occurs to you), and restrict the space only to tax returns until you are finished. You may have to put up signs and barricades, but you'll thank me for this advice later.

Clearing a space for your tax work serves multiple purposes, including the following:

- ✔ You're less likely to lose all the documents and receipts you collected for this process if they are not mixed in with personal stuff like your midnight, April 15 party invitations.

- ✔ If you shove your tax stuff in a drawer or a box each night after you finish plugging away at it (and beating your head against a wall or whatever else you do to help cope with the process), it's really easy to just leave it all there until the last minute. Keeping everything out where you can see it serves as a constant reminder of a job that you need to complete.

- ✔ Displaying your neatly organized tax papers makes you look very thorough and efficient.

Get on the Phone

As soon as you realize that you are missing some information for your tax return, pick up the phone and start making calls. Call your boss, call your bank, call the doctor, call your stockbroker, call your mother, call anyone at all who is supposed to send you information and tell him or her that you need it *now!*

If someone can't send you copies of statements that you need for your tax return, get the amounts that you're looking for over the phone. If you need the printed copies of statements (like a 1099 form), arrange to get them, even if you have to drive somewhere or send someone else in order to pick them up.

The IRS doesn't care that someone didn't send you the forms or statements you need. Getting all the stuff necessary for preparing your tax return is *your* responsibility.

Eat, Drink, and Be Merry

Tax time doesn't need to be a somber event (I said *somber,* not *sober*). Prepare yourself a feast! Surround your tax table with good snacks in order to keep your spirits (and your energy) at a high level.

Consider rewarding yourself with a cookie, a scoop of ice cream, a handful of pretzels, or whatever your junk food of choice may be each time you complete another form or section of the TurboTax Interview. On a diet? Then surround yourself with low-fat snacks. Or give yourself a different kind of reward. Maybe you can tape a favorite television show or have a good book nearby. Reward yourself with ten minutes of reading or watching your show each time you reach a tax return milestone.

Put a vase of spring flowers on your tax return desk. Turn up the lights. Play some music. Invite a friend over to keep you company. Give yourself a party atmosphere and the whole process will be a lot more bearable.

(Right.)

Chapter 18

Ten TurboTax Things Everybody Wants to Know

Will My Computer Run TurboTax?

You need the following things on your computer in order to make a go of this year's TurboTax program:

✔ Microsoft Windows Version 3.1 or higher (Windows 95 is okay)

✔ At least 4MB of RAM (the more RAM, the better the program runs)

✔ Any 3 ¹/₂- inch floppy disk drive or a high-density 5 ¹/₄- inch floppy drive. If your disks don't match the drive size on your computer, take your disks back to your friendly computer store and ask for the size you need; alternatively, you can call TurboTax at 520-295-3100, and they'll arrange to make the switch for you.

✔ One of the following printers or a printer compatible with one of them: HP LaserJet Series II or higher, HP DeskJet, Epson 9 or 24 pin, IBM 9 or 24 pin, Apple LaserWriter, LaserWriter Plus, Laser Writer II, or a compatible PostScript printer.

If you don't have this stuff, you're going to have a problem running this program. You can bypass the printer problem by preparing your return on your machine, copying your program onto a disk, and printing on a friend's machine if that friend has one of these printers and has TurboTax.

Will My Printer Print TurboTax Forms?

See the preceding section about hardware for a discussion of printers. If you have one of the printers listed there, your printer will print the nice-looking forms that make your tax return look like it was prepared professionally.

Can I Use Last Year's TurboTax Program This Year?

Not if you want to prepare this year's tax return. Each year, TurboTax comes out with a new program, and the forms that it prints correlate to the current tax year. This is the 1995 tax year (even though you are probably reading this book in 1996). All the forms you get with this year's version of TurboTax say 1995 on them. The IRS gets pretty upset if you try to use last year's program, which prints 1994 tax forms for this year's tax return.

On the other hand, if you are still working on your 1994 tax return, then you *do* want last year's TurboTax program. Check the TurboTax box or look on the form that appears on-screen when you go into the program to see which year's program you are using.

You can have more than one year's program on your computer at a time — that's not a problem. When you install TurboTax, it puts itself in a unique directory on your hard drive, calling itself TAX95W (last year it was TAX94), so it's unlikely that the two programs could overlap on your computer.

When Will I Get the Final Version?

If you haven't registered, probably never.

This is the single most frequently asked question about TurboTax each January. The answer is, of course, *as soon as the TurboTax programmers are done writing it.* Those folks work around the clock to finish the program as early as they can after the first of the year and start sending it out as soon as it is finished.

Don't get too antsy if you haven't received the program by the middle of January. Give Intuit a little while to process the orders. However, if January is about to be a memory and you *still* haven't received the Final version of your program, it's time to take steps.

If you sent in your card from a HeadStart version, called in your registration, or ordered the TurboTax Final version by mail through a flyer that you received at home or work, expect to receive the Final version in mid-to-late January. The later you send in your card, the longer it takes the company to get the program out to you. If you haven't received your program by the end of January, call the TurboTax Customer Service department at 520-295-3100 and make sure that your name is on file.

Will the IRS Accept the Forms That TurboTax Prepares?

Absolutely. Some sort of secret arrangement has been made between the IRS and TurboTax, ensuring that all the forms that your TurboTax program prepares are acceptable to the IRS.

What about My State Tax Return?

TurboTax now has tax programs for all the states that have an income tax. (Finally! Hooray!) Purchasing the TurboTax federal income tax program does *not* get you a state program, however. The state program is a separate program and a separate purchase.

You can probably pick up the state tax program at the same store where you purchased your federal TurboTax program. If you can't find the state program there, call around to other computer stores or just call TurboTax at 520-295-3100 and order it directly from them. The TurboTax Customer Service department will be happy to take your order.

You can also purchase TurboTax state tax programs online if you subscribe to CompuServe. GO CHIPSOFT while in CompuServe and follow the on-screen instructions for downloading. You will be charged $19.95 per state. *Note:* State tax returns aren't available online until the Final versions are in the stores sometime in January.

Can TurboTax Make Mistakes?

Well, um, it's actually the person typing the information who makes many of the mistakes. It's so easy to transpose figures, enter something twice, or just plain leave something out. TurboTax can't read your mind, so if you make a mistake inputting your tax information, chances are that you will have a mistake on your tax return.

As far as TurboTax itself making mistakes goes, the people who write the program certainly hope that won't happen. If you're convinced that the program made a mistake, however, contact TurboTax Customer Service at 520-295-3100 or Technical Support at 520-295-3090 and tell the person who takes your call what happened. He or she will hook you up with someone who can figure out the problem.

The makers of TurboTax warrant the accuracy of the calculations on the tax forms. If TurboTax causes a mistake by failing to compute something accurately, the company will take the responsibility for paying any penalty you incur. (Don't expect them to do your jail time, though.)

What if I Find More Receipts After I Complete My Tax Return?

There are two possible scenarios here. First, you find more receipts, but you haven't yet mailed your tax return. If that is the case, go right back into your TurboTax program and open your tax return file. You can enter additional information in one of three ways:

✔ From the Interview, click the Interview Navigator and find the item(s) that you want to change in the list of My Tax Data. Click the topic that describes where your additional information should go, click Interview to go right to the questions about that topic, or click Forms to go directly to the tax form. Enter your new information.

✔ If you are in the Interview and want to go to the forms, you can click the Go to Forms button. Once in the Forms method, click the Forms button on the toolbar, double-click the appropriate form, click the line where you want to enter your information, and then type the new numbers.

✔ If you are not sure which form should receive your new information, go to the File Cabinet (in the Forms method, choose Tools⇨File Cabinet or click the little yellow file cabinet button at the top of the screen), select the alphabetical listing that most closely matches the new information you have, and then click Select. TurboTax then leads you to the proper form.

After you add the new item(s), print out a new copy of your tax return and throw the old one away (or, better yet, think "green" and recycle it).

Alternatively, if you have already mailed your tax return to the IRS and then find something worth changing, you need to *amend* your return, putting in the change and filing new forms with the IRS. See "Changing Your Tax Return After You File It" in Chapter 12 for particulars on amending your return.

When amending a tax return, think in terms of the tax value of the item causing the amendment. If you find a receipt for a $1 contribution to the Salvation Army, the net change in your tax liability probably won't even pay for the stamp that you need to mail your amended tax return to the IRS.

Can I Prepare More Than One Tax Return with TurboTax?

You can prepare as many tax returns as your computer and assorted disks will hold with this one little TurboTax program. The trick is to give each new tax return its own name. When the program first asks you to save the tax return, you give it a name. This name distinguishes this particular tax return from any other return that you may have saved previously or may save in the future.

If you've already finished preparing one tax return and want to start a new one, choose New Tax Return from the File menu. TurboTax makes sure that you've saved your old tax return and prompts you to do so if you haven't, and then it lets you start over with a brand new return.

See "Finished for the Day" in Chapter 5 for more information about naming your tax return.

Chapter 19

Ten Reasons to Send Roses to the Person Who Sold You TurboTax

You Can Do Your Taxes Even If You Flunked Math (Twice)

Wow! Magic! Change a number anywhere on your tax return either by going back to a form in EasyStep or by selecting a specific form in the Forms method, and — presto! — TurboTax updates your entire tax return to reflect the change. No more erasing until you have holes in your paper. No more frantically wondering whether you managed to find every place on your tax return where a particular number appears. This number-changing feature is one of the main reasons for buying this computer program.

The Program Helps You Plan for Next Year

TurboTax's planning features help you get ready for next year. In the Review section of EasyStep (click the number 4 tab, labeled Review), you can check the Tax Saving box to learn key tax concepts that may help you in future years.

TurboTax chooses the ideas it presents based on your particular tax situation and offers the ones that should be specifically helpful to you. Get to this point from the Forms method by choosing Final Review from the Tools menu.

Another planning feature is TurboTax's *Plan Mode*. While using the Forms method, choose Plan Mode from the Tools menu. In Plan Mode, you can actually begin preparing your 1996 tax return, starting with income and expenses from 1995 but applying 1996 tax rates. Change these amounts to reflect anticipated income or expense activity for 1996. Experiment with different scenarios, testing the potential income tax on your financial situation under various circumstances. For example, how will your exemptions change if you have a child during 1996? How will your new raise affect your taxes? What will be the tax effect of selling your house?

For a more detailed analysis of how these planning features work, see "Tax Saving Suggestions" in Chapter 15.

Note: Tax Saving ideas and Plan Mode are not available in the HeadStart version.

TurboTax's planning tools for next year are based on the current knowledge of 1996 tax laws. Tax law changes that occur during 1996 will, of course, be incorporated into next year's TurboTax program, but these planning tools can utilize only facts that were in place at the end of 1995. As you plan for your 1996 income taxes, keep in mind that income tax rates, the value of exemptions, and other tax laws may change.

The What If? Feature Lets You Compare Tax Situations

Have you ever wanted to play around with your tax return, wondering what your income tax would be if you won the lottery or how much you'd get to claim in exemptions if all your children had been twins? A feature new to TurboTax this year is the *What If?* comparison. *What If?* lets you experiment with these different tax scenarios, comparing the different situations side-by-side. For example, what would your tax be if you filed Married Filing Separately as opposed to Married Filing Jointly? Take a look at the two scenarios and decide for yourself. Chapter 2 has more information about this new feature.

You Don't Have to Know a Schedule C from a Form 8606

Let TurboTax figure out which forms you need. How nice to not have to worry about all these different documents! Just answer the EasyStep questions, and TurboTax gets the forms and puts your income and expense numbers right where they belong. Answering some simple questions is lots easier than having to run out to the IRS office or phone for forms to be mailed to you. Not to mention that you don't even have to know which forms you need to have in your tax return.

You Can Transfer Information from Quicken and Other Programs

Quicken is a personal finance program that allows you to enter and then summarize income and expense information from your checking, savings, and investment accounts. You can transfer this information to TurboTax so that you don't have to enter it twice. See the "Quicken and Other Transferable Programs" section in Chapter 5 for particulars on performing this transfer business.

Other programs on the market work similarly to Quicken, and TurboTax can read information from them, too. TurboTax makes a bigger deal about Quicken because the two programs are made by the same company. Pretty sneaky, huh?

TurboTax Makes Beautiful, Professional-Looking Forms

This feature may not seem like such a big deal, but you can't help but like it when professional-looking forms come spitting out of your printer. Further-more, the IRS likes it. Forms prepared by TurboTax are easy to read and come out of the printer in the order in which they should be filed. (I'll bet you didn't know that there was a special order in which your tax return forms should be put together. See "Putting the Package Together" in Chapter 12 for clues to the secret IRS tax form order.)

You Can Work in the Comfort of Your Home

It's the end of the work day, and you've chosen this day to begin work on your tax return. Picture these two scenarios:

- ✔ You're still at the office. You get out your box of receipts, which you brought from home, you shove your work files aside on your desk trying to make room for your personal tax papers, you fire up your TurboTax program on your office computer, and you wave good-bye to coworkers who are returning to the comfort of their homes. Meanwhile, you try to fly as quickly as you can through the tax information you brought with you, anxious to return home at the end of an extremely long day.

- ✔ You drive home from the office, slip into some sweats or other comfortable clothes, and get out your neatly organized receipts. (They *are* neatly organized, right? If not, go back to Chapter 16 and "Get Organized!") You pour yourself a cold drink and order a pizza or whatever else you've decided to enjoy for your tax-preparation meal (see "Eat, Drink, and Be Merry" in Chapter 17). You flip on a little music, turn on the computer, and relax, knowing that you can get up and take a break whenever you need one.

Which would you choose?

You Can Take a Vacation with the Money TurboTax Helps You Save

Just think of all the money you are going to save on this tax return! You don't have to pay a professional preparer fee, and, because TurboTax takes the time to remind you of deductions you otherwise may have missed, your income tax is as low as it can be. Because you've saved all this money, why not celebrate? Take a little trip to reward yourself for money saved and time spent efficiently.

You'll Make Nerdy New Friends

Preparing your own tax return puts you in a position to communicate with a new echelon of potential friends: those who prepare their own tax returns. Find yourself dropping into your casual conversation such phrases as *electronic filing, charitable contribution deductions, disks, estimated payments, error messages, depreciation, technical support,* and *filing systems.* Suddenly, you are just as much in the know as all those other people who eschew professional tax return preparers and try to go it alone. Who knows, you may have so much fun talking taxes and tax software with new-found friends that you'll just have to throw an end-of-tax-season party, just like the professional tax preparers do.

Chapter 20

Ten Keyboard Shortcuts
for Tired Mice

In This Chapter

▶ Starting a new tax return

▶ Opening an existing tax return

▶ Printing your tax return

▶ Making choices on-screen

▶ Fixing mistakes

▶ Using the hallmarks of all Windows programs: Cut, Copy, and Paste

▶ Making itemized schedules

▶ Going from the Forms method to EasyStep and back again

▶ Closing files and programs

*T*he people who make TurboTax have worked hard to improve the ease with which you can get around by using the keyboard. So if you're in the mood to let your fingers do the walking rather than relying on your mouse, consider using these keyboard alternatives.

If you are pressing a key combination that includes the Ctrl or Alt key and a letter, it doesn't matter whether you type the letter in uppercase or lowercase.

Ctrl+N: New Tax Return

Had enough of this tax return and want to start a new one? Maybe you're ready to prepare your children's tax returns, or maybe your mom just walked in with a W-2 form in her hand. Whatever the reason, you can close the tax return you're currently working on and start a new one by holding down the Ctrl key and pressing the letter N. TurboTax gives you the chance to save your current tax return before it presents you with a fresh, new one.

Ctrl+O: Open Tax Return

When you're working on one tax return, you can open a different tax return (one that you've already started and previously saved) by pressing Ctrl+O. TurboTax asks whether you want to save the tax return that's currently on-screen, so you won't lose any changes that you've made to that return. Then that tax return closes and the one that you have requested opens, taking the place of the original one on-screen.

Ctrl+P: Print Tax Return

This combination prints the tax return currently on-screen. Pressing Ctrl+P brings up a screen like the one shown in Figure 20-1. You can print the form that you're working on (for example, if you are working on your Form 2119, Sale of Your Home, pressing Ctrl+P and then pressing Alt+P for Print prints the Schedule A). To print the entire tax return, press Ctrl+P, press Alt+R to activate Tax Return for Your Records, and then press Alt+P for Print. To choose certain forms, press Alt+L for Selected Forms and then press Alt+C to choose the forms you want. Hold down Ctrl and click the forms that you want to print from the list of available forms. Then click OK and press Alt+P to Print. For more detailed information about printing options, see the section "See It in Print" in Chapter 12.

Figure 20-1:
Press Alt with an underlined letter to choose a printing option, and then press Alt+P to print.

On-Screen Options

Choose from a variety of on-screen options right from your keyboard. You can select any of the buttons on your screen in EasyStep (Help, Summary, Calculator, and Go to Forms, as well as Next, Back, TaxLink, Itemize, Skip, and Interview Navigator), as indicated in Figure 20-2, by holding down the Alt key and pressing the underlined letter in the word.

Figure 20-2:
The EasyStep screen. Hold down Alt and press the underlined letter to activate one of the buttons.

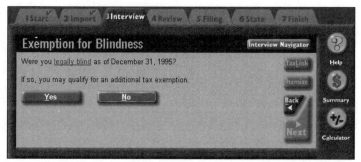

In EasyStep, you can press the underlined letter of a word or button on-screen to answer a question or move to another place. For example, respond to a question that requires a Yes or No answer by pressing Y or N.

If TurboTax is waiting for you to enter information — the taxpayer's name, for example — and you type the underlined letter of one of these buttons, TurboTax won't understand that you want to select a button. In that case, you must press the Alt key while pressing the underlined letter. If information, rather than a blank space for you to fill in, is on-screen, then you can just press the underlined letter without the aid of the Alt key.

Whether you're working in EasyStep or working directly with the forms, you can access menu choices by holding down the Alt key and pressing the underlined letter of the menu name.

Ctrl+S: Save Tax Return

Don't wait for lightning to strike your electrical outlet and shut down your computer. And don't just wait for TurboTax to ask whether you want to save your work. From time to time, press Ctrl+S to save your tax return.

TurboTax assumes that you want to save your tax return on your hard drive. Just to be extra sure, get yourself a floppy disk and save the return there as well. See "Save This Year's Tax Return on Disk" in Chapter 21 for more information about saving.

Ctrl+Z: Undo What You've Done

When you are using the Forms method, you can go back one step by choosing Undo from the Edit menu. The usefulness of this command is somewhat limited, however. For example, if you type some information on a line of a tax form and immediately decide that you don't want it there, you can press Ctrl+Z to make it go away (or to return to what was on that line before you started typing). But if you type something and then move on to another line, TurboTax turns off this Undo feature, and you can't use it. The moral of this story is this: *Undo what you've Done as soon as you've Done it, or consider it Done.*

Ctrl+X, C, and V: Cut, Copy, and Paste

If you've used other Windows programs, you're probably familiar with the Cut, Copy, and Paste commands. They work pretty much the same in TurboTax, the exception being that you really don't need these commands in TurboTax. I've used this program for several years, and I've never once found an occasion to use them. But if you stumble across a reason for using them, here's how they work.

Type something. Select the text that you just typed by clicking and dragging your mouse across the text. The word(s) or number(s) that you select is outlined in dark blue. If you want to remove the item and place it somewhere else, then you want to *cut* it. If you want to leave it where it is but also place it somewhere else, then you want to *copy* it. Ctrl+X does the job of cutting, and Ctrl+C copies.

Both procedures place the selected item in the *Windows Clipboard,* a general holding place that is accessible to all programs running in Windows. You can access anything residing on the Windows Clipboard by pressing Ctrl+V while in TurboTax (or choosing Paste from the Edit menu). So click the place where you want that number to appear and press Ctrl+V to paste. Information that you place in the Clipboard, either by cutting or copying, is also accessible from any other Windows program through the Paste command in that program.

Ctrl+I: Itemize to Provide Detail of an Amount

Press Ctrl+I to open up a statement form on which you can give details about a particular amount that you enter. For example, suppose that when filling out Schedule A, Itemized Deductions, you are ready to enter real estate taxes that you paid on your personal residence. Maybe you changed lending institutions during the year and thus made payments to two different places, and you want to spell out how much you paid to each place. Whether you are using EasyStep or the Forms method, there is room for only one number on the line on which you report the Real Estate Tax on your personal residence.

No matter which method you use, you have the opportunity to *itemize* the information that you put on this line by pressing Ctrl+I before entering the amount of your deduction. TurboTax pops up a statement that you can use to fill in the details. You can prepare this statement for your personal records, or you can send it with your tax return to the IRS.

Ctrl+R: Go from Forms to EasyStep and Back Again

Wander at your leisure through the Forms method or the EasyStep method, and then switch quickly back and forth between the two. Pressing Alt+G in EasyStep takes you to the Forms method. Pressing Ctrl+R in the Forms method takes you back to EasyStep.

Ctrl+F4 and Alt+F4: Put Everything to Bed for the Night

Even your tax return needs rest from time to time. When using the Forms method, close a particular form (the one on top, if several are open at once) by pressing Ctrl+F4. Shut down the entire TurboTax enterprise by pressing Alt+F4. When you exit TurboTax with Alt+F4 (or any way short of turning off the computer with your tax return still glaring at you), you are asked whether you want to save any changes that you have made. Choose Yes or No, depending on whether you care to save your most recent changes. TurboTax makes the save if you pick Yes, and the program then closes properly.

Say you enter something in error and want to get rid of it. It's too late for Edit⇨Undo (Ctrl+Z), but you saved the tax return fairly recently. Consider closing the program by pressing Alt+F4 and electing *not* to save your changes. The next time you tune into TurboTax, the program presents you with the undefaced version of your tax return, the way it was before you entered stuff that you didn't want.

"The first thing we should do is get you two into a good mutual fund. Let me get out the 'Magic 8-Ball' and we'll run some options."

Chapter 21

Ten Ways to Save Time and Money Now on Next Year's Tax Return

*Y*ou can continue to get by year after year, waiting until April 14 to find out how much you're going to pay in taxes and then wishing that you had done a little planning in advance, if for no other reason than to be able to anticipate what to do with your big refund.

Or you can get busy now and prepare to lower next year's tax bite by doing the following:

✔ Figure out how much next year's taxes are going to be (both federal and state).

✔ Organize your records so that you won't be running around at the last minute like one of those weird headless chickens.

✔ Plan your tax activities around certain dates.

✔ Set up a savings plan.

Look through the items in this chapter and do as many of them as you can. You'll thank yourself (or me!) come next April.

Save This Year's Tax Return on a Disk

Don't wait for your computer to crash before you think about backing up your tax return on a floppy disk — by then it will be too late. And computers *do* crash. In fact, some people think that the frequency of computer crashes is in direct proportion to the sensitive and important nature of the data stored on the machine.

Instead of giving a dumb piece of equipment the chance to thumb its mechanical nose at you, find yourself an available disk and use it to save your tax return. To accomplish this feat, follow these steps:

1. **Put your floppy disk in the computer's disk drive.**

2. **Press Alt+F4 to close TurboTax (or choose Exit from the File menu).**

3. **Open the Windows File Manager by double-clicking the little yellow file cabinet icon.**

   You'll find File Manager in the Main group window on the Program Manager screen.

4. **In File Manager, click the letter of the drive in which your TurboTax program is stored (probably the C:\ or D:\ drive).**

   I can't see how many drives you have, so I have to feel my way in the dark here.

5. **Click the TAX95W directory on the left side of your screen. (Take a look at the File Manager screen in Figure 21-1.)**

   You should see a bunch of filenames on the right side of your screen (if you don't, click the View menu and choose Tree and Directory).

6. **On the right side of your screen, find your tax return filename and click it.**

   (It should have *TAX* as the last three letters of its name — see Figure 21-1 again. The default tax return name is MYFED.TAX — but yours will probably have a different name.)

7. **Choose File⇨Copy.**

   That filename appears on the top line of the dialog box that opens.

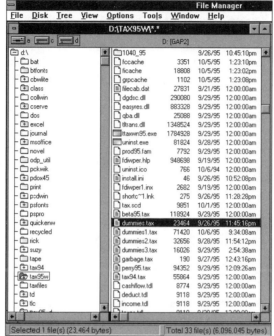

Figure 21-1:
The
TAX95W
directory is
on the left,
and the
*.TAX files
are on the
right on the
File
Manager
screen.

8. **Type** A:\ **on the bottom line (use** B:\ **if you will be using your computer's** B:\ **drive or if you tried** A:\ **and it didn't work). Then click OK.**

   File Manager copies your tax return file to your floppy disk.

9. **Choose** File➪Exit **to leave File Manager.**

10. **Label your disk something appropriate, like** 1995 Taxes, **and put it away in a safe place so that you can reference it later if you need to.**

Start Organizing Your Tax Information Now!

Don't wait until next spring to start looking for receipts for your tax return. Get your act together now and start an organized system for keeping track of important tax information. See Chapter 16 for some organization guidelines.

Estimate Next Year's Taxes

If you really like surprises and want to wait until you prepare next year's tax return to figure out how much tax you owe, then be my guest. But might I suggest that if you don't happen to like what you uncover next April, it may be a little too late to change things.

By estimating your tax liability *now*, over a year in advance of next year's tax return deadline, you can buy yourself lots of time to exert some control over that tax. See "Calculate Next Year's Taxes Now" in Chapter 15 for an explanation of how to figure out what you're going to owe. See the next section for tips on controlling when taxable events occur.

Figure Out Ways to Shift Income and Expenses

If you think that one year will produce a higher income tax than another — maybe your income is going to be much higher one year than the next, maybe you're expecting some large medical bills in one year, or maybe you know that the tax rates are going to change significantly next year — you may want to consider shifting income or expenses out of one year and into another. This trick is most easily accomplished in December and January, when events fall close to the change in the tax year.

If your income comes in the form of a paycheck from an employer, you may not have a lot of control over when you receive it. Paydays are paydays, and they are usually set on particular days. In fact, asking your employer to hold onto your check at the end of the year and give it to you in January doesn't affect when you pay tax on the income. You were entitled to receive the money in December; therefore, it gets taxed in the year that includes December. Alternatively, if you want more income in this year instead of next, you may be able to cajole your employer into giving you the first January check in the end of December. Because the money is yours in December, you pay tax on it with your other income for the year that includes that December.

Deductible expenses that you would normally pay in January can most likely be paid in December, thus generating more expense in the earlier tax year. Alternatively, you may be able to hold deductible December expenses until January if the deduction will do you more good next year. See "Tax Saving Suggestions" in Chapter 15 for more discussion on shifting income and expenses.

Sometimes you know in advance what is going to happen with the tax rates. Tax laws already in place that adjust rates may have a significant effect on the way you want to report income or expenses. As of the end of 1995, it appears that Congress may do some serious futzing with the tax laws and tax rates in 1996. You'll just have to wait and see what happens to the tax laws in the coming year.

Don't Forget Your State!

When estimating income tax, don't forget to include your state income tax. Doing so is especially important for people who have just moved or who anticipate a move in the coming year. State tax rates vary from state to state — sometimes drastically. Find out the income tax rates in your state and prepare yourself accordingly.

If most of your income is derived from employment and your employer withholds for state income taxes, your state tax liability may be covered by your state tax withholding, even if you move to a new state. Knowing the state tax rates in your state and doing a little calculating to see whether you are covered can never hurt, however. The goal is to avoid a surprise in April.

Mark Your Calendar!

Being aware of important tax dates throughout the year will benefit you a great deal. Mark your calendar so that these dates won't creep up and catch you unawares. To begin with, remember the estimated payment dates. Federal estimated income tax payments (see "Pay as You Go: Quarterly Estimated Taxes" in Chapter 15) are due on the following dates:

- ✔ **April 15, 1996**
- ✔ **June 17, 1996**
- ✔ **September 16, 1996**
- ✔ **January 15, 1997**

Your state quarterly estimated income tax payment dates may correlate with those federal dates, or they may not. Check your state income tax instructions or call your state Department of Revenue if you plan on paying quarterly state estimated income taxes and need to know the due dates.

Other important dates are as follows:

- ✔ **January 31, 1996:** You should receive all your 1995 W-2 and 1099 forms by this date. If you are missing forms, start making phone calls.

- ✔ **March 15, 1996:** K-1 forms from partnerships and S-Corporations in which you own an interest should arrive by this day. More phone calls are in order if some of these forms are not in your hands.

- ✔ **April 16, 1996:** Have a big after-tax-return party. Invite the neighborhood.

Save Money for Uncle Sam

People who pay estimated taxes (see "Pay as You Go: Quarterly Estimated Taxes" in Chapter 15) must come up with money four times a year and send it to the IRS and also to their state revenue department. Making four payments a year is probably better than waiting until April 15 and having to cough up everything at once. But even four payments a year can be daunting.

Consider instead putting aside $1/12$ of your taxes each month in a special bank account (or at least keep track of it and don't spend it!); then just draw from that account each time a payment is due. Saving this way may make the quarterly tax bite easier to swallow.

Save Some for Yourself, Too

While you're in the mood to save money for Uncle Sam, you may as well think about your own savings plan. Putting something aside for yourself each month is a good habit to adopt.

Look at Your Life through Tax-Colored Glasses

Many aspects of your daily life provide opportunities for tax deductions; you just have to be aware of them. Look over the sections about deductions in this book for some ideas: "Business deductions for people who run their own businesses" in Chapter 7 and "Have Deductions, Will Itemize" in Chapter 8.

Then, as you go through the year making the odd purchases here and there or driving your car for one cause or another, think about the effect of these events on your tax return. Little expenditures add up to large deductions and significant tax savings. Saving receipts and documenting incidents that may be tax related is worth your time.

Chapter 22

Ten Tips for Facing an Auditor

*1*t hardly seems fair. You did such a good job of following all the rules, and you feel certain that all the amounts on your tax return are correct. So why an audit? And why you?

The truth is that anyone can get audited. Entering all your information properly on the forms and using a program like TurboTax that makes everything easy to find and professional-looking is a great start, but the IRS doesn't really care about all that when it chooses tax returns for audit. Sure, some returns are chosen because they appear to have inconsistencies or maybe even false information in them. But the scary thing is the random audit. Each year, the IRS chooses a random collection of tax returns to audit. Returns from normal citizens who follow all the rules and never break the law. The selection process for random audits is completely arbitrary, so don't feel as if you've been singled out if you get chosen. Just keep your chin up and go to the audit. But don't forget to take these tips with you.

Get a Grip

Auditors get suspicious of taxpayers who sit across the desk from them and whistle, scratch themselves, tie and untie their shoes, shift in their seats, stick fingers in their ears and nose, and generally look like they're trying terribly hard to hide something. Sure, acting naturally is difficult in a situation as unnatural as an IRS audit, while a complete stranger dissects your financial life as if it were a high school biology project, but you have to try. The more uncomfortable you act, the more it looks like you have reason to be uncomfortable. So here are a few pointers for reaching a state of un-ruffled tranquillity as you face the IRS auditor:

- ✔ Think about something pleasant (silently, please) — plan a nice dinner or a trip to the dentist — as you wait for the auditor to sift through your receipts and ask you prying questions.

- ✔ Be confident. Remind yourself continuously that you didn't do anything wrong. Even if there's a mistake on your tax return — say you completely forgot to record that $20,000 grand prize vacation you won last November — mistakes happen and can be corrected. Keep telling yourself that you're the good guy.

- ✔ Know that this too will pass. The clock keeps ticking, and soon you will be outside in the sunshine again and that nasty auditor will be stuck behind his or her metal desk, staring at green walls.

Double-Check Your Figures

When you receive notice of an audit, the first thing you'll probably want to do is consider relocating to another country. After that urge passes, you should get out your tax return (the one being audited) and look over all the items that the IRS plans to examine. Verify that you agree with all the numbers you put on the tax return forms. Go back to your records and find the places from which those numbers originated. Re-create in your mind the process of filling out the tax return, and remind yourself of what on earth you were thinking when you took that deduction for the cost of your new backyard swimming pool. (Calm down! Of course it was for physical therapy, and you had every right to claim it as a medical deduction.) Basically, you have to relive the preparation of your tax return (I know — living through tax preparation once is bad enough . . .) so that every item that is under examination on your tax return is fresh in your mind.

You don't want to sit in the audit fumbling around, scratching your head, and saying, "Got me! I don't know where that number could have come from." Aside from the questionable grammar, your statement will make you sound like someone who doesn't care what the auditor decides. Instead, you want to be able to say, "See, it's right here. This is how I got that number." Not only will the audit go more smoothly if you are on top of all the numbers on your tax return, it will be over with more quickly.

Find Your Receipts

The notice you receive in the mail that tells you about your audit will also describe exactly what the IRS wants to see when you go to the audit. Carefully gather all the documentation you need to support the numbers that are under attack. The IRS likes to see canceled checks, dated receipts for payments, signed statements, diaries and journals (the kind in which you record trips and business-related adventures, not the kind in which you write about what happened with that cute girl you took to the movies last July), calendars, logs (the kind that record dates and amounts, not the kind you put in your fireplace), ledgers, bank statements, testimonials from third parties — whatever you can dredge up to provide support for the deductions you took on your tax return.

The trick here is to be efficient. Don't bring too much in the way of support to the audit, or you'll be there all month wading through paperwork. Walk in with your son's Radio Flyer heaped with dusty boxes of grocery store receipts, and the friendly IRS agent is going to experience a rapid increase in heartbeat rate — and guess who's going to pay? Take what you need, but don't bring three documents to support every deduction.

Dress for the Audit

It's a good idea to choose your wardrobe carefully for the audit. Just like lawyers can dress a hardened criminal for his court appearance and make him look like the Prince of Wales, you should strive to appear as something you're not when it comes to the audit. What you *are* is nervous and shaky, a bit scared, and wishing that you could trade places with anyone. You *want* to appear calm, in control, comfortable, and confident.

Dress nicely, but don't overdress. Don't try to impress the auditor with expensive clothing — she'll just think you have some hidden source of income you didn't report on your tax return. You'll end up feeling uncomfortable, which will show in your demeanor at your audit. Dress the way you do for your job, or dress the way you dress when you're comfortable. Don't wear an excessive amount of jewelry. Don't try to impress the auditor either with your wealth or with your lack thereof. Auditors are on to all sorts of tricks — the businessman who makes $300,000 a year and dresses for his audit in ragged clothing needing of repair in order to look like he can't afford to pay any more tax isn't going to fool anybody.

I've heard stories of people wearing the same clothes for weeks, not bathing, not shaving, and not brushing their teeth in preparation for their audit. The theory is that the more disgusting you are, the more likely the auditor will be to want to finish the audit in a hurry and get you out of the office. You have to decide for yourself if this approach is right for you. Personally, I think it would just alienate the auditor and make him or her want to nail you with every unfavorable adjustment possible.

Be on Time

Think of what a nice impression you'll make if you keep your auditor waiting for your appointment. Let him know just how much you care about the audit by showing up an hour or two late, and he'll be sure to let you know just how much he cares about listening to your stories about missing receipts. Don't arrive at your audit late — keep that auditor waiting, and you'll have an auditor in a bad mood before the audit even begins. Auditors are on strict schedules, and you're not the only appointment of the day.

On the other hand, don't arrive early. Getting to the audit early gives a sign that you're anxious and therefore must have something to hide. Auditors are really good at reading signs. The trick for you is to try to leave no particular impression at all.

Take the Receipts You Need — Only the Receipts You Need

The audit form asks you to produce documentation to support various items you listed on your tax return. *Don't take anything with you to the audit except the items requested on the audit form.* The auditor cannot expect you to produce anything beyond that which is listed on the audit form, but if you bring extra paperwork, the auditor has every right to examine the things you bring, which can lead to more questions and a lengthier audit.

Should the auditor ask you for something that was not described in the audit notice, you should respond that the item was not requested in the audit and that you did not bring it with you.

Do not take materials with you from other years. Bring only receipts and support for the tax return year that is under examination.

Say the auditor wants to see support for your business mileage and you bring in a calendar on which you had marked the miles you drove to a business meeting, and on the same page of the calendar you had marked the day on which you won the lottery. The IRS now has the right to start questioning you about those lottery winnings, which may open the door to questions about other gambling, which might open the door to those alleged business trips you took at the riverboat casino and . . . In other words, closely examine the records you are about to turn over to the IRS and make sure that you give up only the information that you want the examiner to see.

Don't Be Chatty

Answer only the questions the auditor asks you. Don't offer additional information. Don't ramble on at length. Your answers should be brief and to the point. The more you talk, the more you are likely to talk about something other than the items being audited. As soon as you introduce a new part of your tax return, the auditor has the right to question you about it. Don't give the auditor an opportunity to learn more about you or your tax return than is necessary.

The audit is not a time to make a new friend.

Don't Lie

If you don't know an answer, don't make something up; just say, "I don't know" or "I don't remember." You can tell the auditor that you would be glad to check on that item and get back in touch with him or her. But don't fabricate an answer or say something that isn't true.

Don't try to cover up information. It's too late for that. Once in the audit, you are obliged to tell the truth. You do have the right to not incriminate yourself, just as you would in a courtroom. So if the auditor asks you to identify the source of the rather substantial cash deposit that he or she notices on a copy of your bank statement, and you feel that by disclosing that source you may get yourself into trouble, you can plead the Fifth Amendment. It's probably time, however, to get yourself a lawyer before the audit goes much further.

Call in a Pro

You don't have to face the music alone. You have the right to take someone with you: a tax accountant, a lawyer, a friend or family member, or your pet parrot, for example. The person you bring with you can speak for you in the audit. The IRS agent may have you sign a Power of Attorney form — a document that designates that person as your spokesperson.

Part VI
Appendixes

The 5th Wave   By Rich Tennant

Appendix A

Installing TurboTax on Your Computer

*S*o you've been flipping through the book, looking over the parts that seem interesting to you. Now it's time to plunk yourself down in front of your computer and get to work.

In this appendix, I'll show you how to get the program up and running on your computer, make sure that there aren't any kinks, and give it a whirl.

While you're here, you can learn about all the free stuff you can get from the folks who brought you TurboTax. Lucky you!

What's in the Box?

There's something exciting about opening up a box with a new computer program inside. It's not birthday-present exciting because there's no surprise about what's in the box. It's more like the kind of feeling you get when you open up a new box of cereal. You know that it's fresh and crunchy inside, and you know that you're going to enjoy what you get. Okay, so a computer program doesn't have a whole lot in common with a box of Rice Krispies, but it's fun to open up both kinds of boxes, nonetheless.

So go ahead, pierce that shrink-wrap with a pencil or your fingernail and yank it off. Pull the inner box out of the display box and look at the neat stuff inside.

To start with, you probably notice a lot of air. TurboTax packs a big supply of fresh Utah air in its box, so take a deep breath before it gets away and pretend for a moment that you're somewhere in Utah (unless you actually *are* in Utah, in which case you can just open the window).

The TurboTax manual is included in your HeadStart box. Save it because it goes with both the HeadStart version and the Final version of your TurboTax program.

Some important-looking cards are also inside the box. One card demands immediate attention — the registration card. Pull it out and then do what it says. Sending in this card positions you to receive technical support, and it ensures that you will receive free stuff in the mail (see "Free Goodies" later in this appendix). Most importantly, if you bought the HeadStart version, you must send in this card so that the TurboTax mailroom will hop into action and send you the Final version as soon as it's finished. Register your software now and you won't have to think about it again.

What about sharing your disks? According to the TurboTax license agreement, you are not to loan disks to anyone else. You can give the entire package, disks, manual, and whatever pieces you have left from the box and the stuff that came in it, to another person as long as you haven't used the program yourself for at least 180 days. This pretty much precludes preparing your own tax return and then giving the program to a friend who wants to use it.

A TurboTax Quick Start flyer in your box gives you easy-to-find information for installing your program. Also on this flyer is an illustrated, descriptive list of all the buttons that appear across the top of the TurboTax screen.

So send in the registration card and check your disks. Make sure that each disk has a different number on it (Disk 1, Disk 2, Disk 3). Two or more disks with the same number should be returned to the store where you bought them, post-haste.

No Room at the Inn: Checking the Amount of Space Available on Your Hard Drive

Before you start the installation process, it's a good idea to check your computer's hard drive capacity to see whether it has room for this program. You could wait until you actually begin installing; if you are tight on space, the process will come to a screeching halt and you'll be told to push some programs out of the way to make room. By getting the lay of the land before you start, you may just save yourself a step or two.

In Windows 3.1

The easiest way to find out how much room is on your hard drive involves opening the Windows File Manager. If you aren't familiar with this terrific little program, now's as good a time as any to try it out. File Manager gives you a visual rendition of all the stuff that's lurking on your computer, crawling around inside the metal case, or using the modem to order out for pizzas.

For more detailed information about the File Manager and all the other important and fun goodies that Windows has to offer, chug on down to your local bookstore and find Andy Rathbone's *Windows 3.11 For Dummies,* 3rd Edition. (You've made the switch to Windows 95? No problem. Andy's *Windows 95 For Dummies* will help you find your way to files (and the new games) in that program.)

Find the File Manager (not to be confused with the Program Manager) by locating the little filing cabinet icon in your Main group window. Click twice on the cabinet and you're whisked to the File Manager program. On the left side of your screen, you should see a list of directory names. Make sure that you're looking at the list of the C:\ drive, as illustrated in Figure A-1. If necessary, click the scroll bar until you can see the top of the list and then click once on the C:\ at the top. If some other letter is at the top, click the C:\ drive icon above this list, as indicated in Figure A-1.

Now look at the lower-left corner of the File Manager window. You should see a big number followed by the letters KB and the word *free.* This number should be at least 15,000, and a little more wouldn't hurt. (15,000KB = 15MB, which is to say 15 million bytes.)

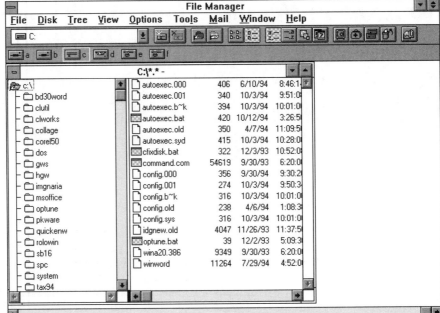

Figure A-1:
The File
Manager
lists the
directories
and files
that live on
your disk
drive.

Figure A-1:
The File
Manager
lists the
directories
and files
that live on
your disk
drive.

In Windows 95

Windows 95 has no File Manager. Instead, double-click the My Computer icon on the Windows 95 desktop. Click once on the drive on which you want to install TurboTax. Then click the File menu and choose Properties. The amount of free space on your disk is listed in the window that appears on-screen (see Figure A-2).

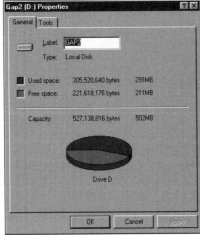

Figure A-2:
The
Properties
window
in My
Computer
shows you
how much
free space
is available
on your disk.

Deleting files to make room for TurboTax

If the number on your screen is smaller than 15,000K (15,000,000 bytes), it's time to get out the knife and start slashing. You need to find some files on your hard drive that are expendable and delete them. To delete a file from the File Manager, click once on the filename and then press the Delete key on your keyboard. Click OK in the following two dialog boxes that pop up on-screen asking whether you're sure that you know what you're doing.

From Windows 95, close the Properties window that was staring at you, double-click the drive icon that you plan to use for your TurboTax installation, and then double-click any folder you think may contain files you no longer need. Click a file you don't need, and then press the Delete key on your keyboard to remove the file. Click the Yes button to confirm the deletion.

When selecting files to delete, don't just haphazardly click the biggest files, the ones that will free up the most space, and then press Delete. Use some judgment here — see the following sidebar for details.

When you're finished with all this File Manager/My Computer stuff, you're ready to get on with installing this program.

Insert Flap A into Slot D and Fold Carefully on Line F, or How to Load TurboTax on Your Computer

Someday, you'll probably just look at your TurboTax disks and say to your computer, "Take these disks, read what's on them, and copy the files to the appropriate place." The 21st century computer will just smile a big, have-a-nice-day smile and — presto! — do what it's told.

Trashing files to free up memory

Delete files that contain stuff you no longer need, like last July's grocery list and every cute drawing your child has made in Paintbrush. You may need to open files in order to see what they contain. Double-clicking the name of a file that contains data or a picture usually opens the program that created the file and displays the file for you. That way, you can see what you're about to trash. Close the program that opened automatically and you're back where you left off at the File

Manager (or at My Computer if you're operating in Windows 95).

One way to make space on your hard drive without deleting files is to move files to a floppy disk. Click the name of a file to select the file, choose File⇨Move from the menu, and then type the disk drive letter (A:, for example) of the floppy drive that holds your disk in the To: box.

Until then, you have to get a little interactive with this installation process. Turn on your computer and start Windows. Pick up the disk labeled Disk 1 and insert it into your computer's floppy disk drive.

From the Windows Program Manager screen, drop down the File menu (click the word File or press the Alt key followed by the F key) and choose Run from the menu (click the word Run or press R on your keyboard). (If you're using Windows 95, see the following section for installation information.) A little box appears on-screen and asks for the Command Line. Resist the temptation to type something like "Finish dinner or no dessert for you!" Instead, type

a:setup

(If your floppy disk drive is the B:\ drive, be sure to type **b:setup**.) Do not put any spaces in that line. It doesn't matter whether you type uppercase, lowercase, or some combination thereof. After you type, press the Enter key.

Just for the record, if you have last year's version of TurboTax on your computer, installation of this year's version does not affect it. Each version is placed in a separate directory on the hard disk, so the files for the old year do not get overwritten with the files for the new year.

If you have the 1994 version of TurboTax on your computer and plan to remove it, be sure not to accidentally remove last year's tax return data files. For 1994 tax returns, the data files were stored in the \TAX94 directory and have .TAX extensions at the end of their filenames. Store these files in a safe place (on a floppy disk or in their own directory on the hard drive) before removing last year's TurboTax program. See "Out with the Old, In with the New" later in this appendix.

First, the TurboTax setup program looks over your computer and makes sure that you have what it needs to load your program. If it comes up short in any area (see "Hardware Requirements" in Chapter 1), it tells you where the short-fall occurs. You may need to remove some other program from your computer to make room, as shown in Figure A-3, or you may have a more serious problem. If you get a message like `Microsoft Test Driver (DS) Error` or some other equally unintelligible communiqué, find a computer guru to help you through this hurdle. (Offer to do his tax return for him if he says that he's too busy.) This isn't a TurboTax problem. You can also call TurboTax technical support and ask for help at 520-295-3090.

Next, you need to verify where you want the software to reside on your computer. All that means is that TurboTax has decided where it wants to put your program. You have the right to say, "No, put it someplace else." If C:\TAX95W is okay, click Install to continue the installation; if it's not okay, change the drive by clicking Select Destination, typing a new drive and directory name, and then clicking Install.

Figure A-3:
Oops! Looks like I need more space on this drive or I need to pick a different drive with Select Destination.

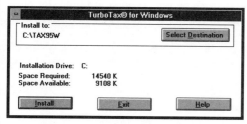

Installing TurboTax in Windows 95

Installing to Windows 95? No problem:

1. Click the Start button and then click Run.

Make sure that you have inserted the first disk in your computer's floppy drive and that drive letter is showing in the window on-screen.

2. Click Browse.

Windows 95 searches your disk for setup-type files and finds two.

3. **Click the file called Setup (see Figure A-4), and then click <u>O</u>pen.**

   Windows 95 takes it from there, prompting you for the information it needs about where to install the program (as described in the section about Windows 3.1 installation earlier in this appendix) and telling you when to switch disks.

Figure A-4:
Click the
Setup
filename
and then
click the
<u>O</u>pen button
to install
TurboTax
on your
computer.

At this point, TurboTax gets the go-ahead from your computer and starts copying files onto your machine.

After TurboTax finishes installing the files on the first disk, you see a message on-screen telling you to switch to the next disk. Eject Disk 1 and insert Disk 2. This process continues until all the disks have been exhausted.

After your computer sucks the last disk dry, the Program Manager reappears on-screen with its new group window, TurboTax® for Windows.

Using a different directory name

For some reason, you may not like the name TAX95W for the name of your TurboTax directory. The most likely reason is that you or someone else has already named a place on your hard drive TAX95W, thinking that you would never have to use that name for anything else. When you see the Select Destination button during the installation of your program, you have the right to override the default name, TAX95W, with any other name of no more than eight letters and/or numbers — UNCLESAM, for example. Doing so does not cause a problem with the program.

Those Cute Little TurboTax Icons

Inside the new TurboTax group window that gussies up the Program Manager after you install the program are several cute icons, as described in the following list.

> ✔ **The TurboTax top hat:** This is the TurboTax for Windows icon, the Fred Astaire icon for preparing your income tax return, as shown in Figure A-5. You need this icon to start the program. You may never use the others. Double-click this hat anytime you want to begin preparing your tax return or review or revise a tax return that you have already started.

Figure A-5:
Double-click
the
TurboTax
top hat icon
to fire up the
program.

> ✔ **Uninstall:** It's summer and your tax return is just another pleasant memory. You also have a crowded computer and would like to make room for some cool games to keep the kids occupied on rainy days. To remove TurboTax completely and safely from your computer, place the TurboTax Disk 1 in the floppy drive, double-click the Uninstall icon (see Figure A-6), and then click <u>Y</u>es.

Figure A-6:
Double-click
this icon to
get rid of
TurboTax.

Don't play around with this icon unless you really want to take the TurboTax program off your computer. This Uninstall process works very quickly. Before you can say, "But I was only kidding," TurboTax will be a thing of the past.

As TurboTax disappears from your computer, it takes the icons from the Program Manager screen with it. If you want to reinstall TurboTax at some point in the future, you'll need to find your TurboTax disks and completely install the program again.

After you uninstall TurboTax, the TAX95W directory remains on your system. Any tax return files you created by using TurboTax remain in this directory — the Uninstall process does not remove the data files that you created while using the program. Whew! Just to be extra cautious, you ought to back up your data files.

✔ **95-1040 Readme:** Computer programmers love to make *readme* files in their spare time. They must have a lot of spare time because nearly every computer program has one of these files. Sometimes it's READ.ME. Sometimes it's README.TOO. Readme files are little files of text material that got left out of the program manual. Occasionally, these readme files contain information that is pertinent to your situation. If you've got nothing better to do, feel free to "readme" by double-clicking the icon shown in Figure A-7. After you finish reading, choose File⇨Exit from the readme window's drop-down menu.

Figure A-7:
Read all about it! You can access late-breaking news by clicking this icon.

Lift Off

After you install TurboTax, you can start the program at any time. Just look for the top hat icon on your Program Manager screen and do one of the following things:

> ✔ Slide the mouse until the mouse pointer is on top of the hat, and then click the left mouse button twice.
>
> ✔ With mouse pointer on the hat icon, click once and then press Enter.

Keep trying until one of those two choices works, and you should find yourself at the starting gate of the TurboTax program.

Taking a Test Drive

Now that you're in the TurboTax program, go ahead and rummage around. You can't hurt anything. Answer some questions, experiment, set up a pretend tax return (you can call it *JUNK.TAX* or something similar), and get the feel of the program. Nothing bad is going to happen, so exercise a little freedom before you get down to the business of actually preparing your income tax return. Poke around in menus, click buttons, fill in fake names, make up some dollar amounts, and make believe you're living the life o' Reilly (or at least of Donald Trump). This is play time.

When you have had enough and are ready to come in from recess, exit TurboTax by clicking the File menu (or press Alt+F on your keyboard) and then clicking Exit or pressing the X key.

Out with the Old, In with the New

You may or may not care about how many years' worth of TurboTax you store on your computer. You may have reasons for wanting to keep last year's program (if, for example, you have not yet filed your prior year's tax return). But most people want to clear the space from their machines.

If you still have last year's TurboTax on your computer and want to remove it, here's how:

1. **Open the File Manager by double-clicking the filing cabinet icon in Program Manager's Main group window.**

2. **In File Manager, make sure that the C:\ drive is the drive that's listed.**

   Just to be sure, go ahead and click once on the C:\ icon, which looks like a miniature disk drive. If you're already looking at the C:\ drive, you haven't hurt anything.

3. **If you want to save tax return files from the prior year, create a new directory for those files and evacuate them to the new location.**

   To create a new directory, click the C:\ at the top of the list of directory names on the left side of the File Manager screen. Then click the File menu at the top of the screen, followed by Create Directory. In the dialog box that appears, type the name of your new directory. You are limited to a maximum of eight letters and/or numbers with no spaces for your directory name. Click OK. Your new directory appears alphabetically in the list of all the directories located on the C:\ drive.

4. **Find the directory titled TAX94 on the list on the left side of the screen and click it.**

   (If you've got really moldy copies of TurboTax around, you may even see directory names like TAX93.)

5. **If you are saving prior year tax return files, locate all the files you can on the right side of the screen that have .TAX tacked on the end of their names.**

   The little icon associated with these files looks like a sheet of paper with writing on it.

6. **Select all the files you want to save by holding down the Ctrl key on your keyboard and clicking each filename with the mouse. Then release the Ctrl key.**

7. **Place your mouse pointer in the highlighted area of any of the selected filenames. Hold down the left mouse button and drag the files over to the name of the directory you just created in the column at the left side of the screen.**

   The new directory name should develop a ring around its collar when you get near it with the mouse. Once the new directory name is surrounded, release your mouse button. The box on-screen lets you know that you are about to move the files.

8. **Click OK, and the files move.**

   The TAX files that were in the TAX94 directory hit the road — they pack up and move to the new directory.

9. **Go back to the TAX94 (or earlier) directory name (on the left side of the screen) and click it.**

   Ready to remove it?

10. **Press the Delete key on your keyboard. Answer OK, Yes, or Yes to All to all the questions you are asked.**

11. **Close the File Manager.**

    Double-click the Control menu, the little horizontal bar in the upper-left corner of the File Manager window, or press Alt+F4 from the keyboard.

Free Goodies

Free stuff?! Sure! Why not? The folks at TurboTax want to do their part in keeping your mailbox free of cobwebs. Just send in the registration card that came with your software; it should be lurking somewhere in the box with the disks and says `TurboTax for Windows Personal/1040 Registration` at the top.

Sending in this card ensures that the following exciting events will happen to you:

✔ If you purchased the HeadStart version, you'll receive the Final version as soon as it is available. It is imperative that you mail this card as early as possible. Remember, you cannot file a tax return prepared with TurboTax unless you have the *Final* version!

✔ You'll be eligible to receive free technical support from the TurboTax techies who sit at telephones all day long answering questions about the program. Talk about an exciting job.

Technical support from TurboTax representatives may be free in that you don't receive a bill for their time. However, the telephone call is not a toll-free call. If you call TurboTax for phone support, try to have a concise question ready and, if logistically possible, call from your desk in front of your computer. That way, you can make a quick, efficient phone call with the least amount of waiting. Also, the TurboTax person will be able to walk you through your problem keystroke by keystroke if you are at your computer.

✔ Hey! More mail! TurboTax will put you on its mailing list so that it can keep you apprised of new developments in its software with its newsletter.

✔ Sometime in the fall of 1996, you will receive notification in the mail of the release of next year's program. You can order from the comfort of your home, and your new program will be shipped to you in the mail. All the modern conveniences.

Appendix B
Form 1040 Cross-Reference

● ●

*T*his appendix serves as a sort of road map to help you get your bearings with the most basic tax form, Form 1040. Turn here whenever you get lost in the jumble of questions that TurboTax asks you.

You can also use this appendix to get help with a specific area of your 1040 form if you're working directly with the forms and not using EasyStep. Find the line or section that's giving you trouble, locate the number of the line that points to it, and turn to the section of the book that's listed for that number. There you'll find information to help you answer the question that that line or section of the 1040 poses.

Form **1040**

Department of the Treasury—Internal Revenue Service

U.S. Individual Income Tax Return **1995** | (99) | IRS Use Only—Do not write or staple in this space.

For the year Jan. 1–Dec. 31, 1995, or other tax year beginning , 1995, ending , 19 | OMB No. 1545-0074

Label
(See instructions on page 11.)

Use the IRS label. Otherwise, please print or type.

L A B E L   H E R E

Your first name and initial | Last name

If a joint return, spouse's first name and initial | Last name

Home address (number and street). If you have a P.O. box, see page 11. | Apt. no.

City, town or post office, state, and ZIP code. If you have a foreign address, see page 11.

Your social security number

Spouse's social security number

For Privacy Act and Paperwork Reduction Act Notice, see page 7.

Presidential Election Campaign ▶
(See page 11.)

Do you want $3 to go to this fund? . . . .
If a joint return, does your spouse want $3 to go to this fund? . . . . . .

Yes | No | Note: *Checking "Yes" will not change your tax or reduce your refund.*

Filing Status
(See page 11.)

Check only one box.

1 Single
2 Married filing joint return (even if only one had income)
3 Married filing separate return. Enter spouse's social security no. above and full name here. ▶
4 Head of household (with qualifying person). (See page 12.) If the qualifying person is a child but not your dependent, enter this child's name here. ▶
5 Qualifying widow(er) with dependent child (year spouse died ▶ 19). (See page 12.)

Exemptions
(See page 12.)

If more than six dependents, see page 13.

6a ☐ **Yourself.** If your parent (or someone else) can claim you as a dependent on his or her tax return, **do not** check box 6a. But be sure to check the box on line 33b on page 2 . .
b ☐ **Spouse** . . . .
c **Dependents:**

(1) First name Last name	(2) Dependent's social security number. If born in 1995, see page 13.	(3) Dependent's relationship to you	(4) No. of months lived in your home in 1995

d If your child didn't live with you but is claimed as your dependent under a pre-1985 agreement, check here ▶ ☐
e Total number of exemptions claimed . . . .

No. of boxes checked on 6a and 6b

No. of your children on 6c who:
• lived with you
• didn't live with you due to divorce or separation (see page 14)

Dependents on 6c not entered above

Add numbers entered on lines above ▶

Income

Attach Copy B of your Forms W-2, W-2G, and 1099-R here.

If you did not get a W-2, see page 14.

Enclose, but do not attach, your payment and payment voucher. See page 33.

7 Wages, salaries, tips, etc. Attach Form(s) W-2 . . . . | 7
8a **Taxable** interest income (see page 15). Attach Schedule B if over $400 . . | 8a
b **Tax-exempt** interest (see page 15). DON'T include on line 8a | 8b |
9 Dividend income. Attach Schedule B if over $400 . . . . | 9
10 Taxable refunds, credits, or offsets of state and local income taxes (see page 15) . . | 10
11 Alimony received . . . . | 11
12 Business income or (loss). Attach Schedule C or C-EZ . . . . . . | 12
13 Capital gain or (loss). If required, attach Schedule D (see page 16) . . . | 13
14 Other gains or (losses). Attach Form 4797 . . . . | 14
15a Total IRA distributions . | 15a | b Taxable amount (see page 16) | 15b
16a Total pensions and annuities | 16a | b Taxable amount (see page 16) | 16b
17 Rental real estate, royalties, partnerships, S corporations, trusts, etc. Attach Schedule E | 17
18 Farm income or (loss). Attach Schedule F . . . . | 18
19 Unemployment compensation (see page 17) . . . . | 19
20a Social security benefits | 20a | b Taxable amount (see page 18) | 20b
21 Other income. List type and amount—see page 18 . . . . | 21
22 Add the amounts in the far right column for lines 7 through 21. This is your **total income** ▶ | 22

Adjustments to Income

23a Your IRA deduction (see page 19) . . . . . . | 23a |
b Spouse's IRA deduction (see page 19) . . . . . | 23b |
24 Moving expenses. Attach Form 3903 or 3903-F . . . | 24 |
25 One-half of self-employment tax . . . . . | 25 |
26 Self-employed health insurance deduction (see page 21) | 26 |
27 Keogh & self-employed SEP plans. If SEP, check ▶ ☐ | 27 |
28 Penalty on early withdrawal of savings . . . . | 28 |
29 Alimony paid. Recipient's SSN ▶ | 29 |
30 Add lines 23a through 29. These are your **total adjustments** . . . . ▶ | 30

Adjusted Gross Income

31 Subtract line 30 from line 22. This is your **adjusted gross income**. If less than $26,673 and a child lived with you (less than $9,230 if a child didn't live with you), see "Earned Income Credit" on page 27 ▶ | 31

Cat. No. 11320B

Form **1040** (1995)

(circled numbers at right margin: 1, 2, 3, 4, 5, 6, 7, 8, 9, 10, 11, 12, 13, 14, 15)

1. Chapter 6: "Name, Rank, Serial Number, Please"
2. Chapter 6: "The Prez Campaign: Will They Call It Off If We All Agree Not to Contribute?"
3. Chapter 6: "Married Filing Jointly, Single Filing Separately, Separate Filing Together — What's the Deal?"
4. Chapter 6: "The Great April 14 Search for Dependents"
5. Chapter 7: "Those Pesky Little W-2 Forms"
6. Chapter 7: "Take It to the Bank: Investment Income"
7. Chapter 7: "Getting Tax Refunds Back in the Mail"
8. Chapter 7: "You're the Boss: Profit or Loss from a Business"
9. Chapter 7: "Selling Stocks and Other Valuable Things"
10. Chapter 7: "Is Nothing Sacred? Reporting Your Retirement Income"
11. Chapter 7: "Reporting Income from K-1 Forms"
12. Chapter 7: "Down on the Farm"
13. Chapter 7: "Unemployment Compensation"
14. Chapter 7: "May I Have the Envelope, Please?"
15. Chapter 8: "Adjustments: The First Step in Reducing Gross Income"

Form 1040 (1995)   Page **2**

Tax Computation (See page 23.)	32	Amount from line 31 (adjusted gross income)	32
	33a	Check if: ☐ **You** were 65 or older, ☐ Blind; ☐ **Spouse** was 65 or older, ☐ Blind. Add the number of boxes checked above and enter the total here . . . . ▶ 33a ☐	
	b	If your parent (or someone else) can claim you as a dependent, check here . ▶ 33b ☐	
	c	If you are married filing separately and your spouse itemizes deductions or you are a dual-status alien, see page 23 and check here . . . . ▶ 33c ☐	
	34	Enter the larger of your: **Itemized deductions** from Schedule A, line 28, **OR** **Standard deduction** shown below for your filing status. **But if you checked any box on line 33a or b,** go to page 23 to find your standard deduction. If you checked **box 33c,** your standard deduction is zero. • Single—$3,900 • Married filing jointly or Qualifying widow(er)—$6,550 • Head of household—$5,750 • Married filing separately—$3,275	34
	35	Subtract line 34 from line 32	35
	36	If line 32 is $86,025 or less, multiply $2,500 by the total number of exemptions claimed on line 6e. If line 32 is over $86,025, see the worksheet on page 23 for the amount to enter .	36
If you want the IRS to figure your tax, see page 35.	37	**Taxable income.** Subtract line 36 from line 35. If line 36 is more than line 35, enter -0- .	37
	38	Tax. Check if from a ☐ Tax Table, b ☐ Tax Rate Schedules, c ☐ Capital Gain Tax Worksheet, or d ☐ Form 8615 (see page 24). Amount from Form(s) 8814 ▶ e _____	38
	39	Additional taxes. Check if from a ☐ Form 4970 b ☐ Form 4972	39
	40	Add lines 38 and 39 . . . . ▶	40
Credits (See page 24.)	41	Credit for child and dependent care expenses. Attach Form 2441	41	
	42	Credit for the elderly or the disabled. Attach Schedule R .	42	
	43	Foreign tax credit. Attach Form 1116	43	
	44	Other credits (see page 25). Check if from a ☐ Form 3800 b ☐ Form 8396 c ☐ Form 8801 d ☐ Form (specify)_____	44	
	45	Add lines 41 through 44	45
	46	Subtract line 45 from line 40. If line 45 is more than line 40, enter -0- . . . . ▶	46
Other Taxes (See page 25.)	47	Self-employment tax. Attach Schedule SE	47
	48	Alternative minimum tax. Attach Form 6251	48
	49	Recapture taxes. Check if from a ☐ Form 4255 b ☐ Form 8611 c ☐ Form 8828 . .	49
	50	Social security and Medicare tax on tip income not reported to employer. Attach Form 4137	50
	51	Tax on qualified retirement plans, including IRAs. If required, attach Form 5329 . .	51
	52	Advance earned income credit payments from Form W-2	52
	53	Household employment taxes. Attach Schedule H	53
	54	Add lines 46 through 53. This is your **total tax** . . . . ▶	54
Payments Attach Forms W-2, W-2G, and 1099-R on the front.	55	Federal income tax withheld. If any is from Form(s) 1099, check ▶ ☐	55	
	56	1995 estimated tax payments and amount applied from 1994 return .	56	
	57	**Earned income credit.** Attach Schedule EIC if you have a qualifying child. Nontaxable earned income: amount ▶ _____ and type ▶ _____	57	
	58	Amount paid with Form 4868 (extension request)	58	
	59	Excess social security and RRTA tax withheld (see page 32) .	59	
	60	Other payments. Check if from a ☐ Form 2439 b ☐ Form 4136	60	
	61	Add lines 55 through 60. These are your **total payments** . . . . ▶	61
Refund or Amount You Owe	62	If line 61 is more than line 54, subtract line 54 from line 61. This is the amount you **OVERPAID.** .	62
	63	Amount of line 62 you want **REFUNDED TO YOU.** . . . . ▶	63
	64	Amount of line 62 you want **APPLIED TO YOUR 1996 ESTIMATED TAX** ▶	64	
	65	If line 54 is more than line 61, subtract line 61 from line 54. This is the **AMOUNT YOU OWE.** For details on how to pay and use **Form 1040-V,** Payment Voucher, see page 33 . . ▶	65
	66	Estimated tax penalty (see page 33). Also include on line 65	66	

Sign Here
Keep a copy of this return for your records.

Under penalties of perjury, I declare that I have examined this return and accompanying schedules and statements, and to the best of my knowledge and belief, they are true, correct, and complete. Declaration of preparer (other than taxpayer) is based on all information of which preparer has any knowledge.

Your signature	Date	Your occupation
Spouse's signature. If a joint return, BOTH must sign.	Date	Spouse's occupation

Paid Preparer's Use Only

Preparer's signature ▶	Date	Check if self-employed ☐	Preparer's social security no.
Firm's name (or yours if self-employed) and address ▶		EIN	
		ZIP code	

✿ *Printed on recycled paper*

Index

(continued)

(continued)

(continued)

• *N* •

• *O* •

(continued)

• U •